POSTCARD HISTORY SERIES

Bethlehem Revisited

On the Front Cover: This rare photograph of early-1900s Bethlehem shows the Lehigh & Lackawanna Railroad train passing by along the bottom of the card. The majestic Central Moravian Church towers over the scene in the background. The next-tallest building, toward the left, is the Eagle Hotel, built in 1794. The Moravian Market House was once located there. The assorted factories, businesses, and residences in the foreground no longer stand. The frequent flooding of the Monocacy Creek made this floodplain problematic for building. (Courtesy of Bill Weiner.)

On the Back Cover: This is Five Points, an important business district in South Bethlehem. It includes Wyandotte Street, Broadway, and Dakotah Street. Directly center is a grocery store. On the far right is a sign for the Five Points Hotel. A trolley of the South Bethlehem & Saucon Street Railway Company makes its way up Wyandotte Street on the far left. The back of the E.P. Wilbur Trust Company Building can be seen on the left on Broadway. It is a busy intersection with people on each corner navigating through the cars and trolleys. (Courtesy of Bill Weiner.)

POSTCARD HISTORY SERIES

Bethlehem Revisited

William G. Weiner Jr. and Karen M. Samuels

ARCADIA PUBLISHING

ISBN 978-1-4671-2239-9

Published by Arcadia Publishing
Charleston, South Carolina

Printed in the United States of America

Library of Congress Control Number: 2014937853

For all general information contact Arcadia Publishing at:
Telephone 843-853-2070
Fax 843-853-0044
E-mail sales@arcadiapublishing.com
For customer service and orders:
Toll-Free 1-888-313-2665

Visit us on the Internet at www.arcadiapublishing.com

This book is dedicated to past, present, and future persons who care and who cherish learning more, understanding their heritage, and sharing with their children—Enjoy!

CONTENTS

ACKNOWLEDGMENTS

We could not have completed this book without the help of the following:

Bill thanks his wife, Sharon; his sons Bill and Paul; and his two granddaughters, Kyley and Charley. Karen is grateful to her husband, John; her sons Teddy and Tommy; and her sister Deborah and brother Richard.

We thank our friends and Bethlehem historians Natalie J. Bock, Ed Cann, Phil Carlson, Chris Eline, Dana B. Grubb, Kathryn Klein, Mark Lampietro, Kenneth F. Raniere, Nancy Rutman, Karol Strelecki, and Drummond B. Taylor. Once again, we thank our editor from Arcadia Publishing, Abby Henry, who was patient, supportive, and always helpful.

Unless noted in the caption, all postcards in this book are from Bill Weiner's collection.

INTRODUCTION

We invite you once again to experience a selection of 213 postcards from the Bill Weiner collection. In our first book, Postcard History Series: *Bethlehem* (2011), you saw a wide variety of postcards that chronicled 20th-century life in Bethlehem. We paid special attention to the photographer Gustav Adolph Conradi, whose postcards are highly collectible because of his attention to detail and his production of crystal clear images. Conradi's work appears in this book as well. Also, the majority of these postcards have not appeared before in any other book. The influence of the Moravians, who settled Bethlehem in 1741, will be seen in many of the images. The Central Moravian Church (1803), Gemeinhaus (1741), Sun Inn (1758), and many other historic buildings set the stage for the first 100 years of Bethlehem. The Moravian settlers were a hardworking, purposeful people, and we continue to enjoy their legacy today. In 1748, as a treat for the students, Moravian teachers built and decorated small Christmas trees. This is the first documented reference to a Christmas tree in America. Bethlehem is now known as "Christmas City," which is illustrated by the images of decorated streets in this book. The images of the buildings that once housed early Moravian industries are included for their importance in Colonial history. George Washington, Martha Washington, John Adams, and many others visited these industries and considered them extraordinary. In a letter to his wife, Abigail, dated February 7, 1777, John Adams wrote the following from his room at the Sun Inn: "They have carried the mechanical Arts to greater Perfection here than in any Place which I have seen."

In Bethlehem, the Lehigh Canal was excavated alongside the Lehigh River between 1827 and 1829. As much as one million tons of anthracite coal was transported down the canal from Jim Thorpe to Easton each year. The quiet religious community of Bethlehem was forever changed when the finished canal allowed outsiders to float by. You can see from the postcards that the canal was constructed within walking distance to the center of town. Everyday life on the canal is on display around Bethlehem's locks Nos. 42 and 44. The canal ceased operating in the 1940s. Today, the canal towpath has been converted into a multiuse trail that runs from Freemansburg through Bethlehem to Allentown. Next came the railroads to put the canal out of business. Railroads were more dependable for moving anthracite, as the canal would frequently freeze during the winter. In the beginning, the companies that serviced Bethlehem were the Lehigh Valley Railroad, the North Penn Railroad, and the Central Railroad of New Jersey. Asa Packer, president of the Lehigh Valley Railroad, established its headquarters in South Bethlehem in 1858.

In 1857, Augustus Wolle purchased 200 acres of the former Luckenbach farm, in South Bethlehem, from Charles Brodhead. Brodhead had convinced Wolle to establish the Bethlehem Rolling Mills and Iron Company near the junction of the Lehigh Valley and North Penn Railroads. The arrival of the railroads encouraged the building of several mills in South Bethlehem. Wolle's iron company has had many names over the years, including Bethlehem Iron Company as well as Bethlehem Steel Company, and eventually settled on the name Bethlehem Steel Corporation, which is the name used throughout this book. Like the Lehigh Canal had an enormous effect upon Bethlehem, so did Bethlehem Steel Corporation. It transformed the small town into a city. Charles M. Schwab, president of Bethlehem Steel, used his influence to consolidate the boroughs of Bethlehem and South Bethlehem in 1917. Schwab was behind the scenes in the building of the Hill-to-Hill Bridge in 1924 and Hotel Bethlehem in 1926. In 1914, Bethlehem Steel was the first US company to receive armament orders from Europe. The need for laborers became intense, and Bethlehem Steel welcomed newly arrived immigrants looking for work. Czech, Slovak, Hungarian, Windish, Polish, Italian, Armenian, Greek, Mexican, Portuguese, and Spaniards soon arrived in Bethlehem. The population increased 65 percent, with 22 percent being foreign born. Bethlehem Steel coordinated with churches and public schools throughout Bethlehem to offer English and Americanization classes for its employees. Bethlehem Steel obtained textbooks and teacher's manuals from the US Bureau of Naturalization. During the years of World War I, Bethlehem Steel produced over 60 percent of the total guns, ammunition, and ships for the United States and Allied countries. After the end of World War I, in 1919, the company employed 32,000 of the town's general population of 60,000. The Bethlehem Steel Corporation executives built their mansions in the Mount Airy section of West Bethlehem as the laborers struggled to find housing in South Bethlehem. When Frederick Law Olmsted Jr. visited Bethlehem in 1917, he observed that "the whole territory is supersaturated so far as housing conditions are concerned." The stark differences in living conditions between management and laborers can be seen in several of these postcards.

Despite the housing problems, the wonderful hodgepodge of ethnic cultures made South Bethlehem an interesting and appealing place to live. As seen in the images in this book, beautiful ethnic churches sprang up on every block. As soon as there were enough residents who belonged to a specific religion, they would organize a church to preserve their religion, language, and customs.

As roads and bridges improved in Bethlehem, residents became enamored with the automobile. There are images of automobiles in this book that have long been forgotten by the general public. People used their cars to transport their families along with overflowing picnic baskets to Oakland Park in Bethlehem Township and the Bethlehem Fairgrounds in North Bethlehem. The fairgrounds contained a horse-racing track, a grandstand, and an exotic midway. Oakland Park offered a large pavilion, countless picnic tables, refreshment stands, and children's rides. The automobile eventually would cause a migration of residents to the suburbs of Bethlehem. The 1950s images in the book captured the last hurrah of the downtown shopping centers. Only recently have people returned to the North and South Bethlehem downtowns to shop in boutiques and eat in exciting new restaurants. The Sands Casino, on the old Bethlehem Steel site in South Bethlehem, has attracted more visitors than any other Pennsylvania casino. People are returning to Bethlehem's downtowns to seek historical charm, cafés, locally grown farmers' markets, and crafts—not the chain stores and restaurants that are offered everywhere else.

One

Downtown Revisited

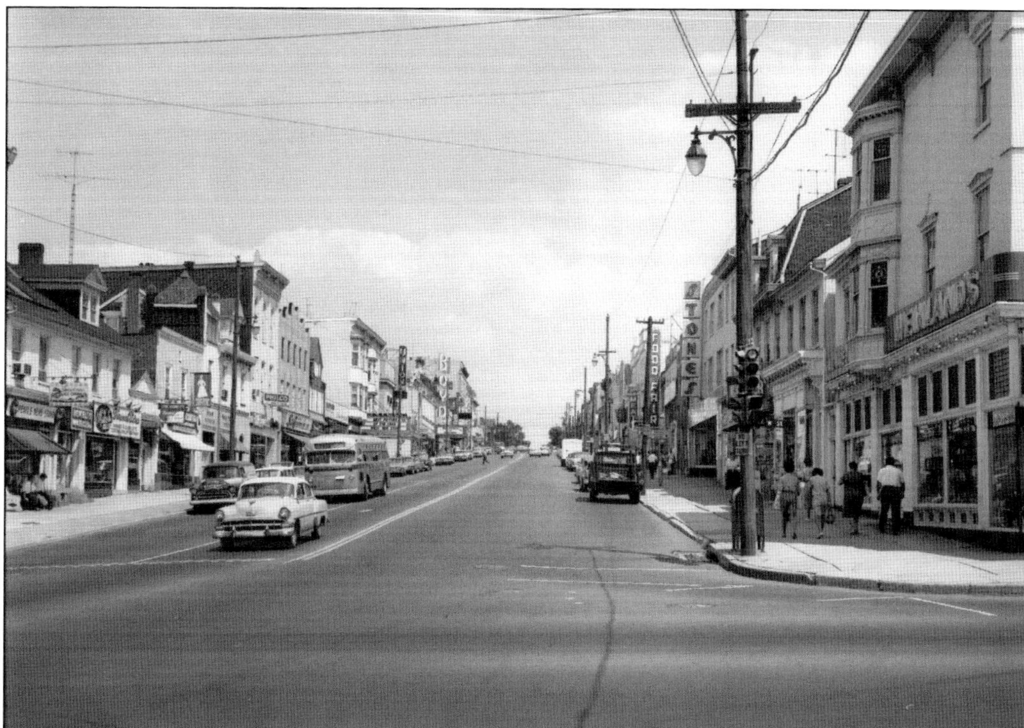

This 1950s view is looking east on Broad Street from Main Street. One can see that this shopping district offered anything a shopper would need. On the far right, at the intersection of Broad and Main Streets, is Weinland's Hardware. This building stood on that spot for 175 years. It was gutted by fire in 2005. Continuing up on the south side of Broad Street are Warner's Drugstore, Stone's, Food Fair, and Reliance Fire Company. On the north side of Broad Street are Pearl's News Stand, Beitel's Music Store, Nile Theater, and the Boyd Theater

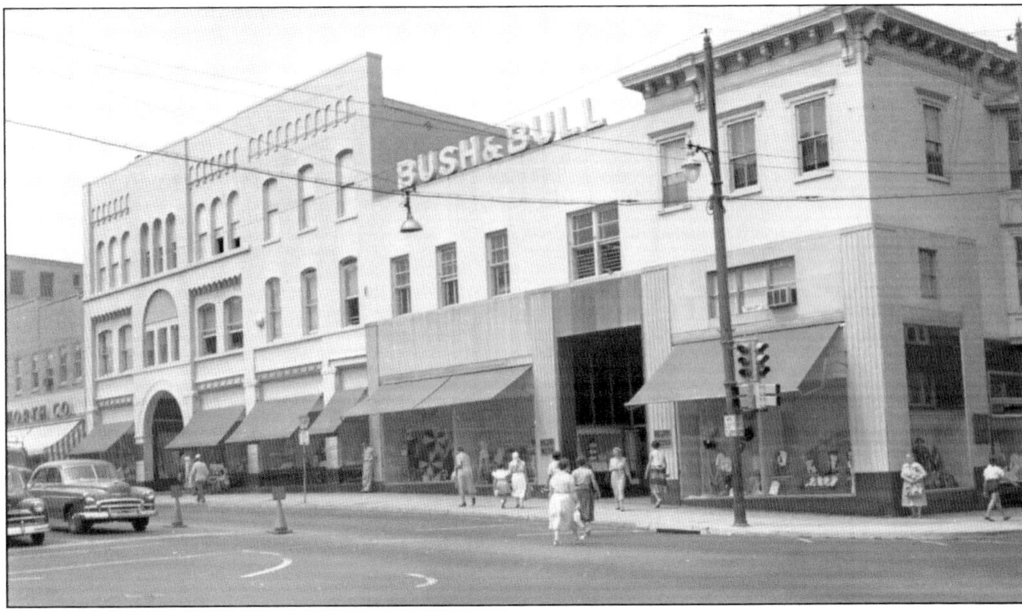

This photograph is of the west side of Main Street, between West Market and Broad Streets. The F.W. Woolworth Company's five-and-dime store and Bush & Bull Department Store line the street. Bush & Bull arrived in Bethlehem in 1908, when it purchased this building from Lerch, Rice & Co. Dry Goods Store. Orr's bought out Bush & Bull in 1955. The Bethlehem Trust Company is on the far right. (Courtesy of Joe Hancaviz.)

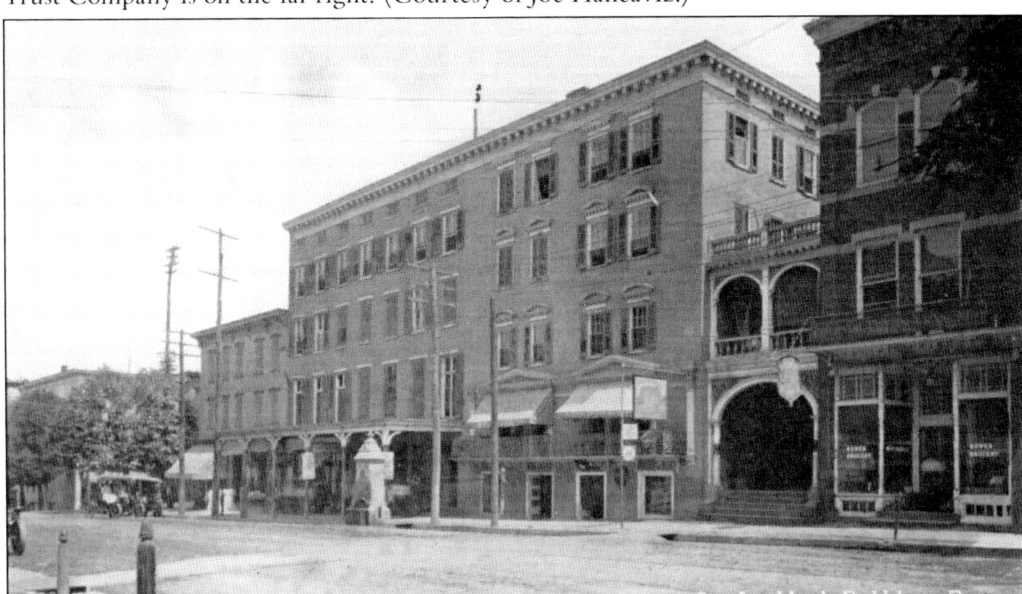

The Moravians built the Sun Inn in 1758 to accommodate the increasing number of "strangers" or non-Moravians that passed through town. The inn was built on the edge of town to keep the guests from interfering with the activities of the Moravian community. Both George and Martha Washington stayed at the Sun Inn on separate visits. When Martha stayed in 1779, she stayed in a two-bedroom suite and expressed great delight upon tasting the fresh strawberries she was served. Fourteen members of the Continental Congress stayed at the inn on September 22, 1777.

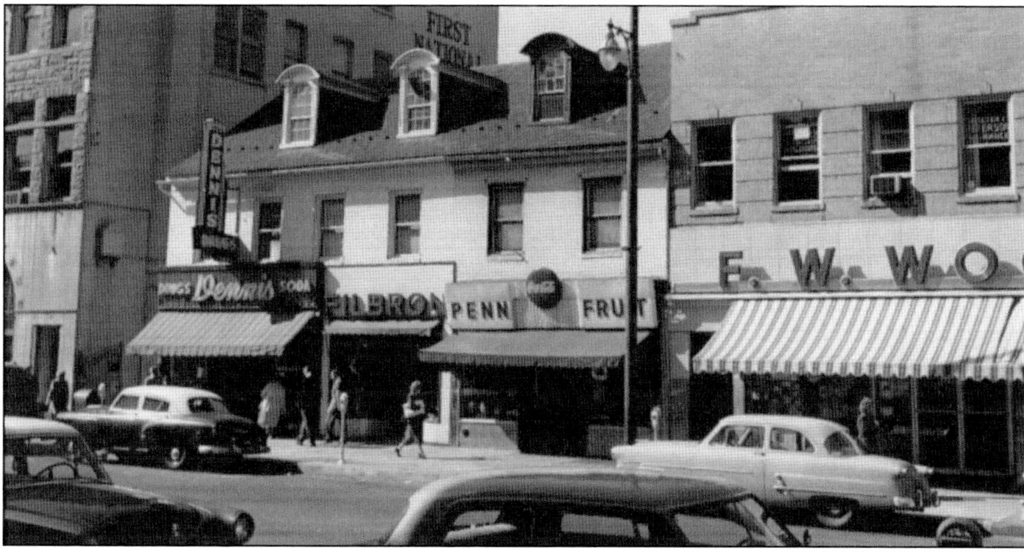

In this 1950s Main Street scene, Dennis Drugstore was in the heart of Bethlehem's business district. Owner Charles E. Dennis specialized in photography. Next-door was Filbrons, a women's clothing store. Penn Fruit was a popular grocery store owned by Fred Donatelli. F.W. Woolworth had arrived at this location in the 1920s. All the buildings were occupied on their upper floors with offices and apartments.

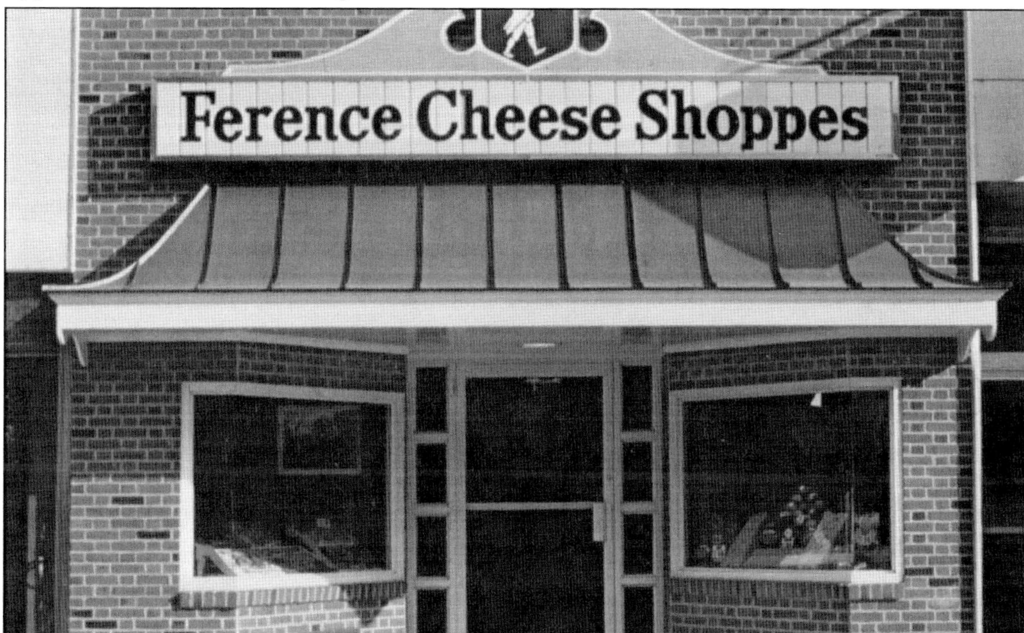

The Ference Cheese Shoppes on Main Street once offered 200 varieties of fine cheese from 17 countries. It opened in 1925 as "The Cheese Lover's Paradise" and sold such items as Appenzeller cheese from Switzerland, Cahill's Irish Porter cheese from Ireland, and medium-aged Gouda from Holland. Students from Lehigh University often would call in for orders of large platters of cheese and crackers. William Ference Sr. founded Ference Cheese and also opened shops in Allentown and Asheville, North Carolina.

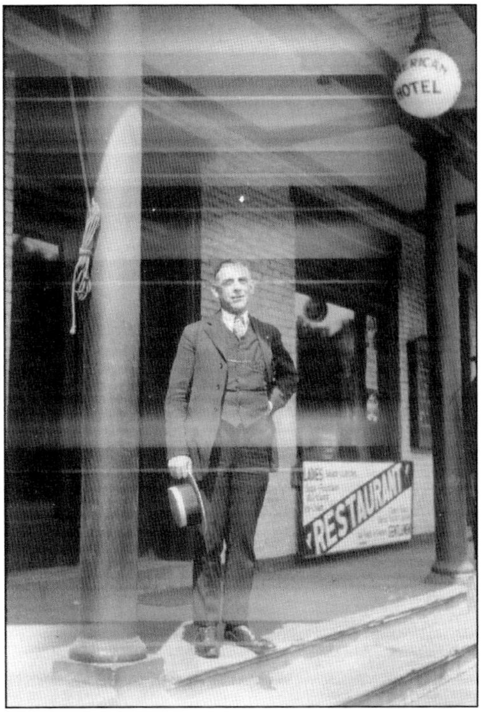

Here is a gentleman well satisfied with his accommodations at the American Hotel at Broad and New Streets. The following was the hotel's slogan: "Home of the traveling man and tourist." According to the sign to the man's left, the hotel also catered to women with a soda fountain and Borden's ice cream. The hotel was originally built in the 1850s as the American House and was enlarged in 1862; it eventually became known as American Hotel. In the 1950s, the location also served as a bus terminal. A quote from the 1956 Lehigh University yearbook said, "A location on top of the bus terminal has helped make the American Hotel a good place to house dates over party weekends."

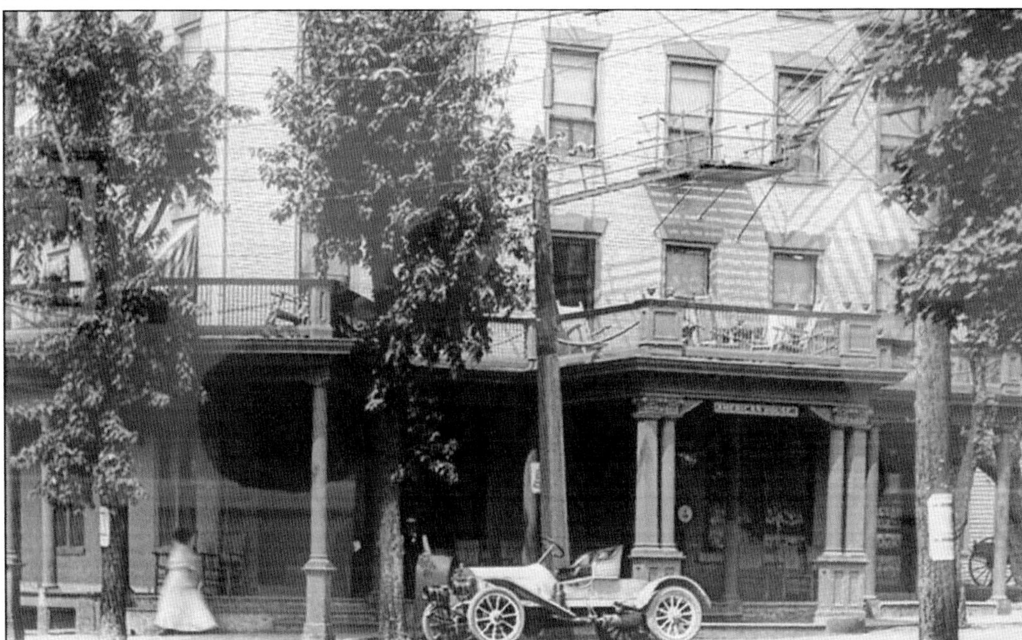

American House had an excellent reputation for comfort, food, and exceptional views. Located at the intersection of Broad and New Streets, a hotel guest could see the Blue Mountains to the north and the lush countryside. A drink at sunset on the roof was greatly anticipated by patrons. The hotel initially was the home of John Levers, who opened up his rooms for boarders. The business expanded into a full-service hotel, eventually taking the name of American Hotel. In 1982, the 126-year-old hotel was razed.

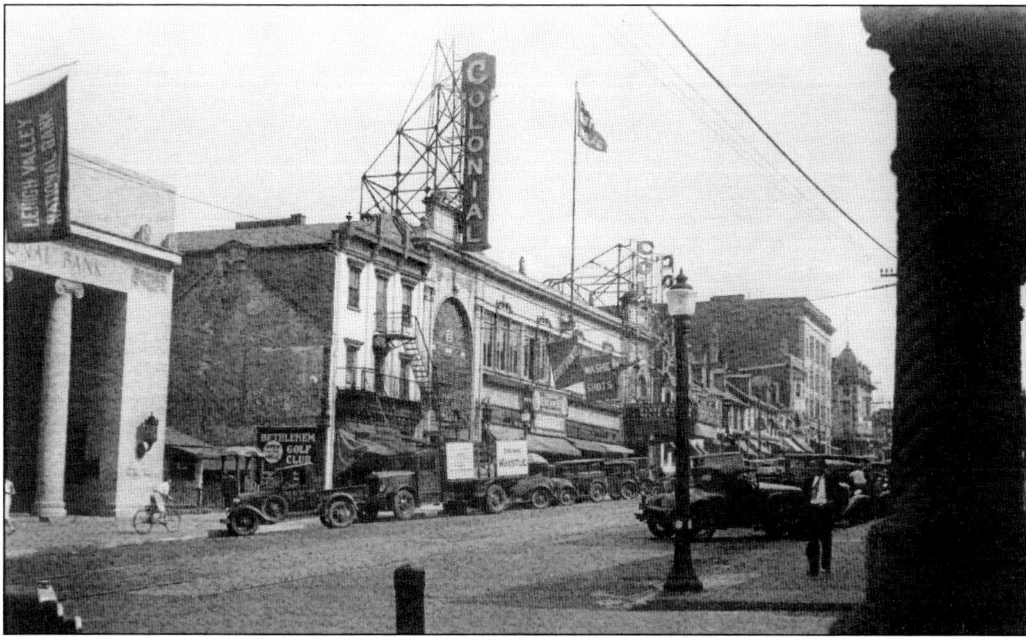

Brothers Charles F. and John Kurtz sold their theater and restaurant to the Wilmer and Vincent Theatre Company in 1924. The new owners changed the name of the theater to the Colonial. Initially, they stayed with the combination of vaudeville acts and silent movies. Sidney Wilmer and Walter Vincent were former vaudeville actors themselves. During the 10 years that they owned the theater, they oversaw the transition from vaudeville to movies as the main draw of customers. Wilmer and Vincent sold the theater to A.R. Boyd in 1934.

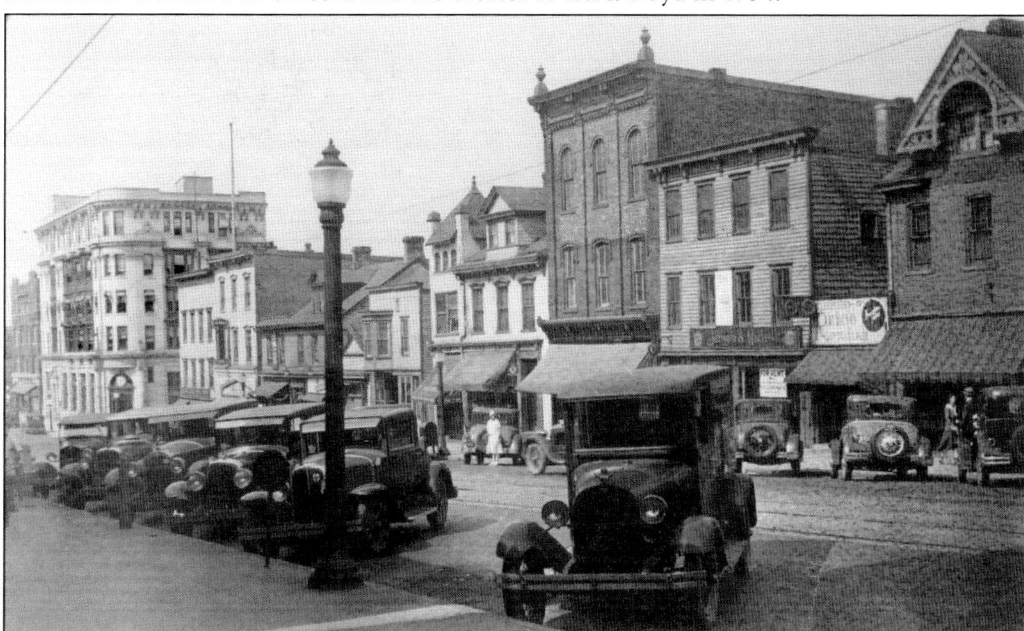

This 1926 photograph is looking toward the northwest corner of Broad and Main Streets. On the far left is the Bethlehem Trust Company. This is a main business street in Bethlehem. Among the hardware, bakery, and clothing shops were opticians and dentists.

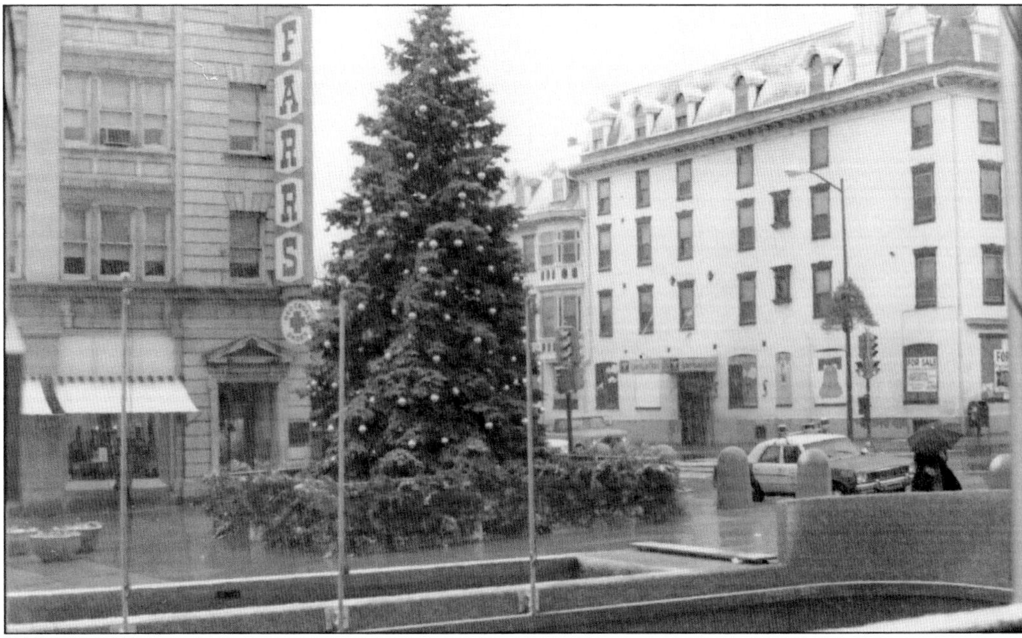

This postcard captures a dreary, rainy day at the intersection of New and Broad Streets. A large Christmas tree has been erected on the pedestrian mall; it did not help to dispel the struggling economic times of the 1970s. Across the street, the American Hotel has "For Sale" signs in its windows. Today, the pedestrian mall has been removed to improve traffic flow, and the American Hotel was demolished in July 1982.

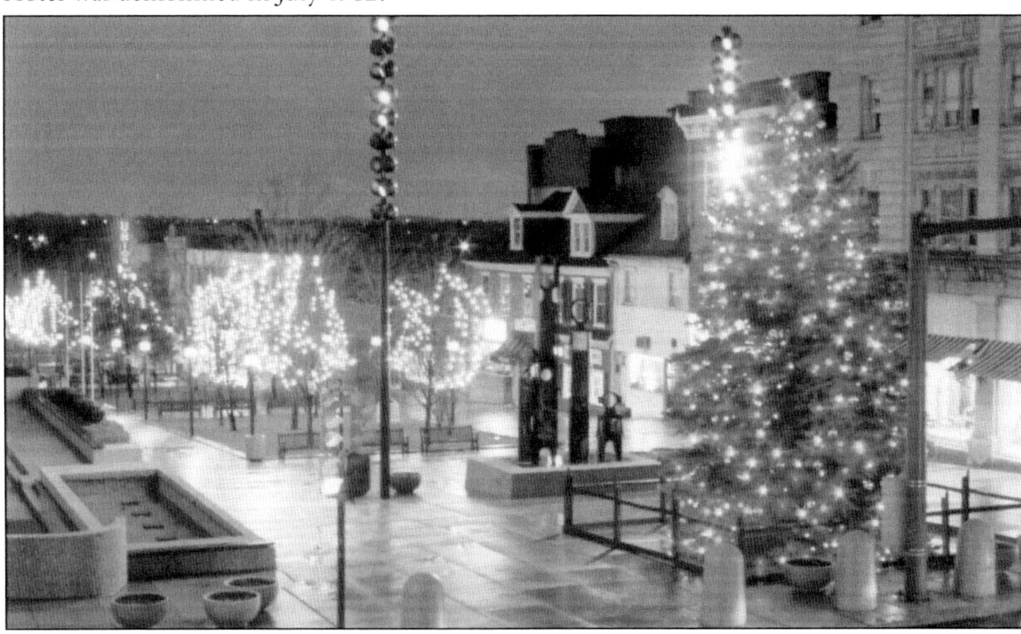

Again, here is the ill-fated Broad Street pedestrian mall, which opened in 1974. The city demolished a block of 19th-century buildings to allow for the closure of Broad Street between Guetter and New Streets. Broad Street was reopened to traffic in 2002. The *Family of Man* sculpture by Paul Remely, shown in the center, was moved into storage.

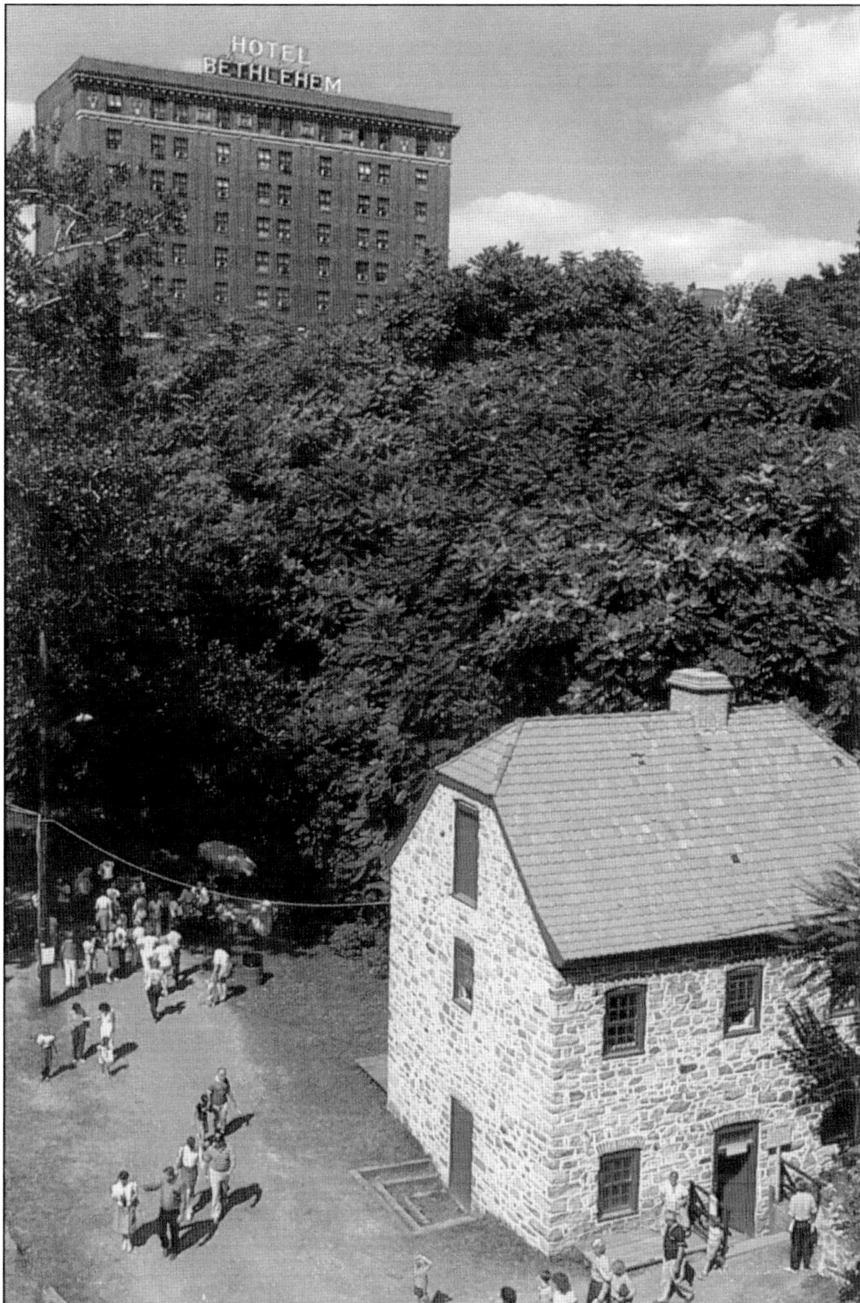

The Bethlehem Waterworks, built in 1762, attracted esteemed visitors such as George and Martha Washington, John Adams, and Gov. John Penn. This two-story stone building, 22 by 30 feet, still stands today. Inside the building were three single-acting iron pumps, cast at the nearby Durham Furnace. The pumps worked by means of a triple crank, which was forged by Bethlehem blacksmith Stephen Blum. The water was pumped, through wooden pipes, 112 feet to a reservoir, located on a wooden tower in the square. Overlooking the historic area is the Hotel Bethlehem, built in 1922. This 1980s postcard shows the beautifully restored waterworks.

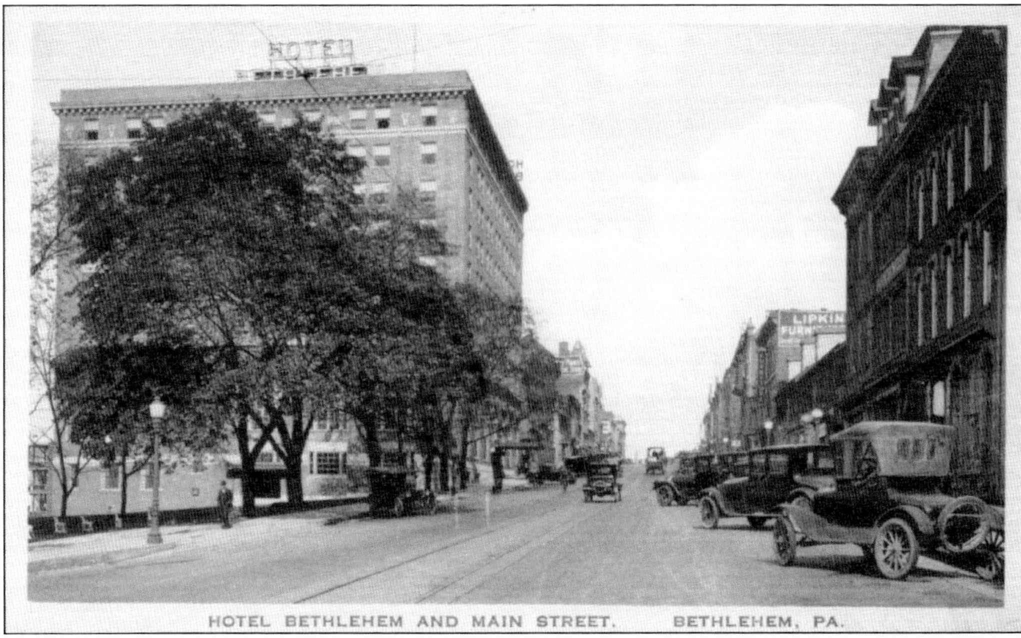

In this 1920s postcard, drivers have parked their cars on Main Street by backing in diagonally. Charles M. Schwab pushed to have a luxury hotel built in Bethlehem to accommodate visiting dignitaries to his company, Bethlehem Steel Corporation, the second-biggest steel maker in the United States. Community bonds were also sold to fund the construction of Hotel Bethlehem, built between 1921 and 1923 as the first luxury hotel in the Lehigh Valley.

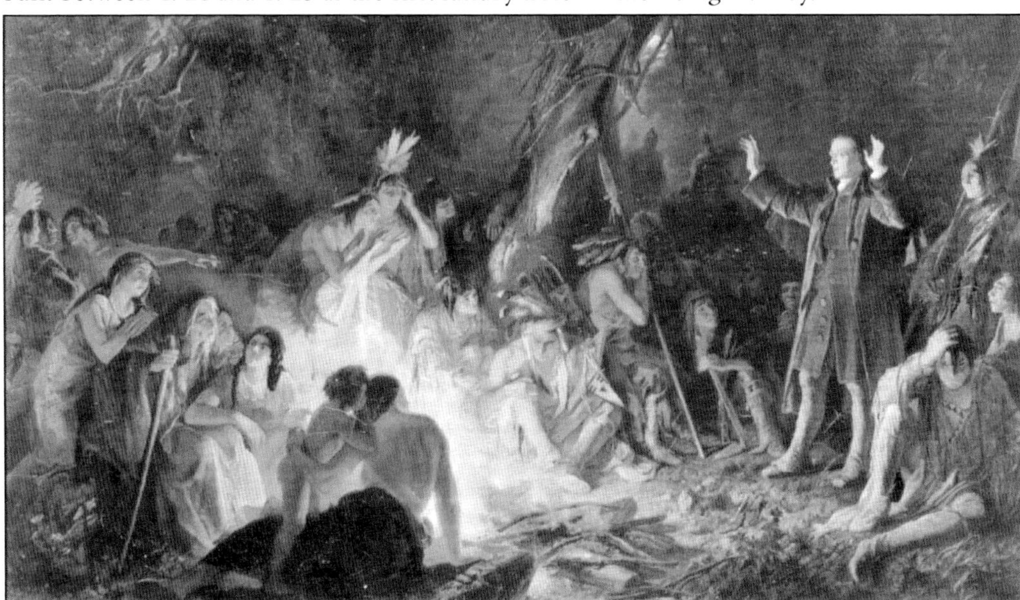

In 1862, C. Schussle painted *The Power of the Gospel.* It represents the Moravian missionary David Zeisberger preaching to the Munsee Indians in Goshgoshink in 1767. He stayed in their village, located on the Allegheny River above Oil City, Pennsylvania. He spent a period of 62 years as a missionary among Native Americans. This painting is held in the Moravian Archives of Bethlehem.

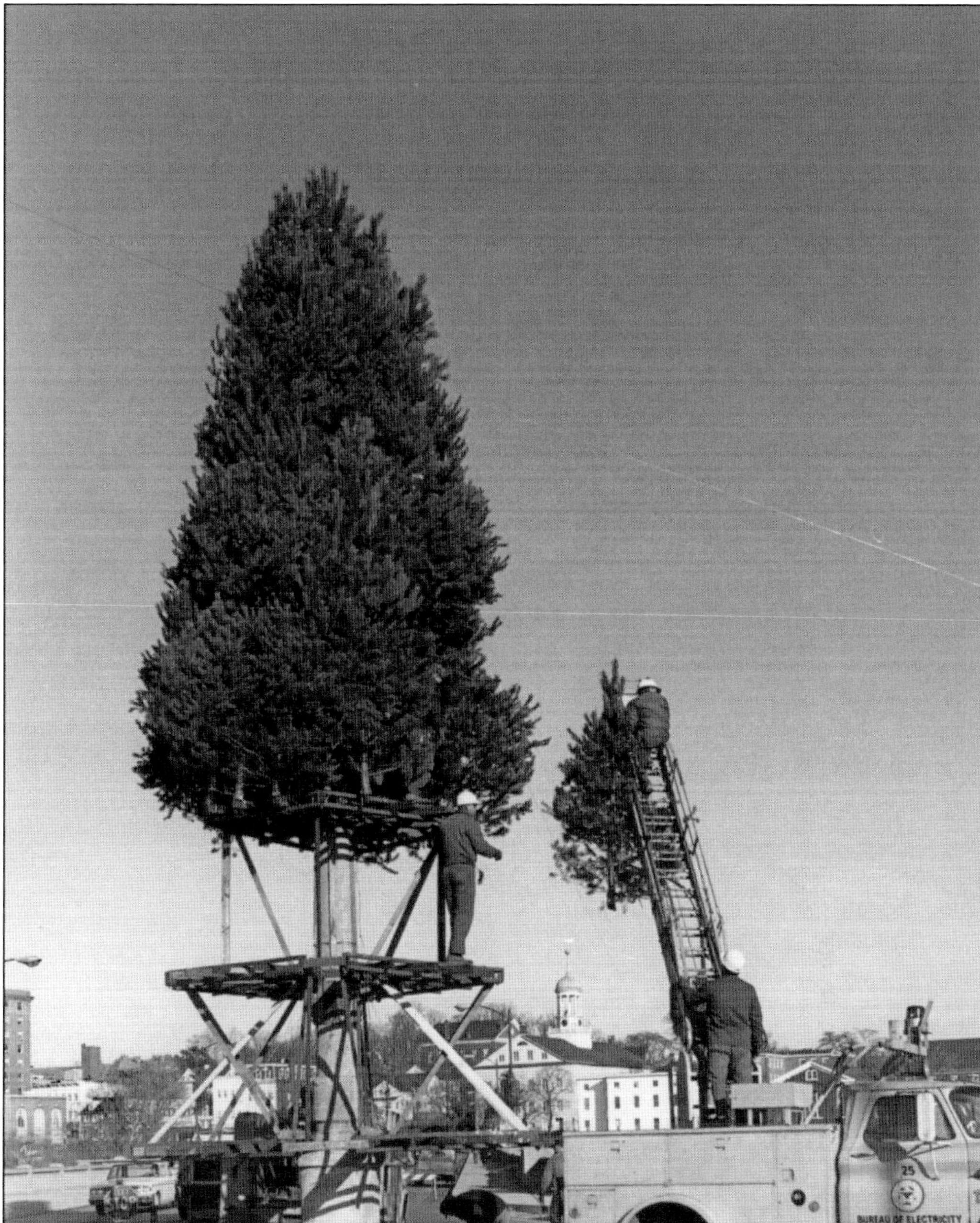

This 1970s photograph shows Bethlehem work crews erecting a giant Christmas tree made up of many smaller trees on the Hill-to-Hill Bridge. Today, a single large tree is placed on the bridge and another at city hall, and also each light pole along the main streets of Bethlehem is decorated with a small tree, requiring a total of 800 trees. It is believed that the first Christmas tree in America was introduced in Bethlehem. On Christmas Day, 1748, Moravian teachers built three-foot-high wooden pyramids for their students. They covered them with evergreen branches to represent Christmas trees. The pyramids were placed on tables and decorated with beeswax candles, cookies, hymn stanzas, and fruit.

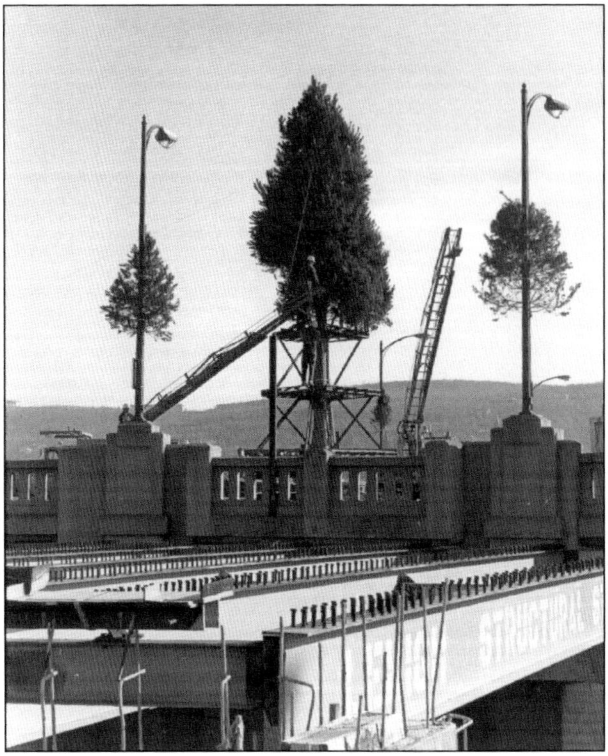

In the foreground is what is left of the central plaza on the Hill-to-Hill Bridge, removed in 1967. When the plaza was removed, Route 378 connected the bridge to Route 22. This bridge was listed in the National Register of Historic Places in 1972 and is a source of pride for Bethlehem residents.

This ramp on the Hill-to-Hill Bridge leads to the central plaza, where the giant Christmas tree is being constructed of smaller trees. This tree has become symbolic of the city's holiday tradition. Although the central plaza was removed in 1967, a tree still is placed on the bridge. Unfortunately over the years, a Grinch twice set the tree on fire.

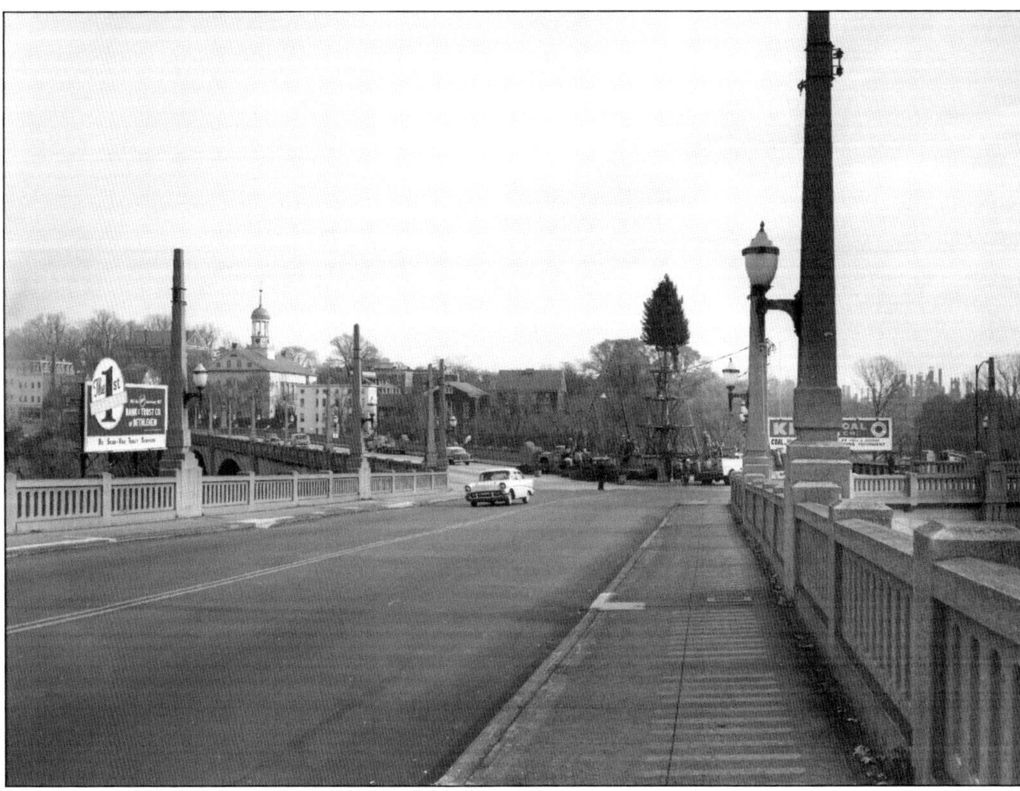

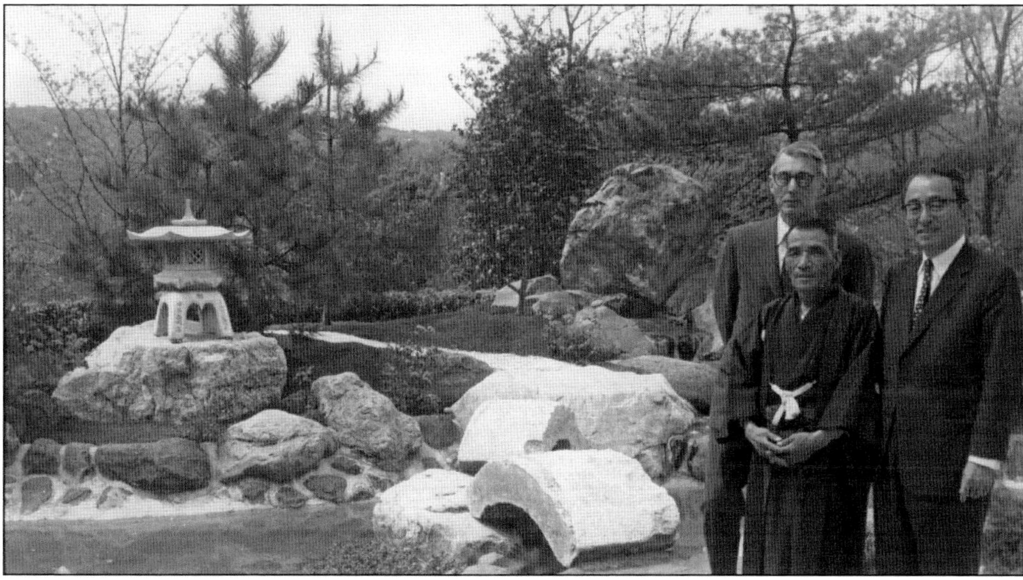

Attending the dedication ceremony in 1971 of the Serenity Garden, located just west of the Bethlehem Area Public Library, was the distinguished Tondabayashi architect Yoshinaga Sakon, on the far left. Through a friendship between Sakon and Mr. and Mrs. Laurence Fenninger of Bethlehem, Sakon was inspired to design the garden and tea house at his own expense. Today the garden is a popular place for tourists and weddings. The Bethlehem Tondabayashi Sister City relationship dates back to 1959, when Rev. Kenneth Heim began a cultural exchange program with the city.

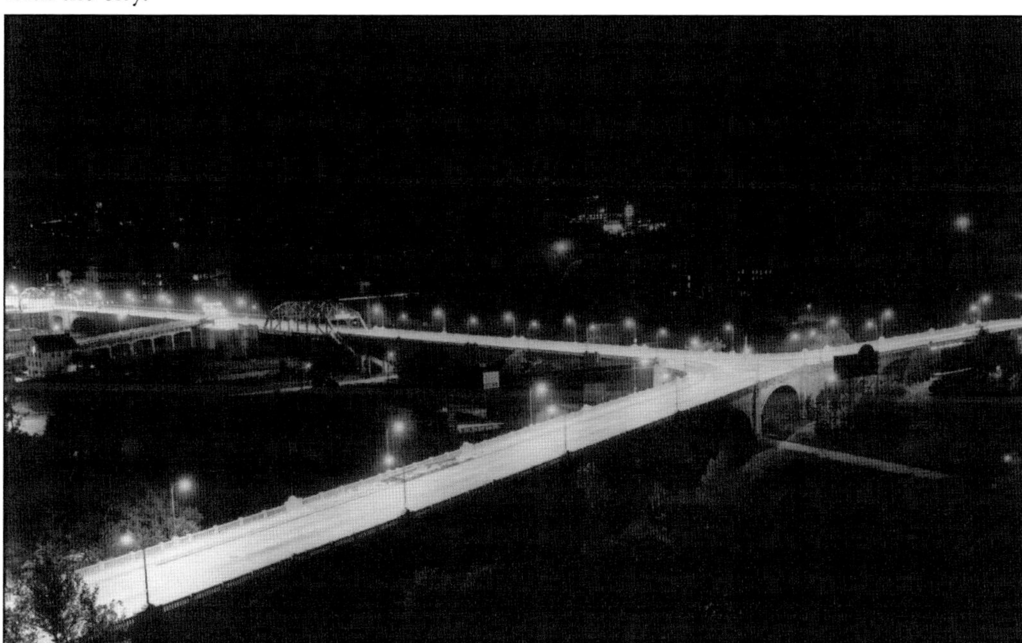

This nighttime photograph shows the Hill-to-Hill Bridge, built in 1924 for automobiles. The photograph is dated before 1967, when the bridge connected with Route 378. The four-lane bridge normally carries 25,000 cars across the Lehigh River daily.

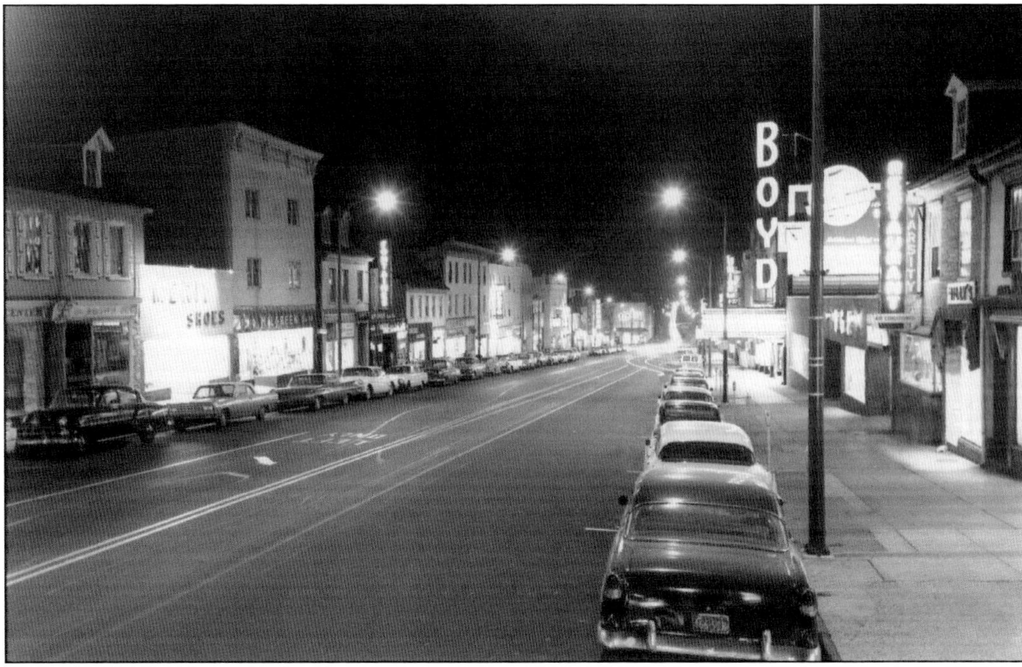

Here is another nighttime view of Broad Street but this time looking west. The Boyd Theater dominates the scene on the right. Across the street are Merit Shoes, H.L. Green Five and Dime, and Fontaine's Dry Goods (curtains and draperies).

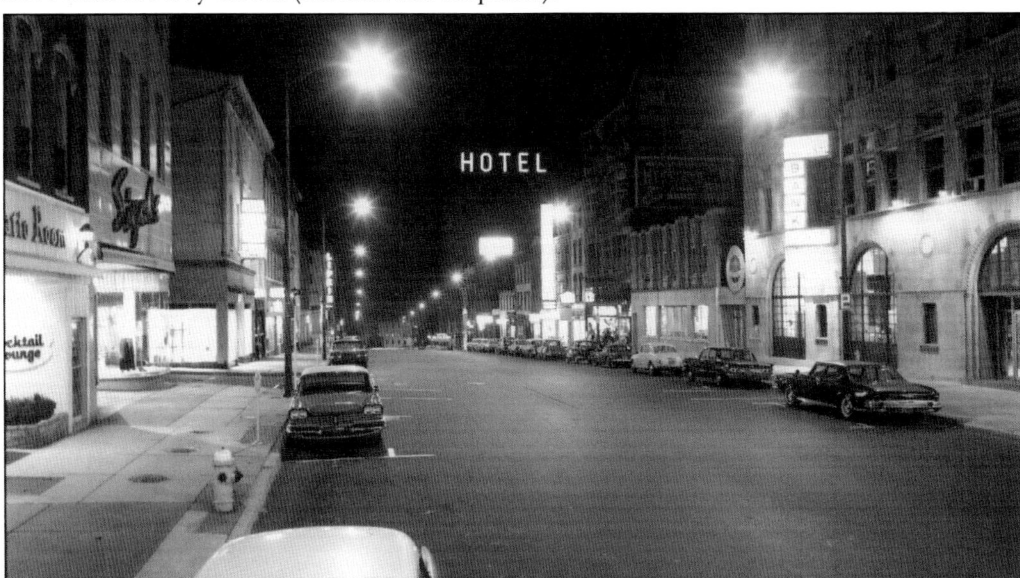

A nighttime view of Main Street shows on the far right the First National Bank and Trust Company. Across the street is Sigal's Women's Clothing Store. Farther down Main Street on the left is Lipkins Furniture Store. One cannot miss the Hotel Bethlehem sign in the distance. The sign on the south side of the hotel, not pictured, read, "Hotel Bethlehem;" this sign still exists today. In the past, Lehigh University students enjoyed turning off some of the letters to spell "HOT__ _ETHLE___."

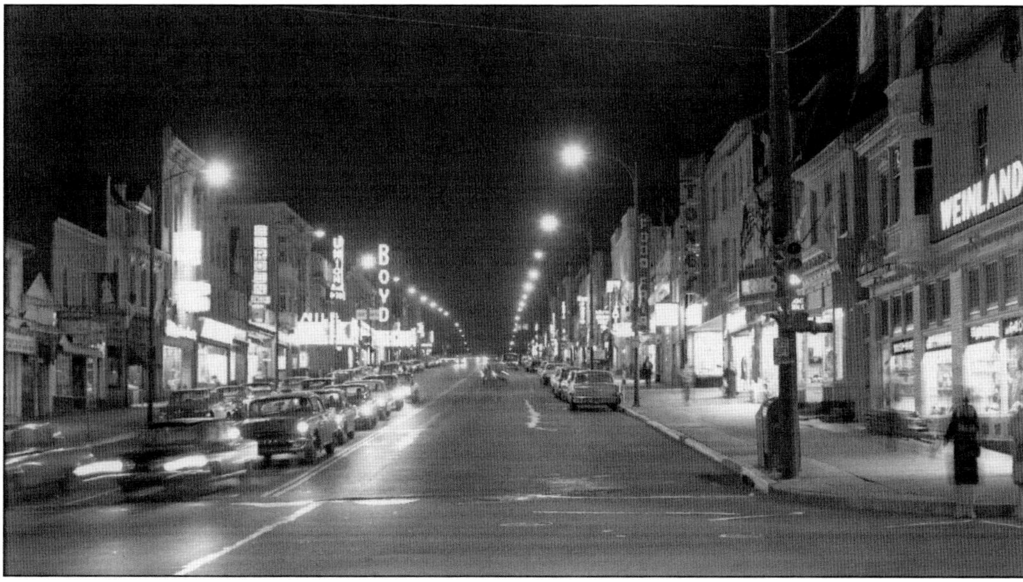

Here is a nighttime photograph of Broad Street, near the intersection of Main Street, looking east. This 1950s photograph shows a vibrant shopping district. The first mall in the Lehigh Valley, the Whitehall Mall, opened in 1966. The Lehigh Valley Mall followed in 1976. In the years following the 1950s, this stretch of Broad Street would suffer great economic hardship due to the malls. Recently, however, Bethlehem has experienced a population shift back to city living and shopping.

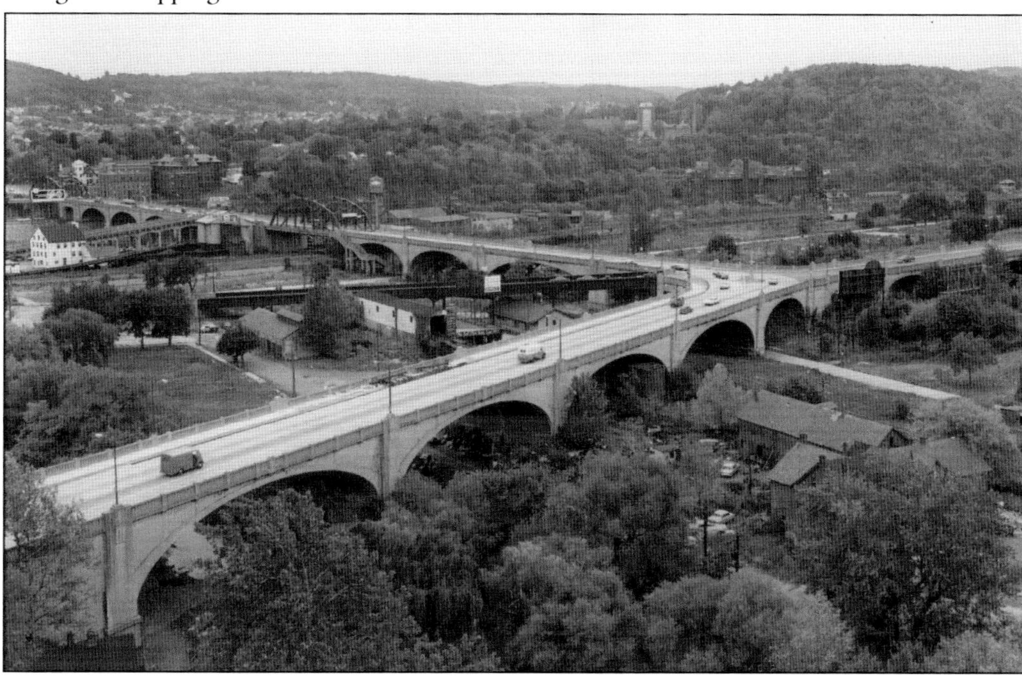

Here is a photograph of the Hill-to-Hill Bridge before it was connected to Route 378 in 1967. The section of the highway north of the bridge (not shown) is an expressway named the Fred B. Rooney Highway, which continues to the Route 22 interchange. South of the bridge, the highway narrows to a city street as it crosses through South Bethlehem.

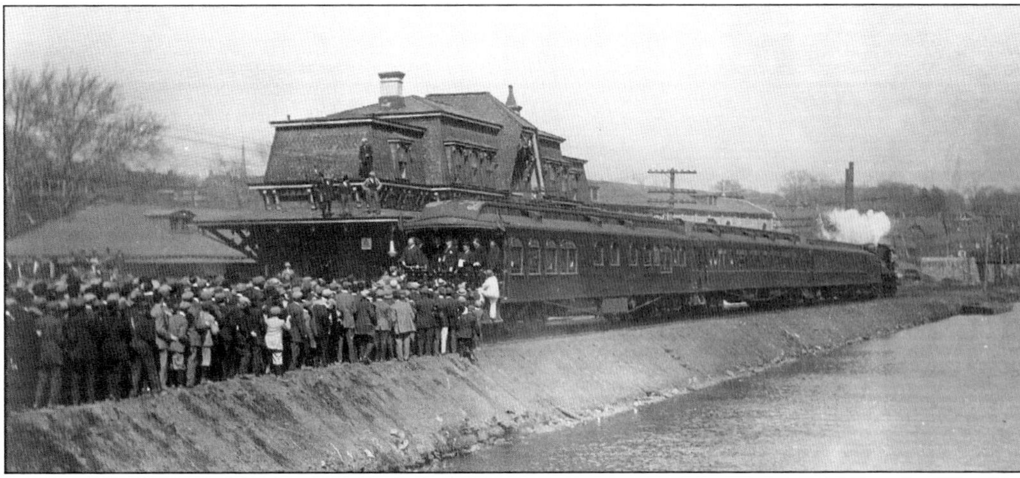

In August 1905, a great crowd had gathered to hear Pres. Theodore Roosevelt make a whistle stop at the Central Railroad of New Jersey Railroad Station on Lehigh Street. Roosevelt traveled extensively by rail across the country. This trip was on a special train that originated on the Eric Railroad in Jersey City, New Jersey. The Lehigh Canal is in the foreground.

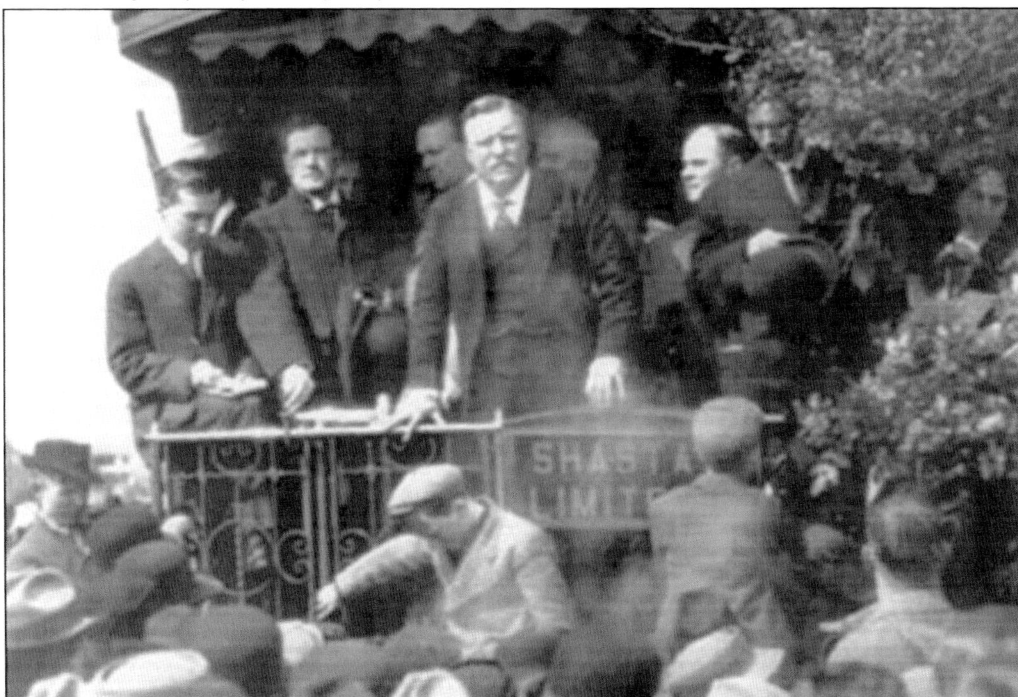

Pictured in August 1905 is Pres. Theodore Roosevelt at the Central Railroad of New Jersey Railroad Station on Lehigh Street. The president's private car was attached to the *Shasta Limited De Luxe*, a special train run by the Southern Pacific Railroad. He is shown here speaking from the rear of his car. For this trip, his car was described as "solid mahogany, velvet plush, and sinkingly-deep furniture. It had two sleeping chambers with brass bedsteads, two tiled bathrooms, a private kitchen run by the Pennsylvania Railroad's star chef, a dining room, a stateroom, with picture windows, and an airy rear platform for whistle-stop speeches."

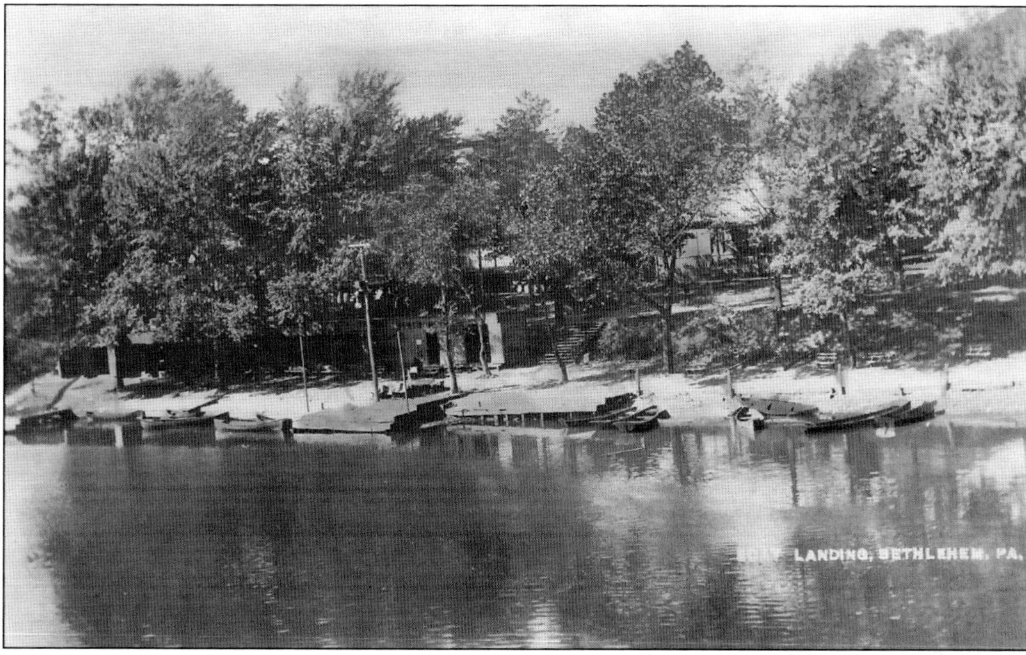

This is a rare early-1900s, hand-painted postcard of George Mack's Boat Landing, which was west of the old covered bridge on the northern bank. At his building near the dock, he rented boats that were used for paddling on the Lehigh River or to visit Calypso Island. Mack also rented sheds to store canoes, as it was popular at the time to own a canoe.

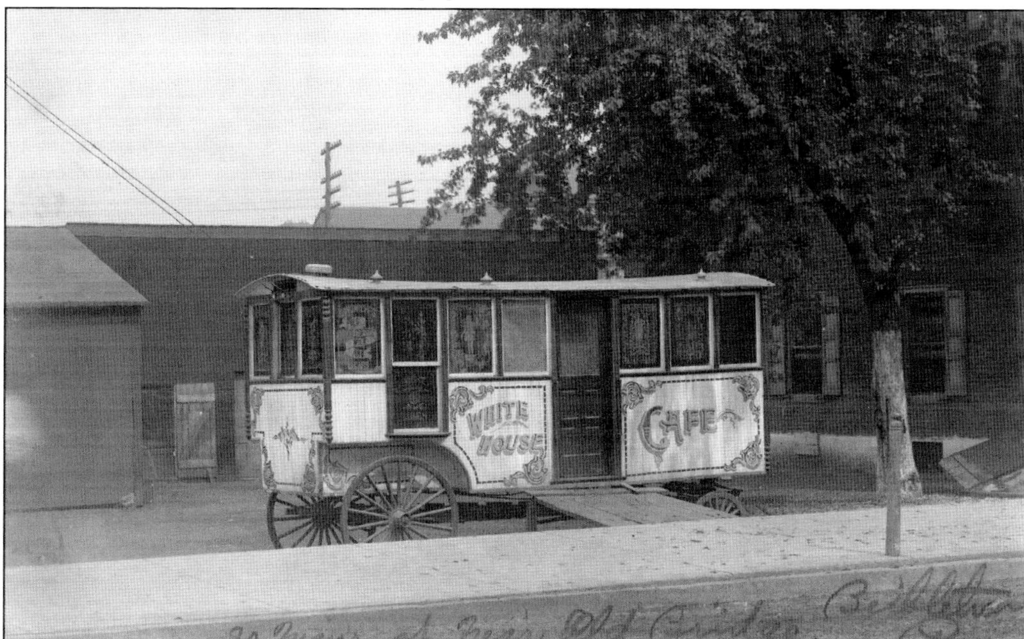

White House Café was a popular lunch wagon located on South Main Street near the old covered bridge. It offered sandwiches, pies, coffee, milk, and cigars to appeal to the laborers employed by the manufacturers on Sand Island, such as the Pettinos Brothers Graphite Factory and Bethlehem Fabricators.

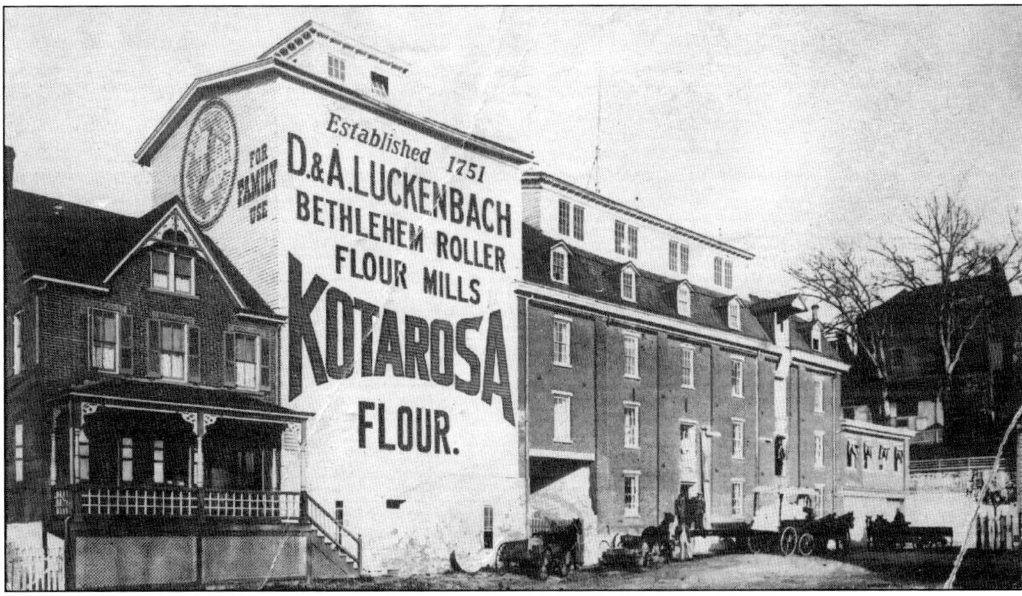

After the Monocacy Creek overflowed in 1747, damaging the first Moravian gristmill, and then a fire destroyed the next mill in 1869, this mill was built on the same foundation within nine months. In 1877, both steam-powered and two Leffel turbine wheels were added. In 1882, the millstones were replaced by the Allis roller system. In 1884, the Lehigh & Susquehanna Division of the Central Railroad of New Jersey built a siding to the mill, which greatly increased distribution of Luckenbach flour.

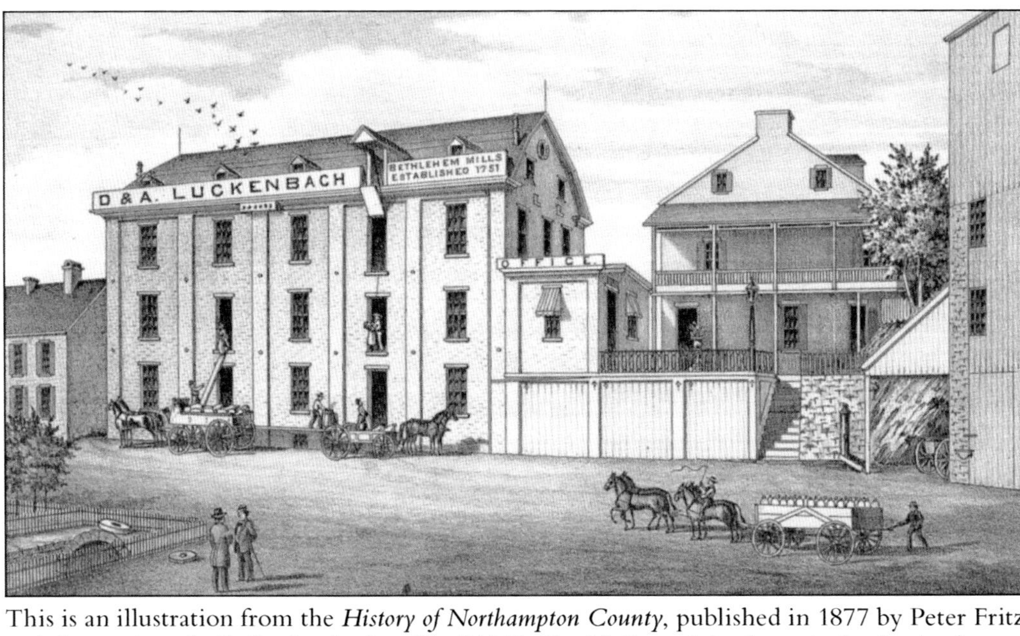

This is an illustration from the *History of Northampton County*, published in 1877 by Peter Fritz, and shows the rebuilt Luckenbach mill of 1869. David O. and Andrew A. Luckenbach were brothers and in the milling business for 42 years together. In 1869, David and Andrew purchased the mill from their father, Charles A. Luckenbach, for $17,000. After their deaths, the mill was left to David's sons, Horace, Robert, and Paul. The mill was the first in the country to mill oats and still stands today.

Far in the background is Flory's Mill, previously known as the Luckenbach Mill, which last operated as a mill in 1951. In 1952, the mill and property were sold to Isaac Kaplin and Abe Glaser, who utilized the property for their car parts dealership. In 1963, Glaser and Kaplin sold the mill to the Redevelopment Authority of Bethlehem for one dollar under the stipulation that the property be used as a park. In 1966, Historic Bethlehem, Inc., leased the mill from the City of Bethlehem for a period of 99 years. It completed the restoration of Luckenbach Mill in 1982.

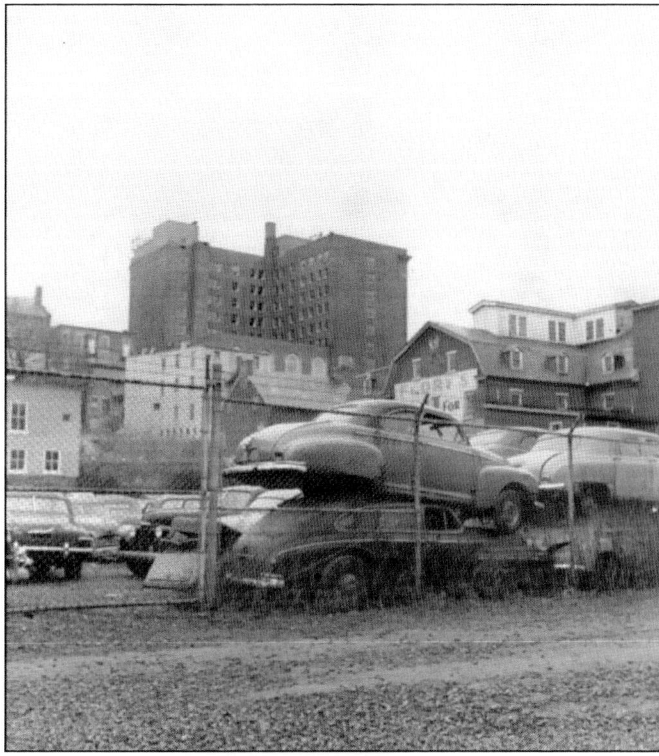

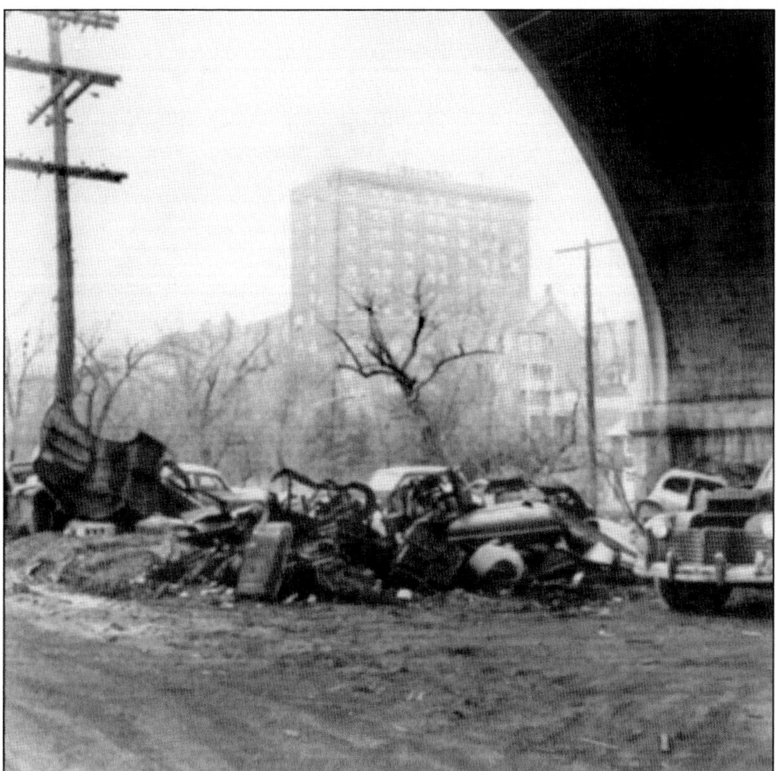

The junk cars from Isaac Kaplin and Abe Glaser's car parts business at the old Luckenbach Mill seemed to be overflowing under the Main Street ramp of the Hill-to-Hill Bridge. In 1963, Kaplin and Glaser generously donated this property to the city when Historic Bethlehem, Inc., developed a plan to bring back the Colonial Industrial Quarter, where the Moravian settlers established a wide variety of industries.

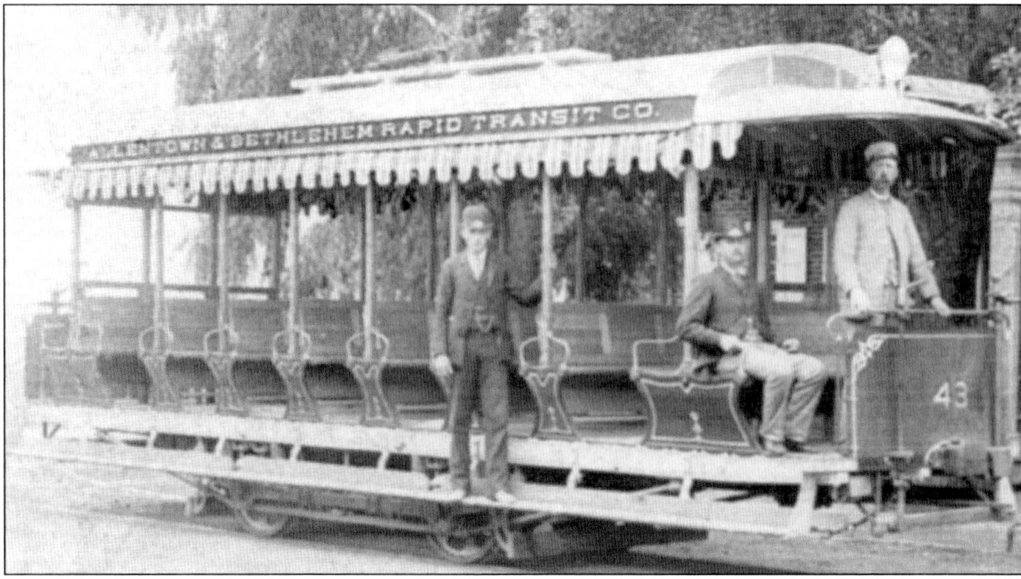

When trolley cars in the Lehigh Valley switched from horse-drawn power to electrical power in 1891, Allentown & Bethlehem Rapid Transit Company was gobbled up, as well as several other local trolley companies, by Albert L. Johnson to create the Lehigh Valley Traction Company. The trolley shown here provided service in Allentown along Hamilton Street, Hanover Avenue in Rittersville, and Bethlehem at Broad and New Streets. The company built a central park in 1892 and a horse race track in 1893, both in Rittersville.

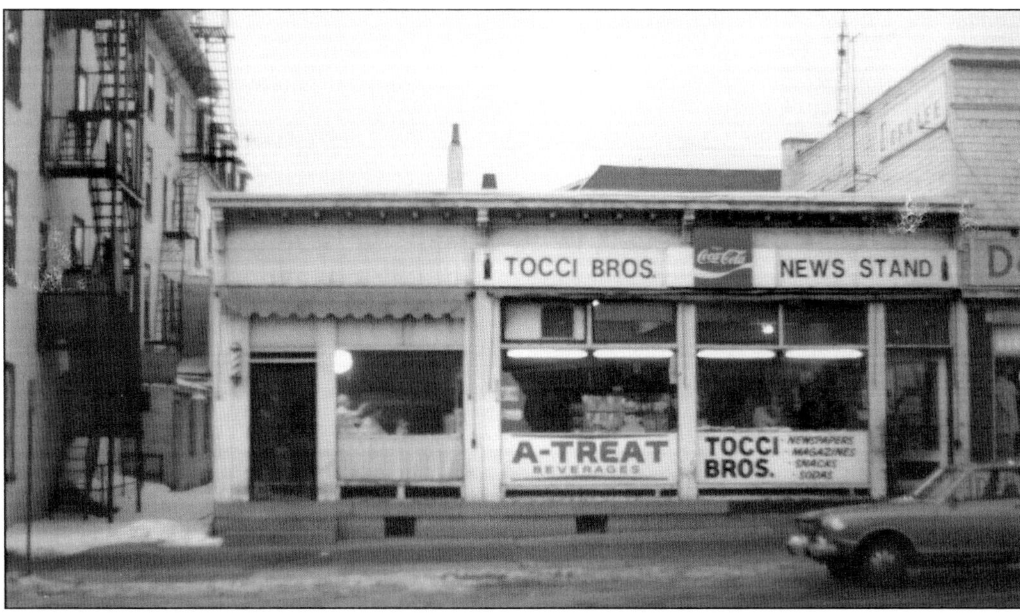

Tocci Brothers News Stand was located at 9 East Broad Street, next to the American Hotel. Salvatore Tocci opened the stand in 1929, and it became the place to hang out for local gossip. Two of his sons, Sal and Richard, continued the business after Salvatore passed away in 1960. If Tocci Brothers News Stand could not locate a newspaper or magazine, it was not to be found in the Lehigh Valley. In 1984, the business closed. The building was demolished and replaced by a parking lot.

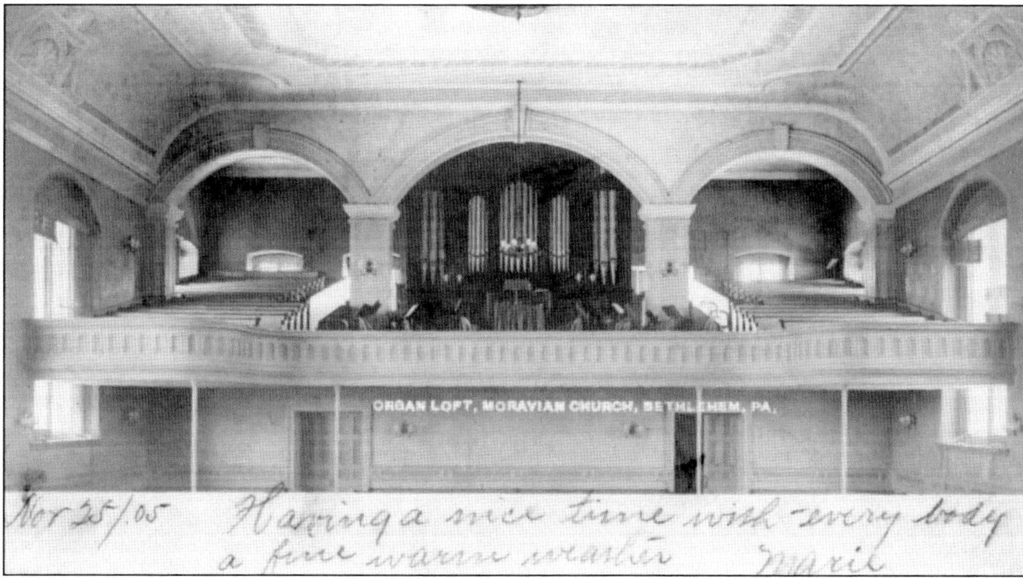

David Tannenberg, the first professional organ builder trained in North America, was commissioned to build the organ for the Central Moravian Church. His plans required the church's roof to be raised four feet higher than called for by the architect. Although Tannenberg died before he could build the organ, the roof was raised to his specifications. Shown here is a George Jardine & Son organ, installed in 1873.

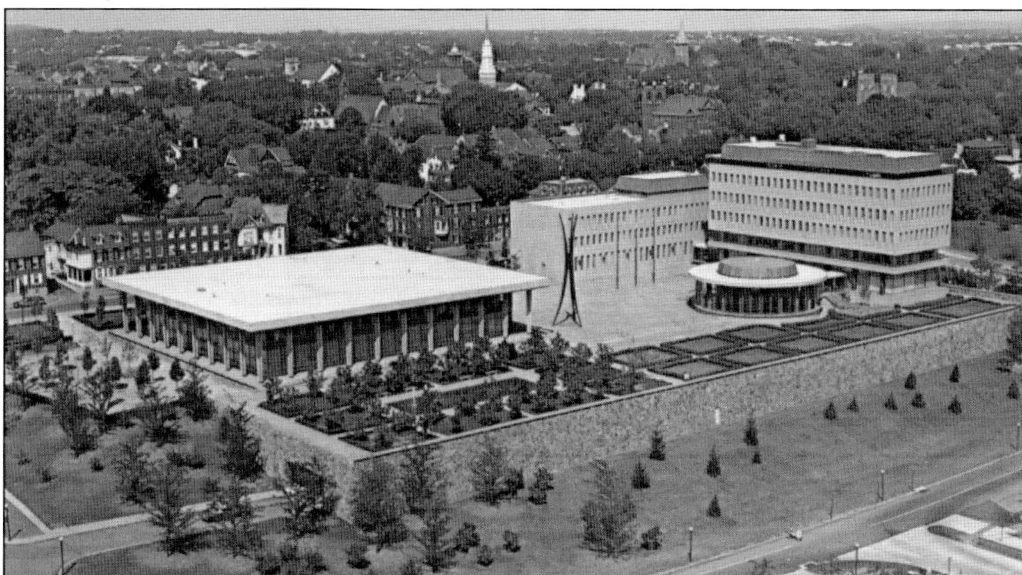

Here is the Bethlehem City Center, which includes city hall, the Bethlehem Police Department, the Bethlehem Area Public Library, and the circular town hall for public meetings. The center was built in 1967. A large Chinook helicopter flew in the 60-foot, 11,000-pound steel sculpture seen in the center of the courtyard. Joseph J. Greenberg Jr. of Philadelphia created the sculpture, titled *Symbol of Progress*. The sculpture consists of three tapered steel arcs that symbolize the various ethnic groups that have formed the city of Bethlehem and the strength in unity of all the people of Bethlehem.

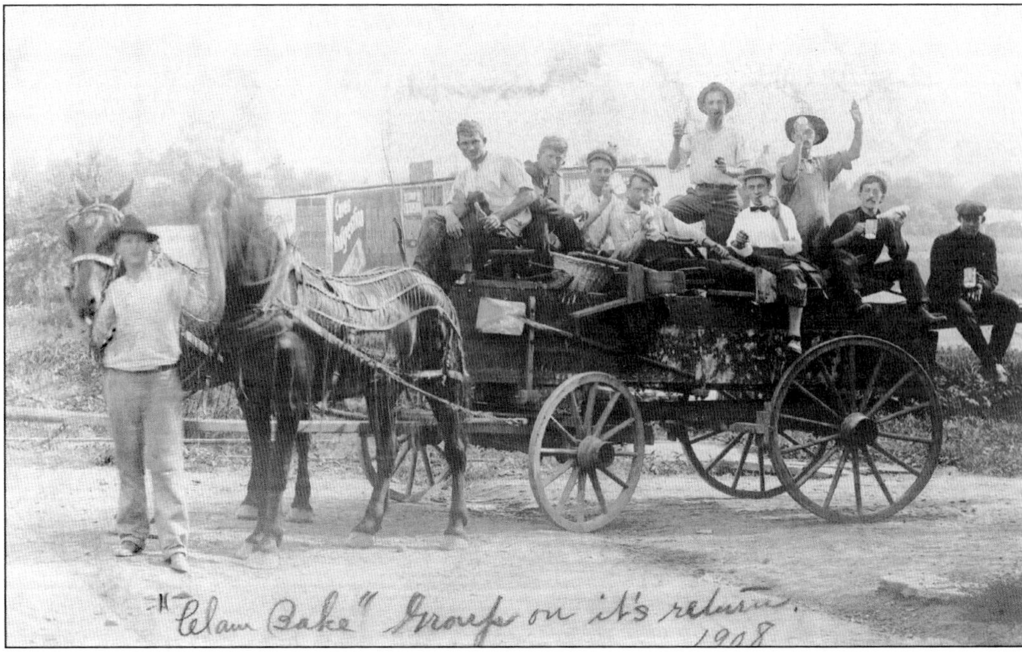

This jovial group of men is returning from a clambake in 1908. They are toasting the photographer with bottles and mugs of beer. A fortuitously placed advertising sign in the background recommends that Adams Pepsin Chewing Gum will cure indigestion. The mode of transportation looks uncomfortable and was not meant for passengers.

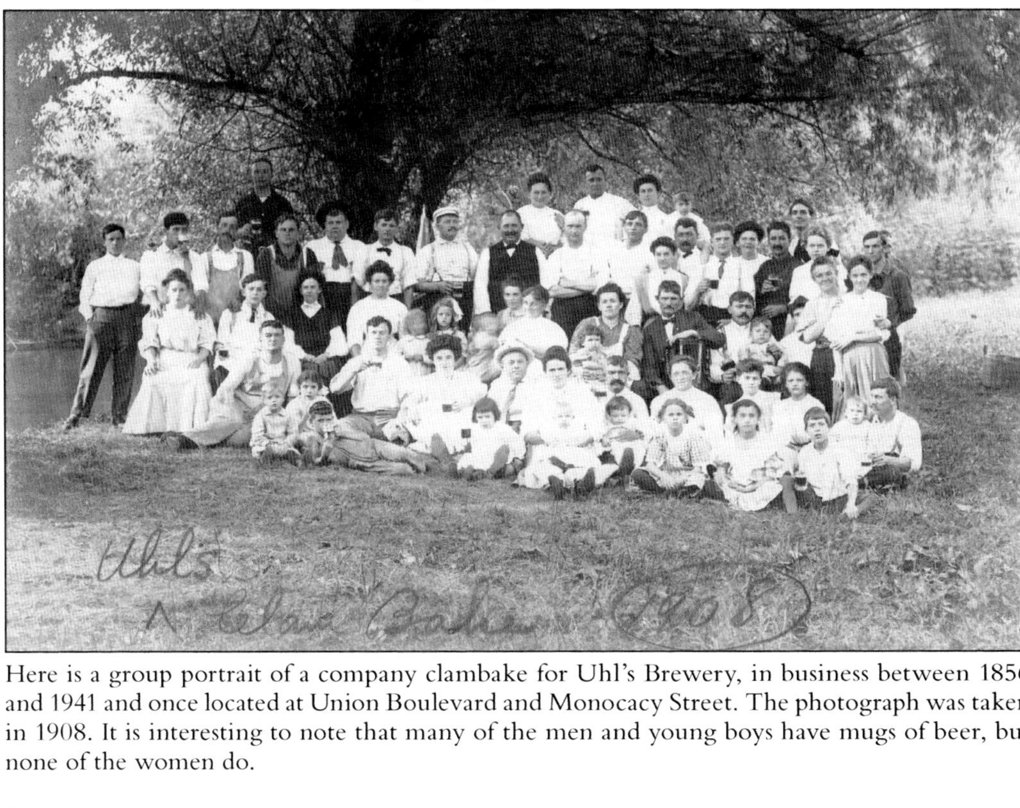

Here is a group portrait of a company clambake for Uhl's Brewery, in business between 1856 and 1941 and once located at Union Boulevard and Monocacy Street. The photograph was taken in 1908. It is interesting to note that many of the men and young boys have mugs of beer, but none of the women do.

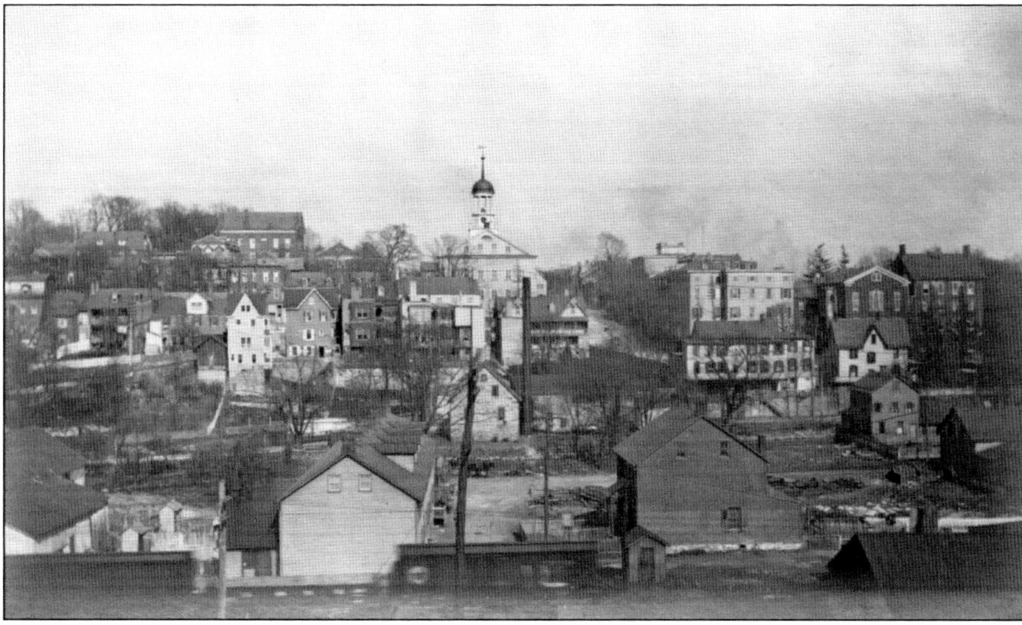

The building of the Lehigh Canal in the 1830s, followed by the railroads in the 1850s, encouraged the growth of the businesses seen in the foreground of this early-1900s postcard. The high density of buildings in this floodplain of the Monocacy Creek would prove problematic. Today the city prohibits new structures in the area.

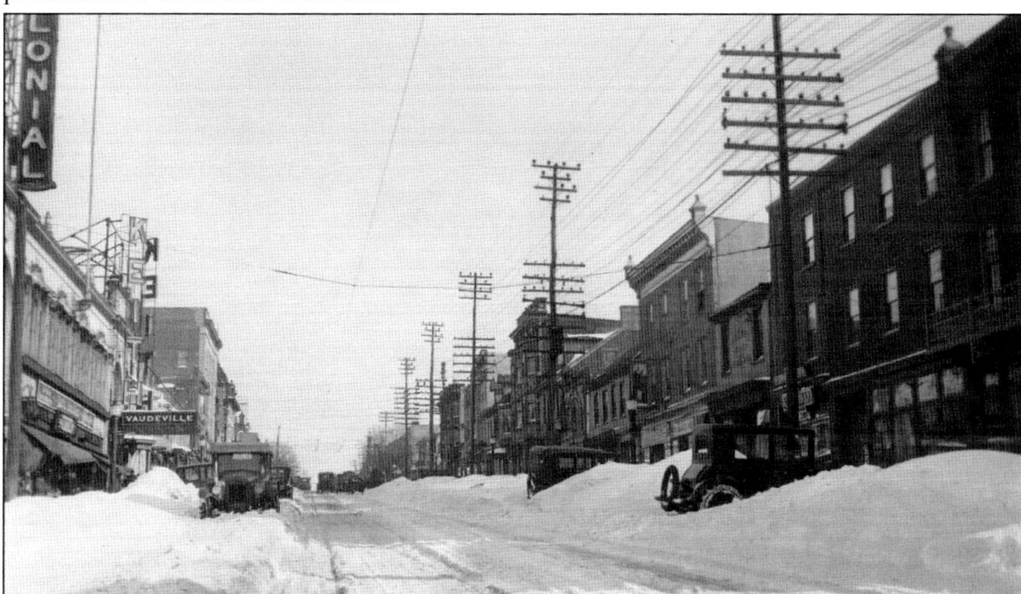

The newspapers were filled with hardship stories in January 1925. During that month, Bethlehem would endure three major snowstorms. An Arctic air mass had settled in the region, and then a nor'easter moved up the coast. Snowfall records were smashed, and automobiles were useless. This is Broad Street looking east between Guetter and New Streets. The Colonial Theatre is on the left and offered the Keith Vaudeville circuit performers. A continuous variety show ran from 10:00 in the morning until 11:00 at night every day.

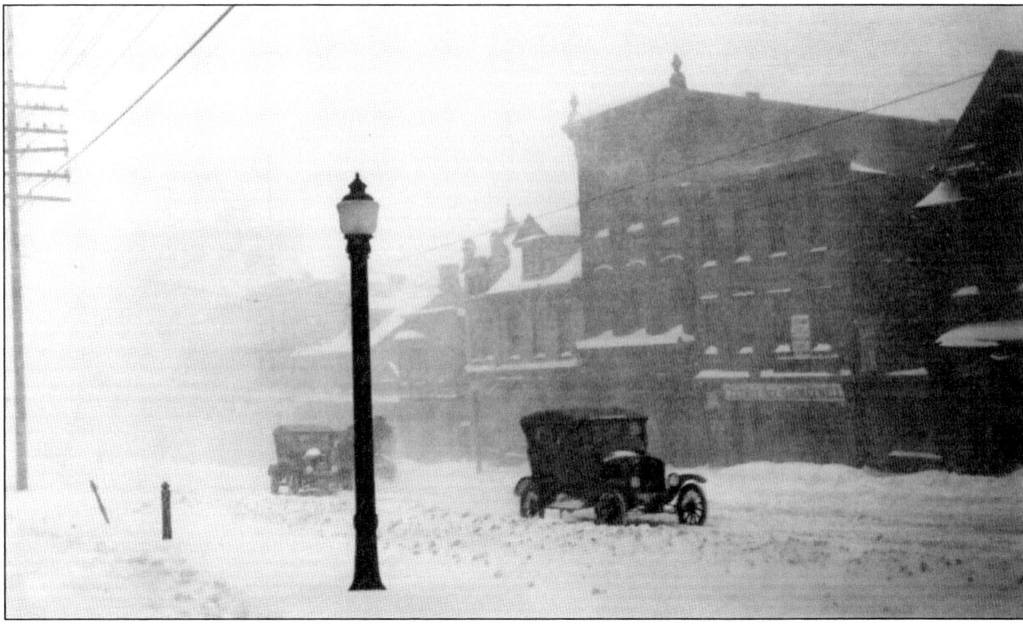

Trolley cars going down Broad Street encountered snow packed so tightly along the lines that they could not make electrical connections and were stranded without power. This photograph was taken on Broad Street between Main Street and New Street.

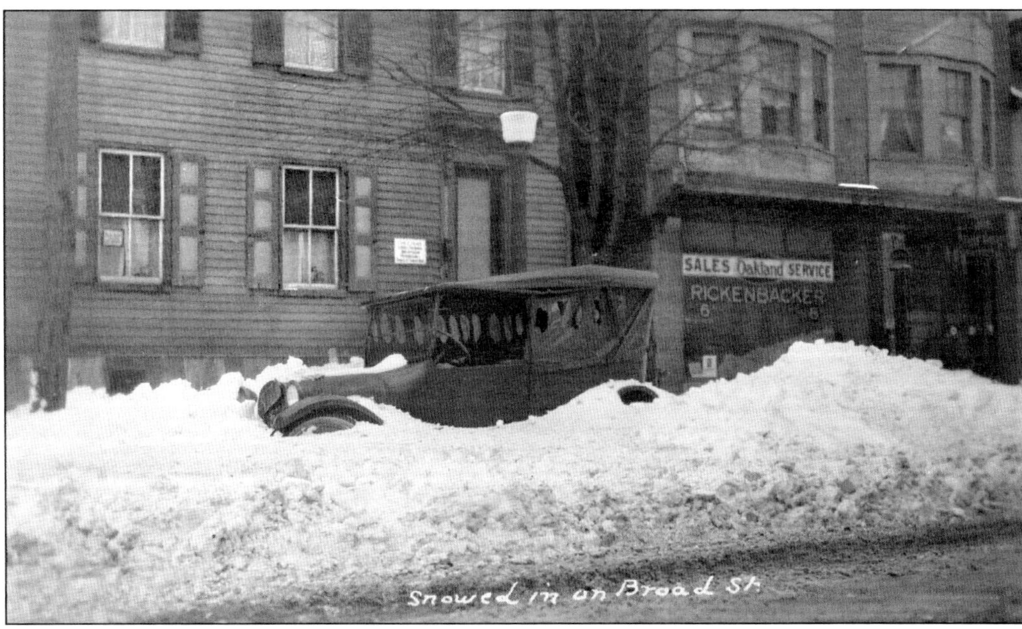

This 1920s automobile is not going anywhere soon. Caught in a snowbank on Broad Street, it probably took the owner several hours of shoveling to free it. The building just behind the car has a sign for Oakland automobiles, which were manufactured between 1909 and 1931 by the Oakland Motors Division of General Motors Corporation.

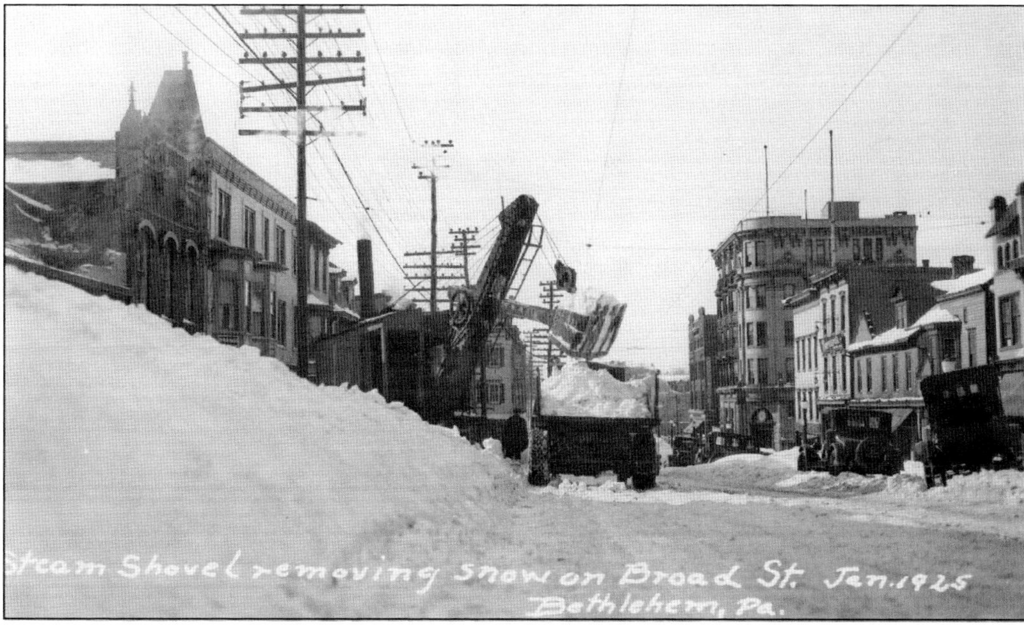

In January 1925, the city needed to contract with someone who had the equipment to move the abundance of snow out of the way. The steam shovel is loading the snow in a dump truck to remove it from Broad Street, one of the busier streets in the city. Looking past the intersection of Main Street, on the right, is the Bethlehem Trust Building and Beck-Wilhelm Decorating Company.

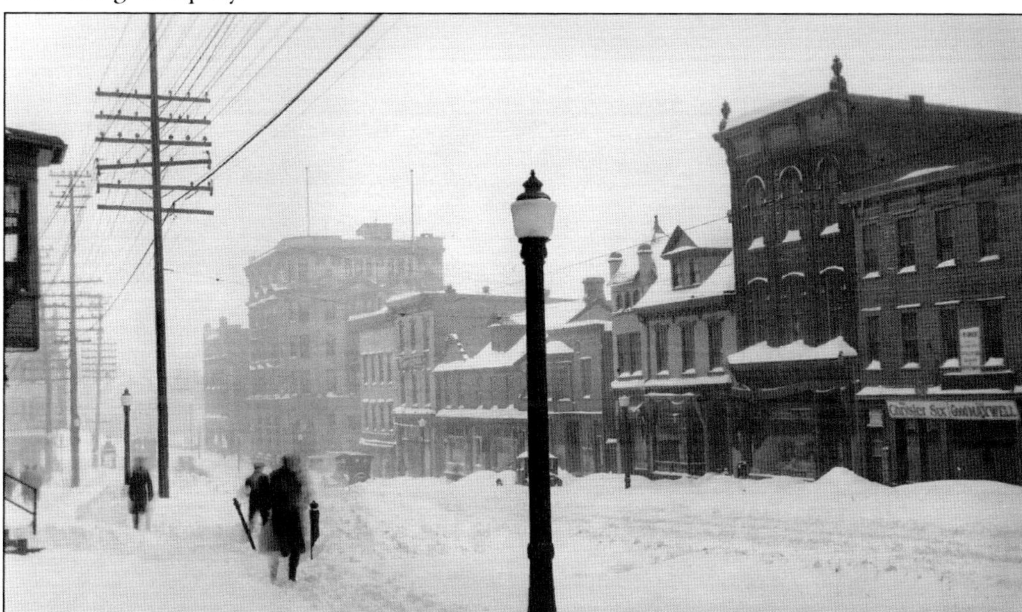

On the far right, a Maxwell car dealership features the Chrysler Six cars, which were built in 1925. These first Chrysler cars had a revolutionary new six-cylinder, high-compression engine with a seven-bearing crankshaft, carburetor air cleaner, and replaceable oil filter. On this snowy day on Broad Street, between Main Street and New Street, the Bethlehem Trust Company is the large building down the block on the right side of the street.

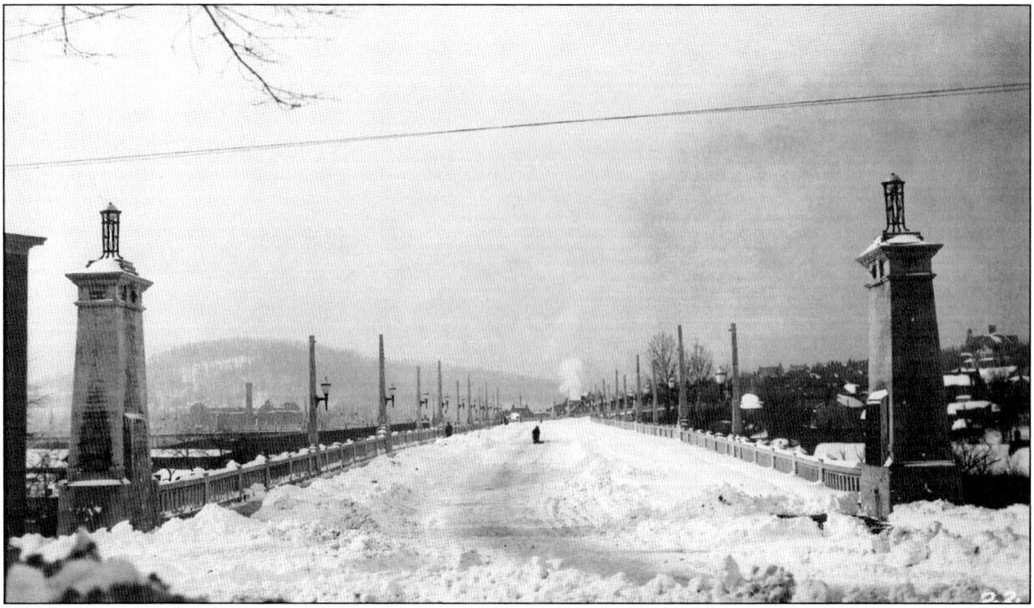

After this snowstorm, the only sure way to cross the Hill-to-Hill Bridge was to walk across it. This is the entrance off of Main Street, and it was quite a long walk. The bridge is 6,055 feet long and was one of the largest concrete bridges in the world when it was completed in 1924.

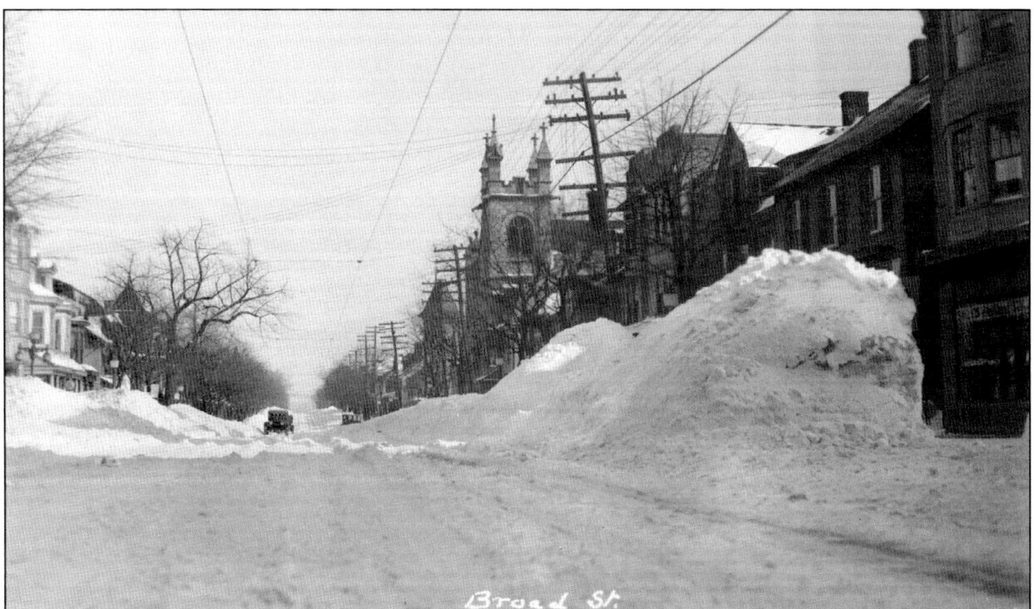

On the right, one can barely see Grace Lutheran Church on East Broad Street behind the snowbanks. The church is located near School Street and, as of 2014, is known as Grace Deliverance Baptist Church. The Model Ts traveling up Broad Street do not have much of a chance of getting through.

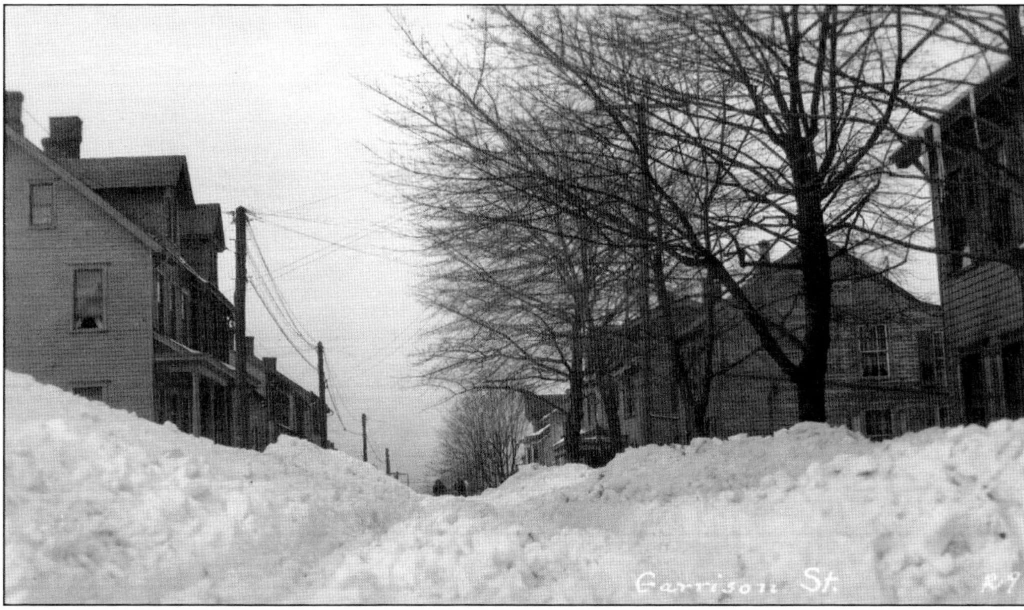

Here is a view of East Garrison Street after a major snowstorm. The residential street traveled east to west across the heart of Bethlehem. An early Bethlehem public school was located at Center and Garrison Streets in 1866. The street was named for Capt. Nicholas Garrison, who crossed the Atlantic Ocean 23 times on the ship *Irene* to transport Moravians to America.

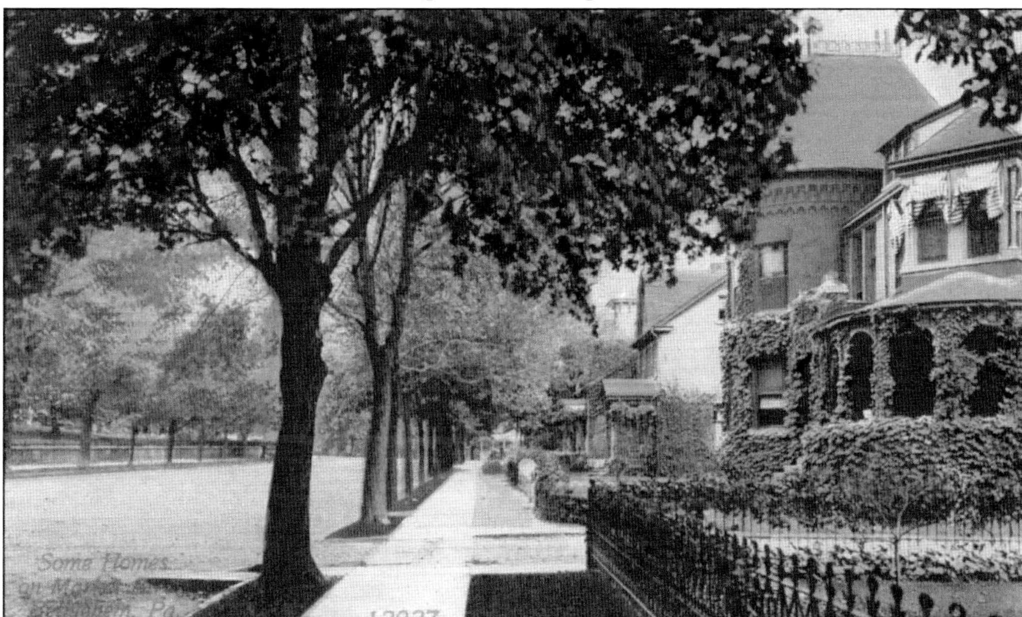

This is a view of the luxurious homes on Market Street. Truman M. Dodson's home is on the far right; it is an immense brick home. Although the street was primarily residential, it received its name for being the location of the first general store in the Lehigh Valley. The Moravians called the store "Strangers' Store," as it was a place designed to sell to people outside the Moravian community. At the time this photograph was taken in the early 1900s, many of the Market Street houses were rented out to Lehigh University fraternities.

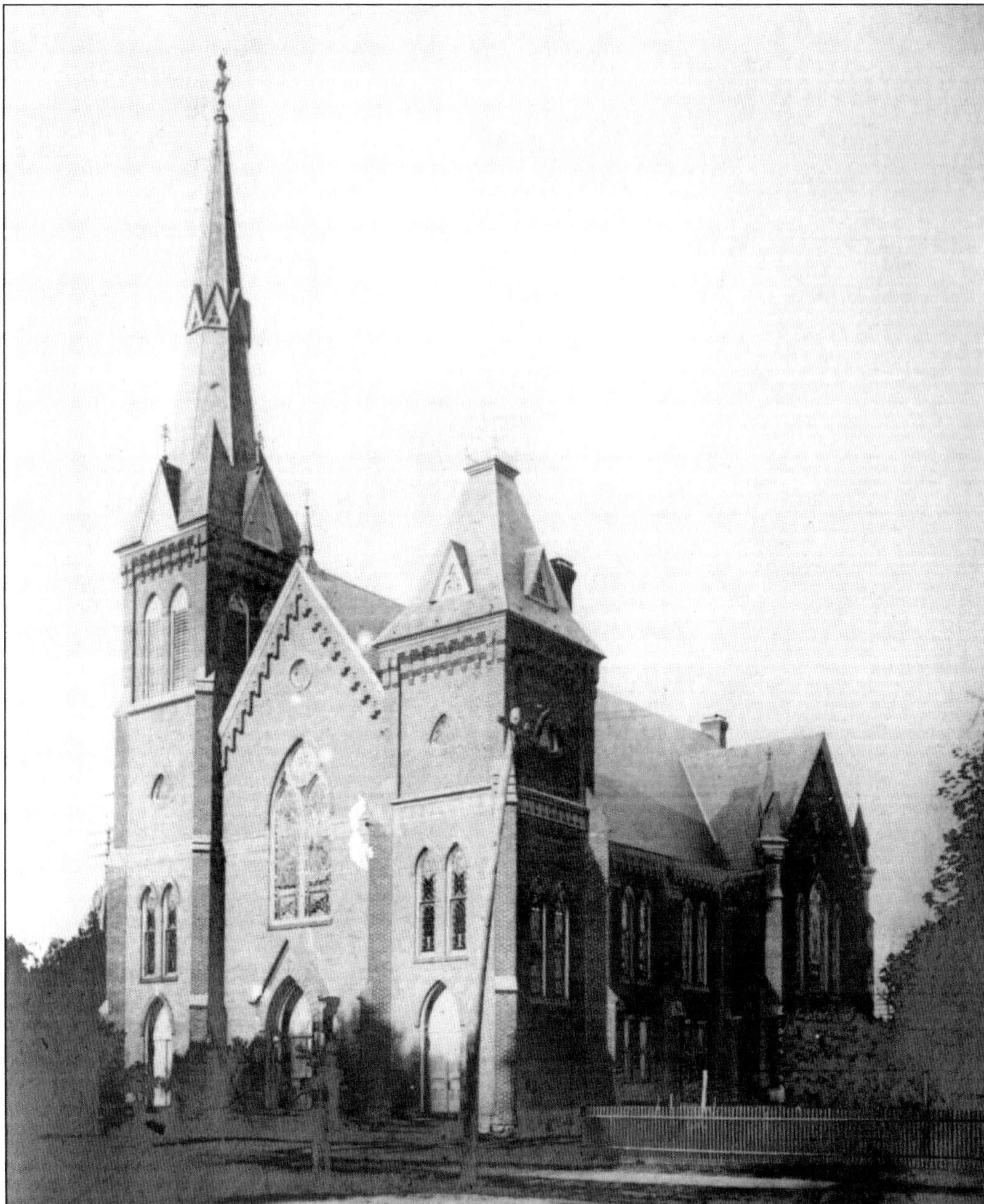

Salem Lutheran Church was founded in 1850 as the first united church for Reformed and Lutheran faiths in Bethlehem. It was located on property purchased from Philip H. Goepp on the west side of High Street near Broad Street. In 1868, the two congregations decided to separate. The church building went to the highest bidder, the Lutherans, for $9,700.

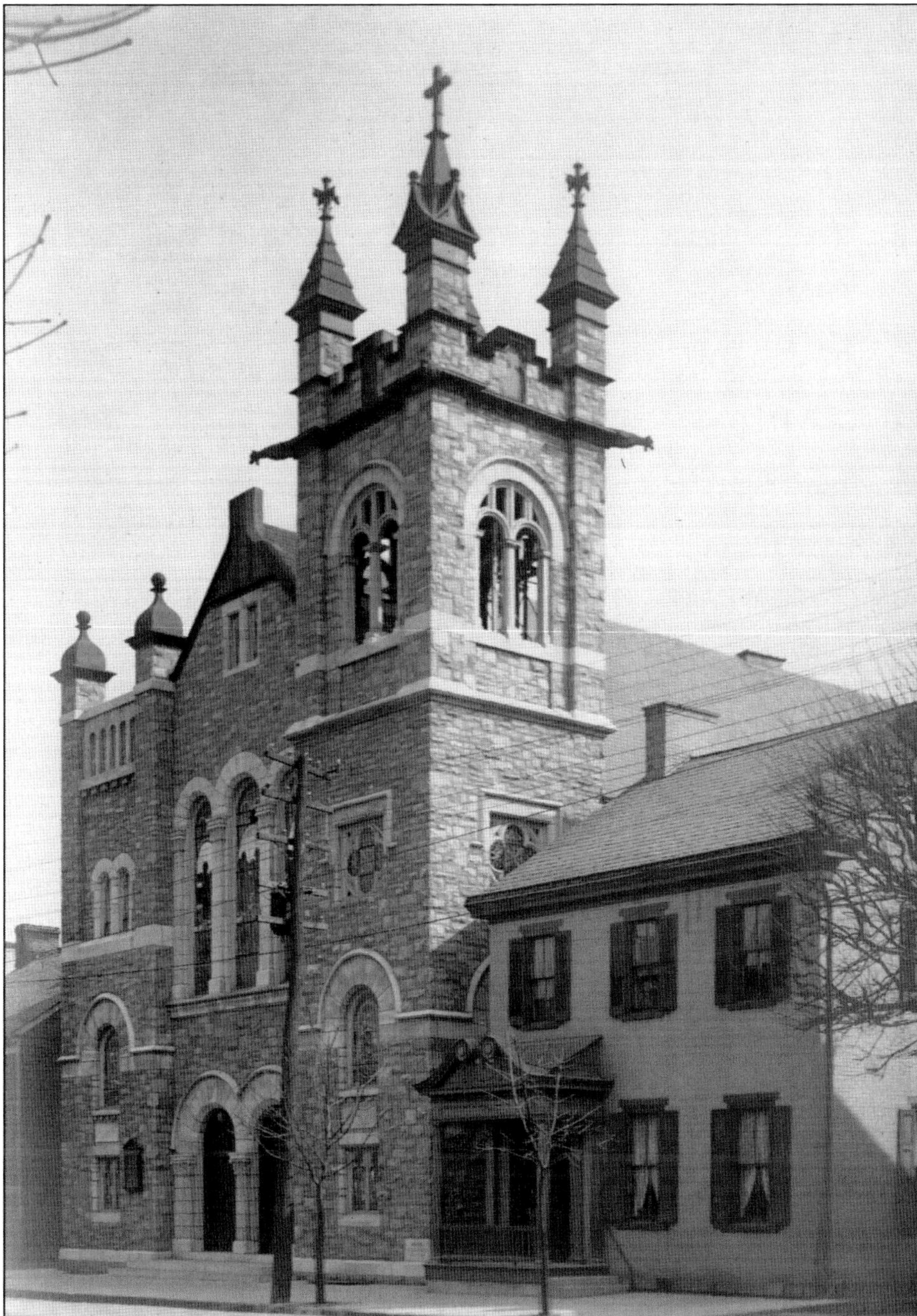

Grace Evangelical Lutheran Church was the first English Lutheran church organized outside of Easton in Northampton County. The Salem Church members raised $10,000 for the construction of Grace English Evangelical Lutheran Church. A property at Broad and Center Streets was purchased for $3,000 in 1872. The cornerstone was laid on August 25, 1872. The new church was formally organized on Reformation Day, October 31, 1872, with 88 members. Bethlehem photographer G.A. Conradi took this photograph.

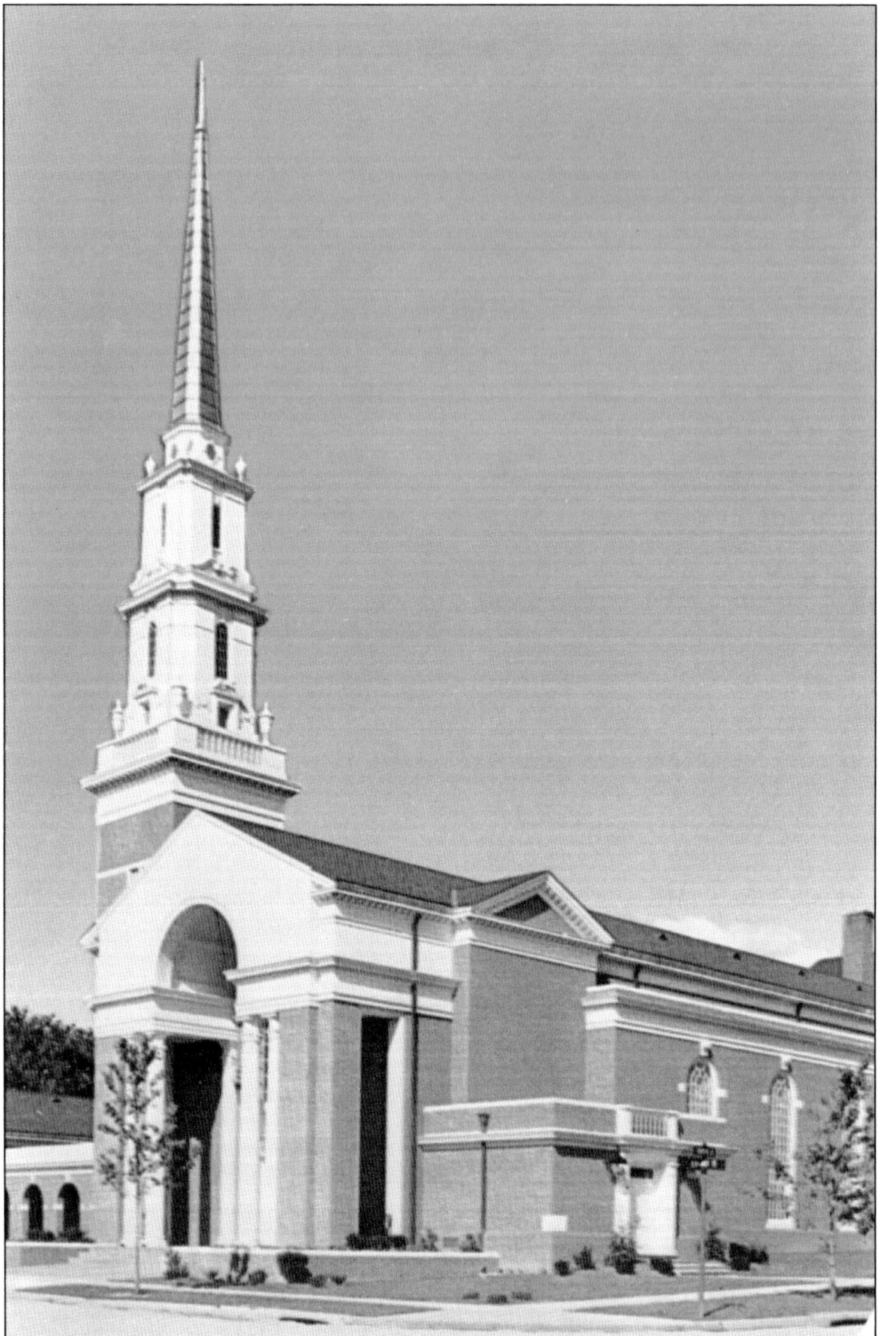

Christ Evangelical and Reformed Church purchased property at the corner of Center and Wall Streets in 1868. It shared this property with the home of John Fritz, which was demolished to make room for the expanded church that today faces Market Street. With mergers at the national level in 1957, the church became known as Christ Church, United Church of Christ. Rev. Gustave A. Schwedes was the first pastor of the new church. He was known as a great speaker in German or English. Shown here is the new church, built at the same location in 1959 and facing Center and Market Streets; it later became Christ United Church of Christ.

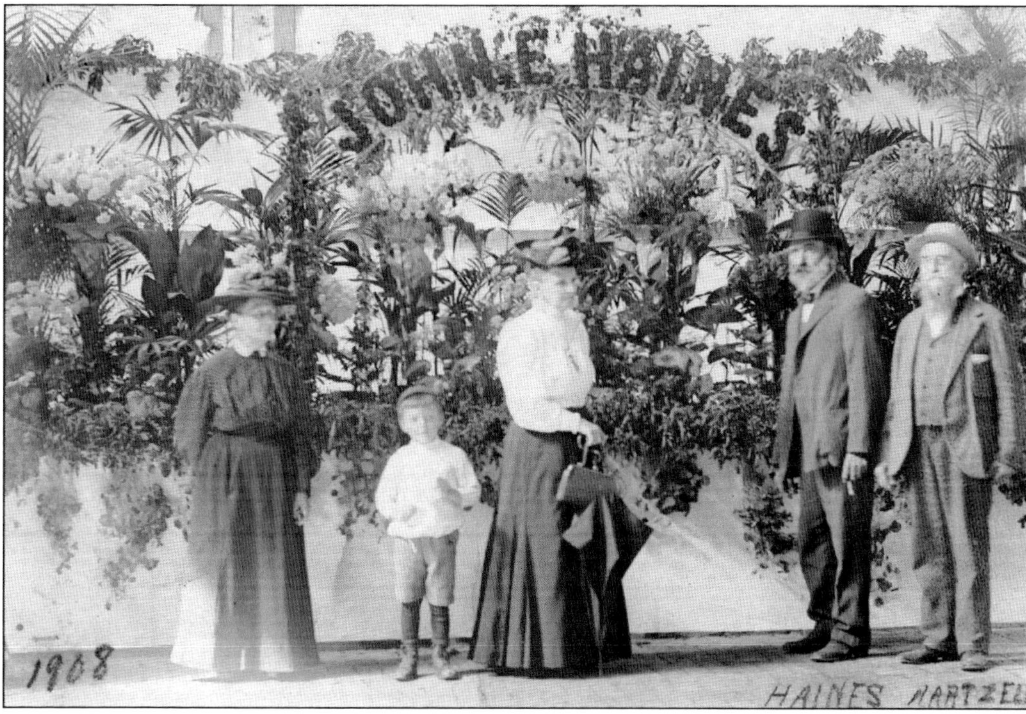

Pictured above, John E. Haines of Bethlehem, second from the right, stands in front of his display at the 1908 National Flower Show at the Coliseum in Chicago, Illinois. It was the first national flower show in the United States and awarded 200 medals for the most beautiful blooms. The huge coliseum was described as a veritable paradise of waving beauty. At the time, flower competitions were considered a hobby for only the wealthiest Americans. The postcard below shows Emma S. Barron, on the left, who was married to Clinton L. Barron of Barron and Cruickshank Booksellers on Broad Street, Bethlehem, visiting the same 1908 flower show. It took two days to travel from Bethlehem to Chicago by train. Emma S. Barron and her friends surely were eager to attend the first national flower show.

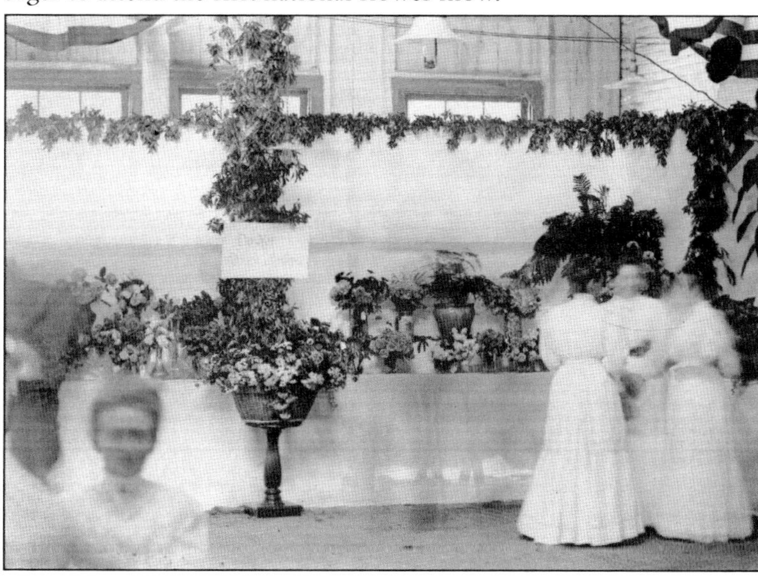

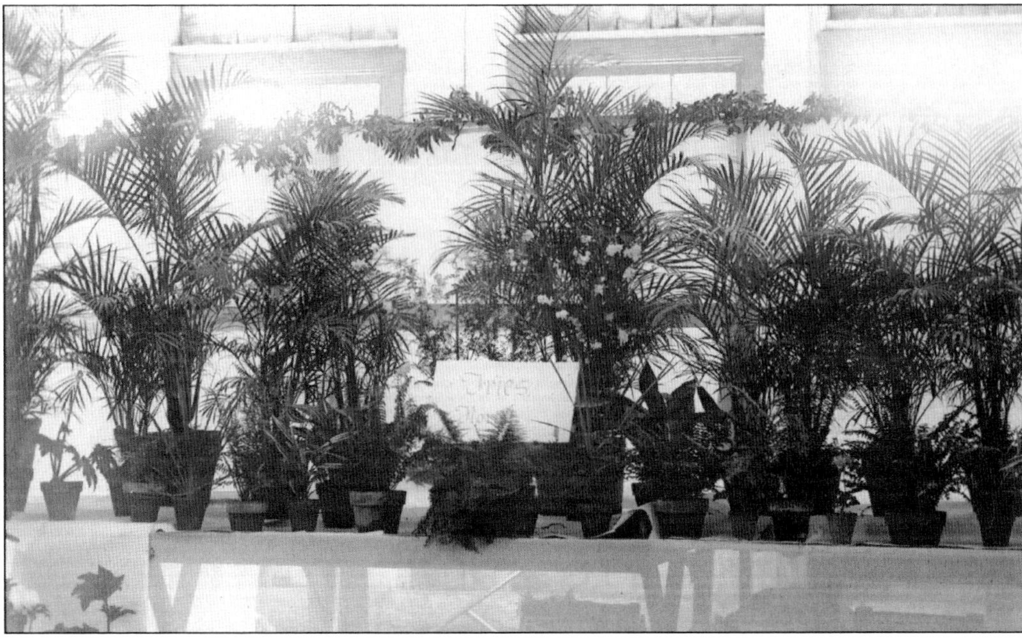

Here, at the same flower show in 1908, John E. Haines won first prize for his pink imperial carnations. For many years following this show, he competed in flower shows across the country and continued to win medals for his carnations. He earned a national reputation as well as a bustling florist business located at 219–223 Laurel Street.

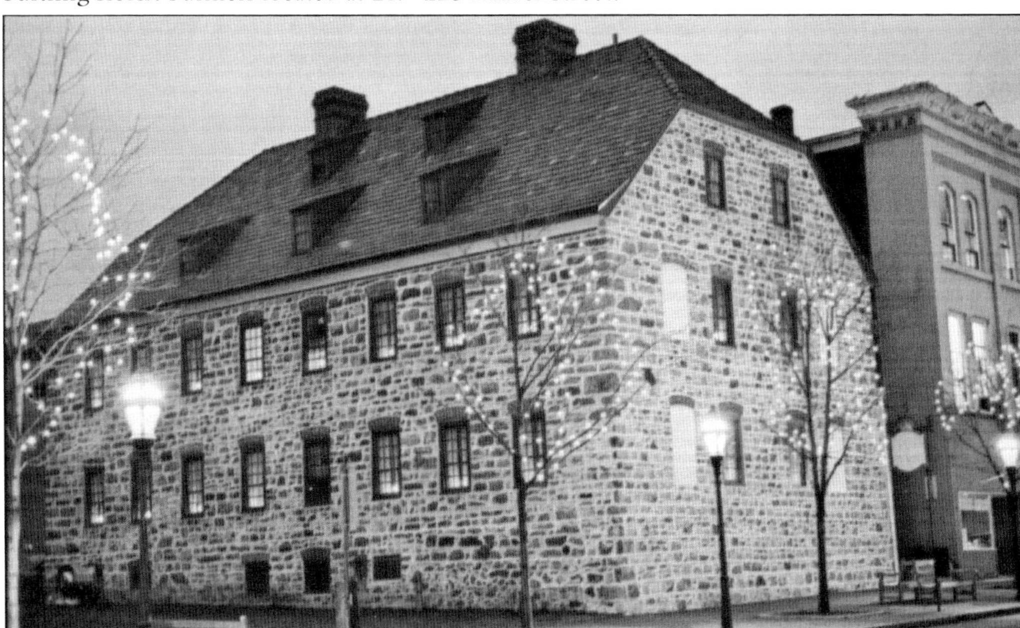

Photographer Tim Gilman took this lovely photograph of the Sun Inn on Main Street in 1982. It was near the end of the renaissance of historic Bethlehem when the Sun Inn was restored to its original appearance in the year it was built, 1758. Today, the inn still decorates for Christmas with Moravian candles in the windows. The city adds the miniature lights in the trees to create a festive scene that draws millions to visit Bethlehem during the holidays.

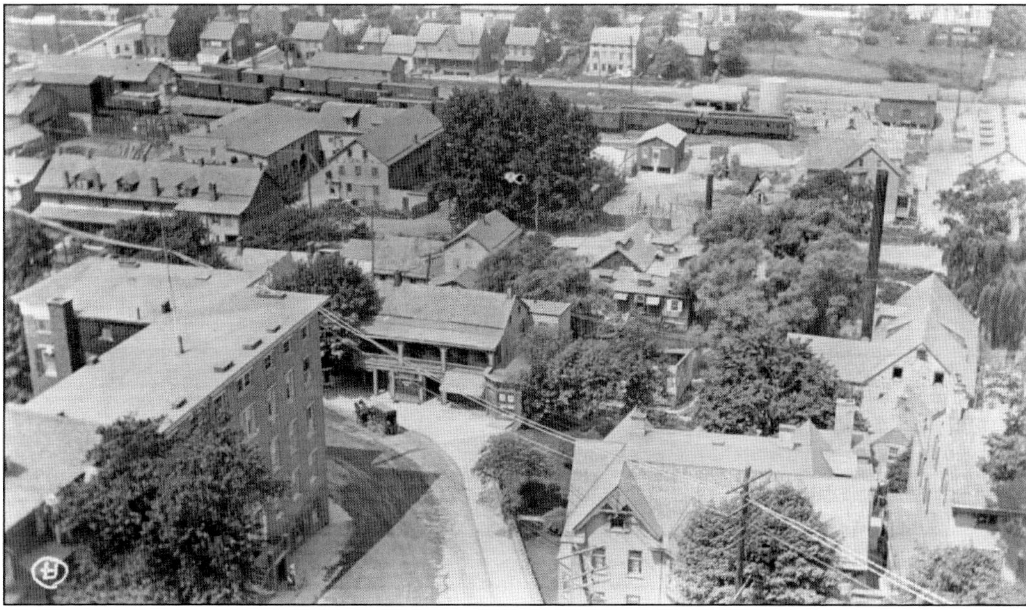

The buggy and horses are winding down South Main Street around the Moravian Female Seminary building on their left. This postcard will surprise viewers who know this area today as a pleasant grassy space with few buildings. The Brown-Borhek Lumber and Coal Company sits on the left below the railroad tracks. The Lehigh & Lackawanna Railroad crosses the photograph horizontally with Conestoga Street just above the tracks.

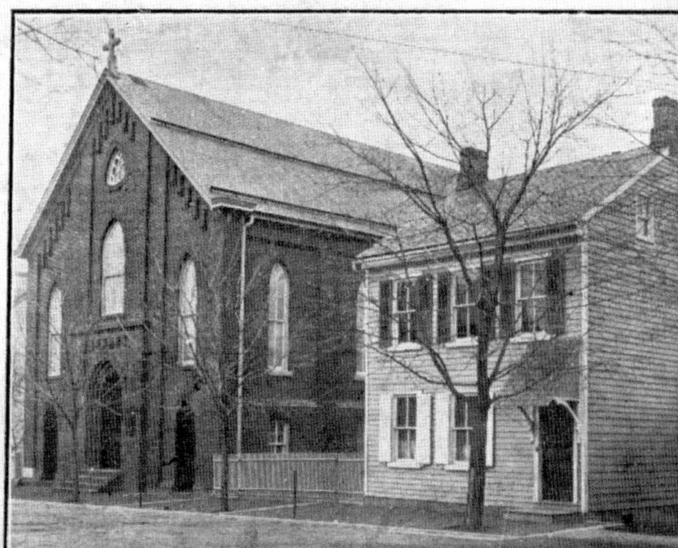

ST. JOHN'S EVANGELICAL CHURCH AND PARSONAGE, NORTH ST., BETHLEHEM, PA.

The evangelical group who built its first church on this site in 1895 was known as St. John's United Evangelical Church. The church was located on North Street. As early as 1847, preachers of the Evangelical Association visited Bethlehem to preach to followers in their homes.

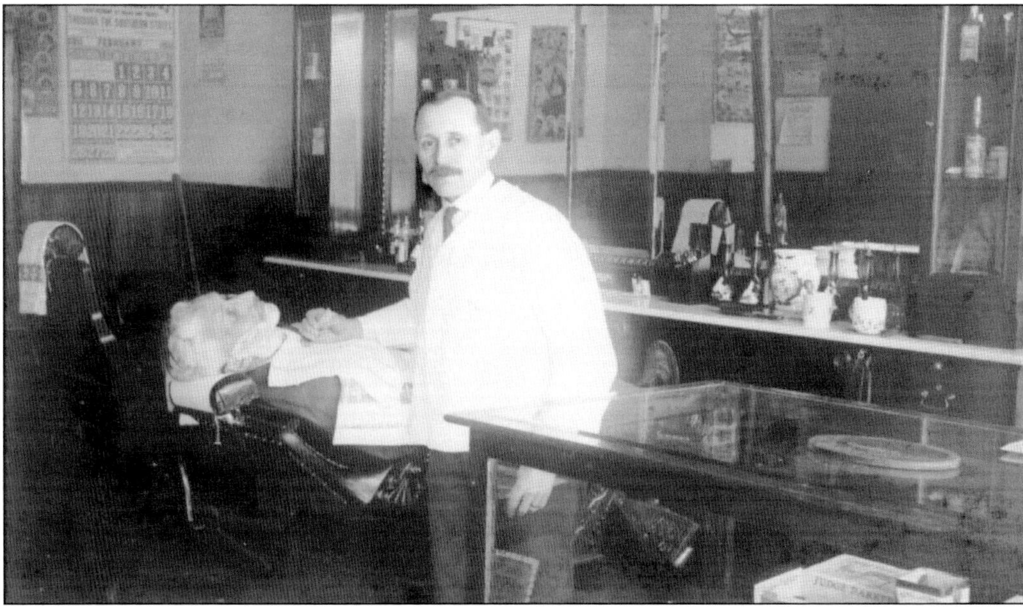

Nine-year-old Angelo Tocci immigrated to Philadelphia from Italy in the 1890s. He married Rose Puppo in Philadelphia in 1895, and 10 years later, they moved with their family to Bethlehem. Tocci operated several businesses on Broad Street—Tocci Movie Theatre, National Poolroom, Tocci Barbershop, and Tocci Restaurant. In this photograph taken in February 1911, Tocci is giving a customer a shave. Angelo and Rose's 12 children all helped out in the Tocci businesses.

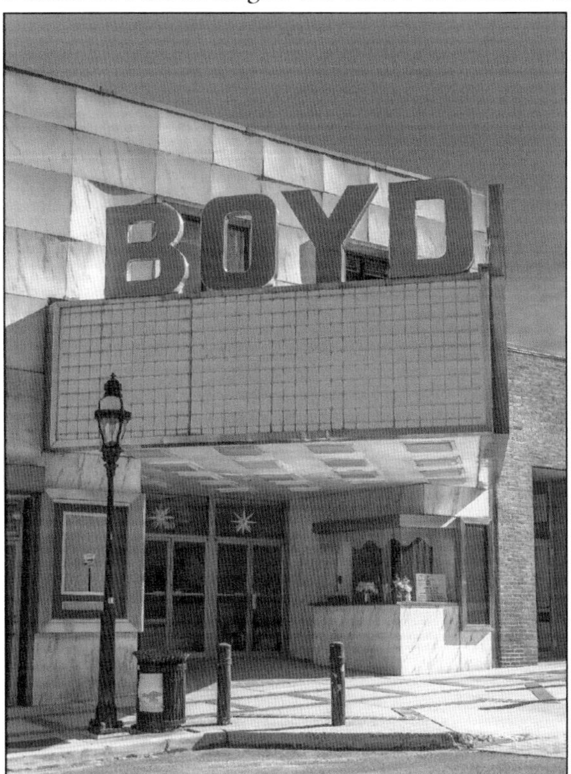

Brothers Charles F. and John Kurtz built the Boyd Theater in 1921. A fire on December 27, 1966, in a nearby retail shop caused damage to the theater's lobby, its external facade, and its marquee. Initially, there was discussion of leveling the theater; urban renewal was the catchphrase of the 1960s. In the end, the owners decided to renovate the 45-year-old theater. Today, the theater still stands, but water damage has kept the theater closed for the past few years. (Courtesy of John DelGrosso.)

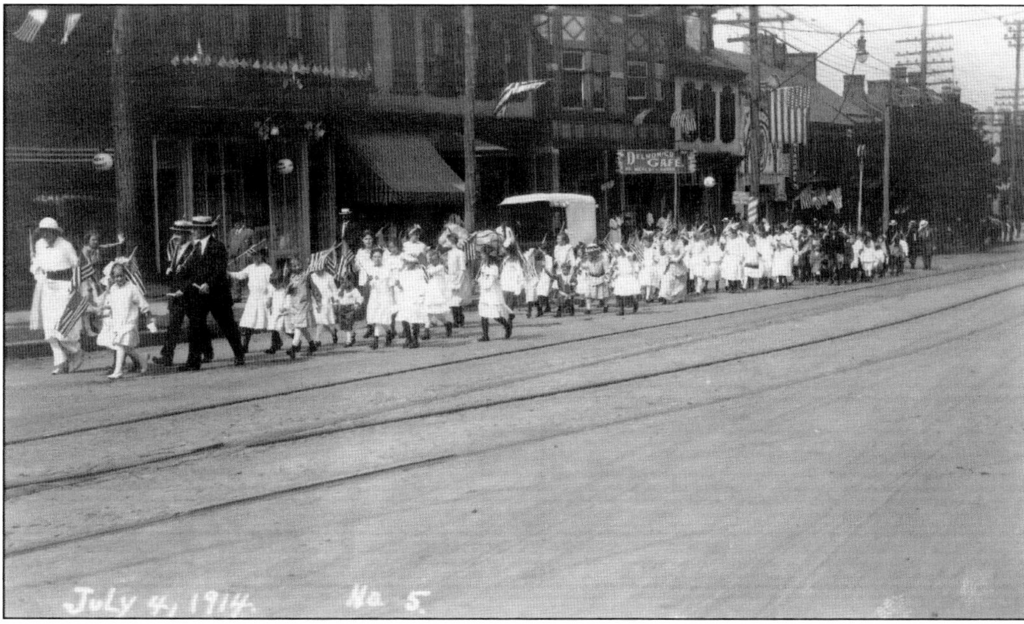

It is the Fourth of July in 1914, and the business owners along Broad Street show their patriotism with flags hung at every address. Young girls are all wearing white dresses with touches of red and blue in their bows and bonnets. The group stays clear of the busy trolley tracks and passes a horse and carriage. They are not tempted by the delicious smells coming from the Delmonico Café at 80 Broad Street, which offered light lunches or regular meals, oysters in all styles, ice cream, and soda all year-round.

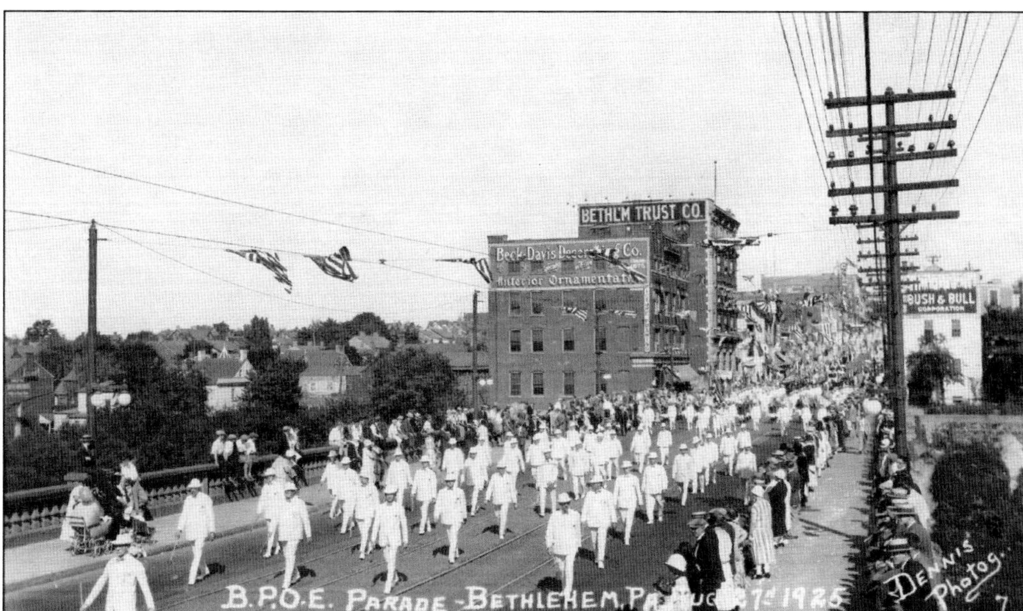

On August 27, 1925, members of the Elks marched in a parade heading west across Broad Street Bridge. The Elks are dressed in matching hats and uniforms. Spectators lined the bridge to enjoy the parade.

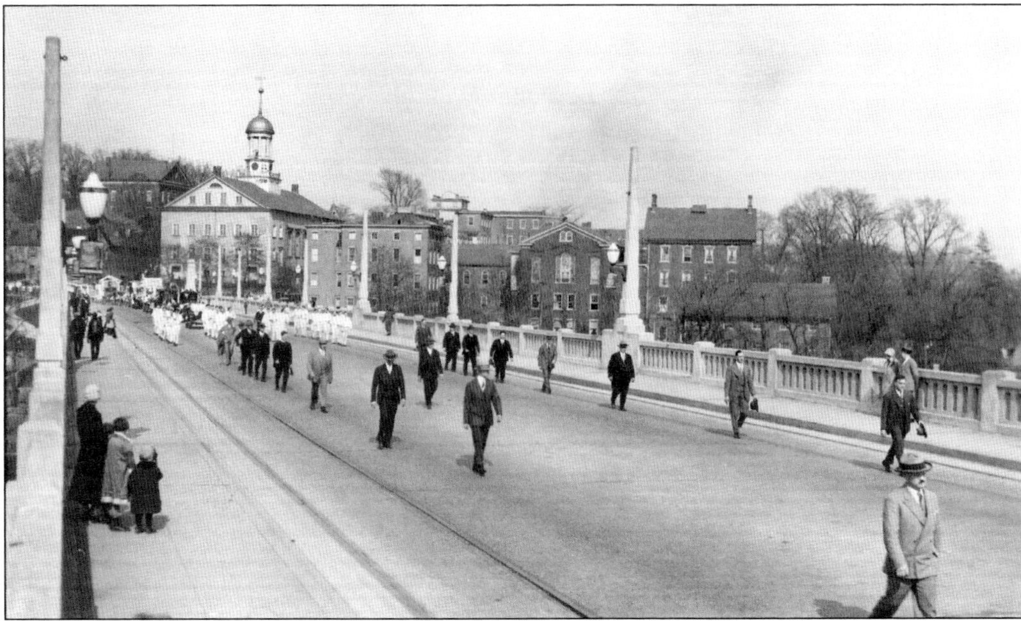

The Elks march over the Hill-to-Hill Bridge in the Easter parade on April 25, 1943. They are followed by an array of floats. The Benevolent and Protective Order of the Elks Lodge No. 191 was founded in 1891 by 25 charter members. Today, they are still an active group with headquarters located on Union Boulevard, Bethlehem.

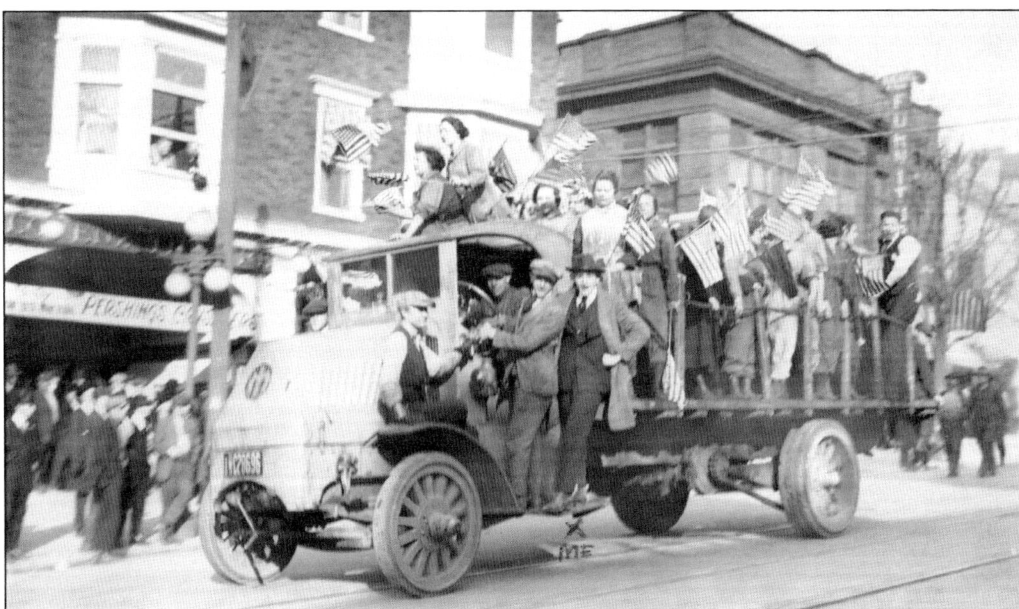

Here is a peace parade to honor Gen. John J. Pershing, commander in chief of the American Expeditionary Forces. Marching behind the truck can be seen World War I vets. The men and women on the Mack truck are joyous to see the return of family and friends from the war in Europe. The parade is on Broad Street and occurred some time between 1918 and 1919.

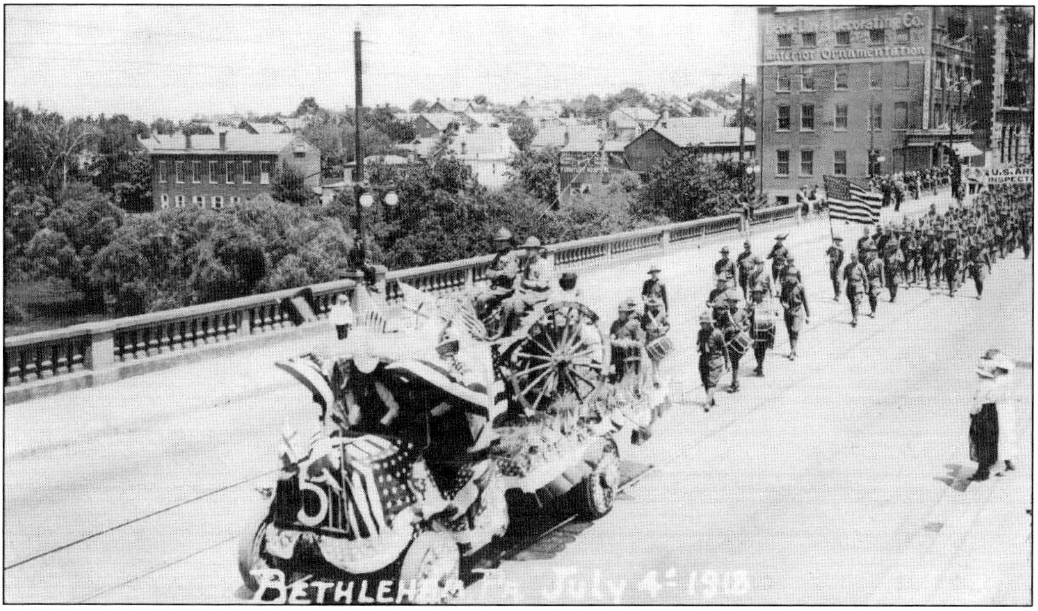

The Fourth of July parade was a must-see in Bethlehem. In this postcard, Army troops march in along the Broad Street Bridge in 1918. The Bethlehem Steel Corporation Machine Shop No. 5 created the float. Writing on the back of the postcard called it the "Monster Parade." The year before, on April 6, 1917, the United States declared war on Germany after learning that it tried to motivate the Mexicans to join the conflict with the promise of Texas, New Mexico, and Arizona as a reward. On the day of this parade, Pres. Woodrow Wilson gave a passionate speech making the case that war was necessary to create a lasting peace.

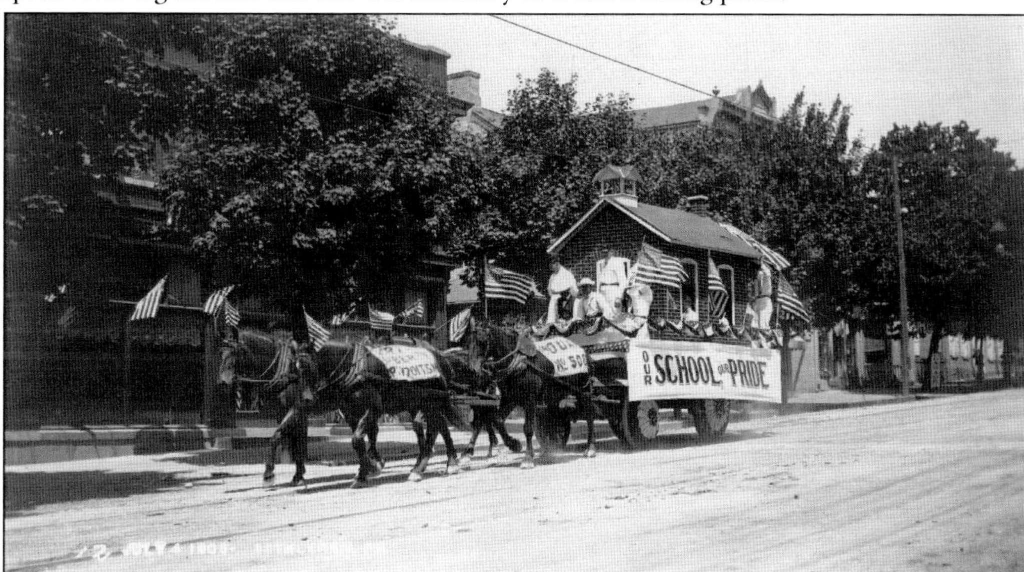

Because of the large numbers of immigrants that came to live in Bethlehem during the first half of the 20th century, Bethlehem schools emphasized patriotism in their curriculum as a way to help families adapt to their new country. This is a photograph of the July 4, 1908, parade. Note the model schoolhouse with flags and banners. Education is of supreme importance in the United States.

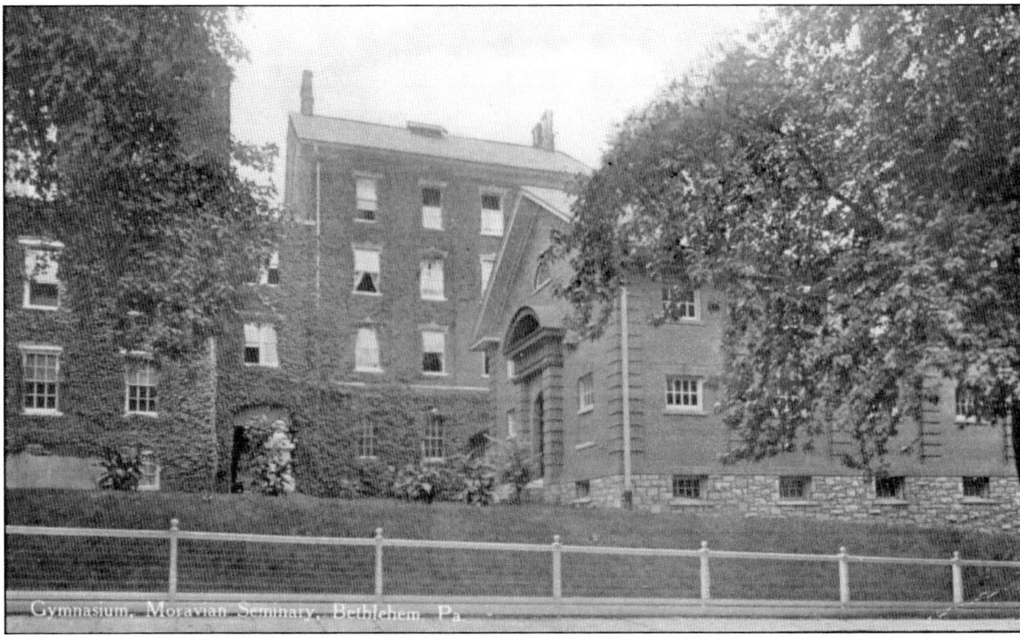

Today these buildings are part of the Priscilla Payne Hurd Campus of Moravian College facing South Main Street. On the left is Peter Hall, and to the right of it is South Hall. The building on the far right was the gymnasium for the Moravian Seminary for Girls, built in 1911. In 1982, the former gymnasium was converted into the Frank E. and Seba B. Payne Gallery.

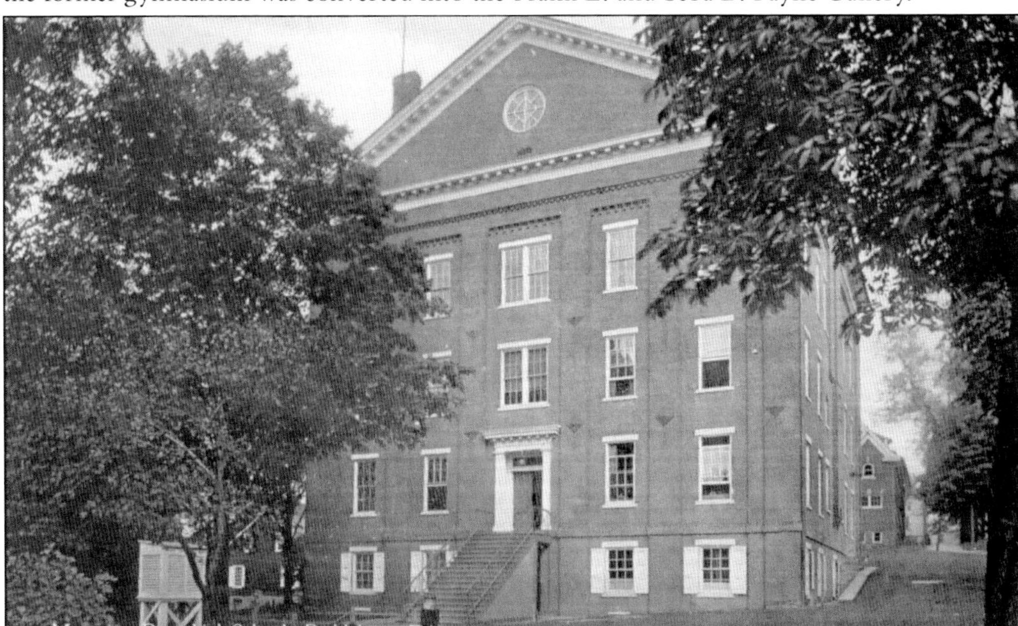

Here is the Moravian Academy Lower School building, which became coeducational in late 1960s, when the Moravian Seminary for Girls merged with Moravian Preparatory School. George Neisser, a teacher at the Moravian Seminary for Girls, founded the preparatory school in 1742. The school shares the same campus with the Moravian Academy Middle School, Moravian College Priscilla Payne Hurd Campus, and the Central Moravian Church.

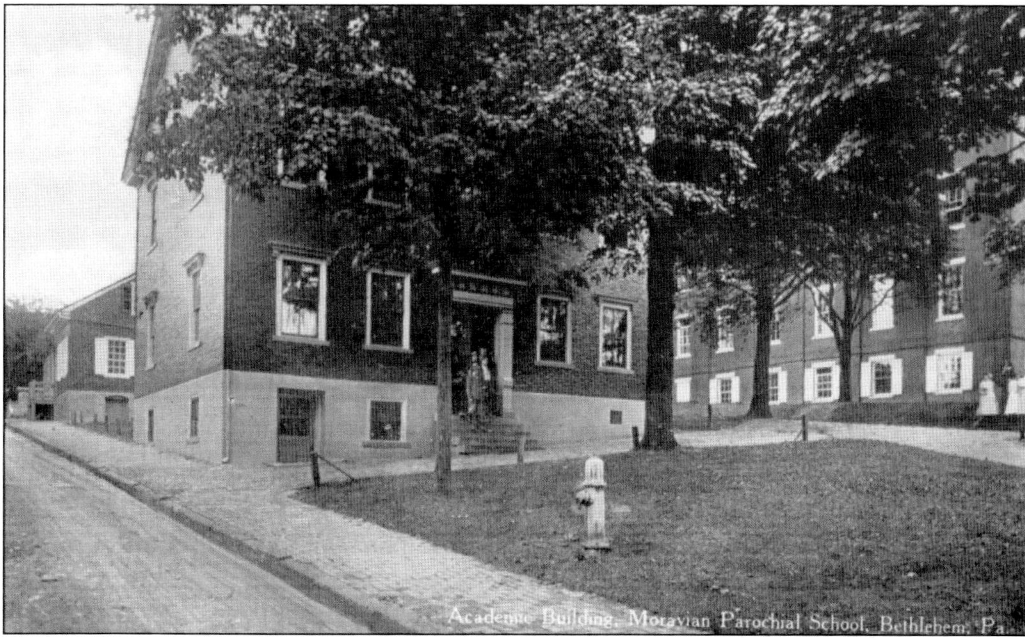

The building on the far left was for many years the home of the sexton of the Central Moravian Church. On the right is the Moravian Academy Lower School building. The academy is the ninth-oldest independent school in the nation. Today, the private school provides education from prekindergarten to the fifth grade.

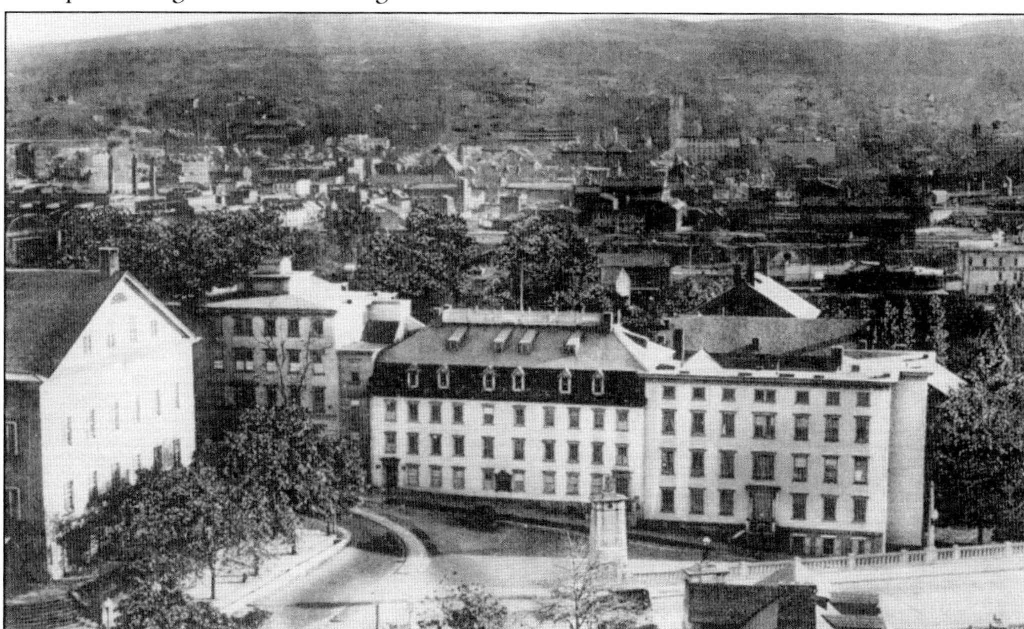

In the foreground is the entrance to the Hill-to-Hill Bridge from Main Street. The two buildings in the center of the photograph were originally used as the Single Brothers Choir House, a Moravian boardinghouse for single men of roughly the same age. The one on the left was built in 1744 and was the first stone structure built in Bethlehem. The brick addition, West Hall, was built in 1858.

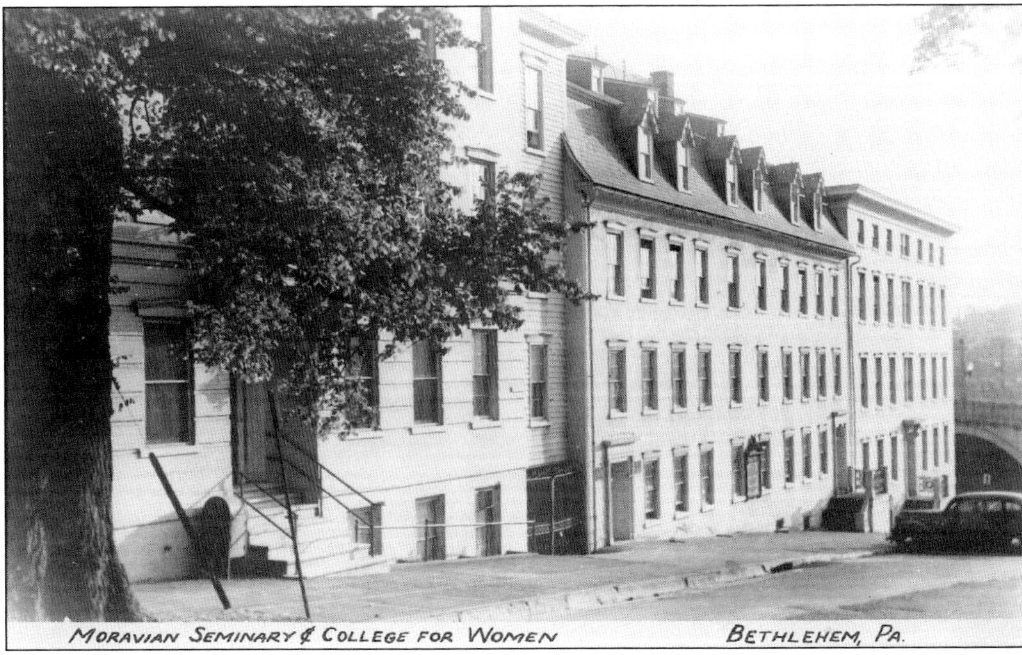

Countess Benigna, the daughter of Count Zinzendorf, founded the Moravian Seminary for Young Ladies (now known as Moravian College) in 1742. The school became the first girls' boarding school in the country. It was the first school to employ a female teacher. On the far left is the Main Hall, which was built in 1854. It was the first building in Bethlehem to be lit by gas. Moravian Academy was incorporated in 1971 with the merger of the Moravian Seminary for Girls and Moravian Preparatory School. These buildings are now part of Moravian College, called the Priscilla Payne Hurd Campus on Church Street, located in the center of Bethlehem's Historic District.

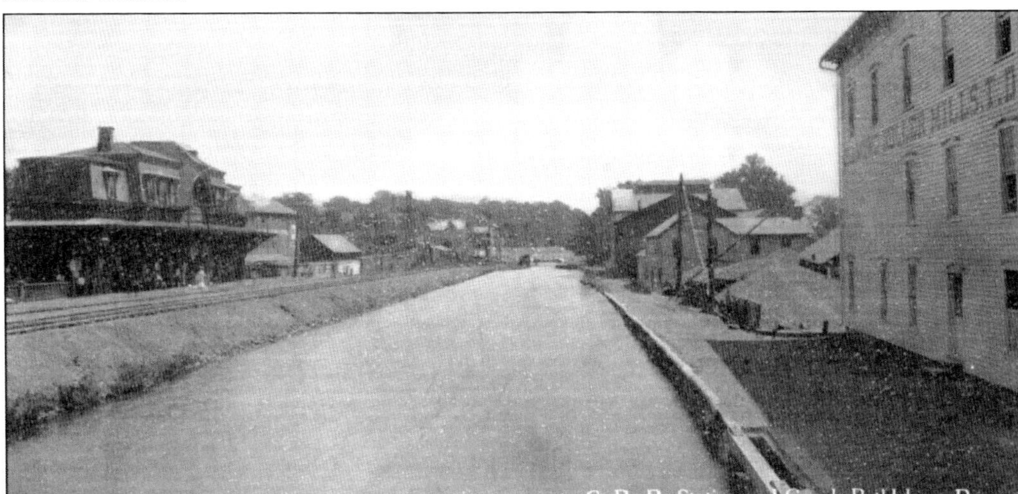

In 1889, Tryon D. Fritch built the T.D. Fritch and Sons Diamond Roller Mills at the corner of South Main and River Streets, seen on far right. The mill had a daily capacity of 200 barrels of flour. The mill was four stories high and 50 by 120 feet. Also pictured here are the Lehigh Canal and, on the far left, the Central Railroad of New Jersey Railroad Station on Lehigh Street, built in 1873.

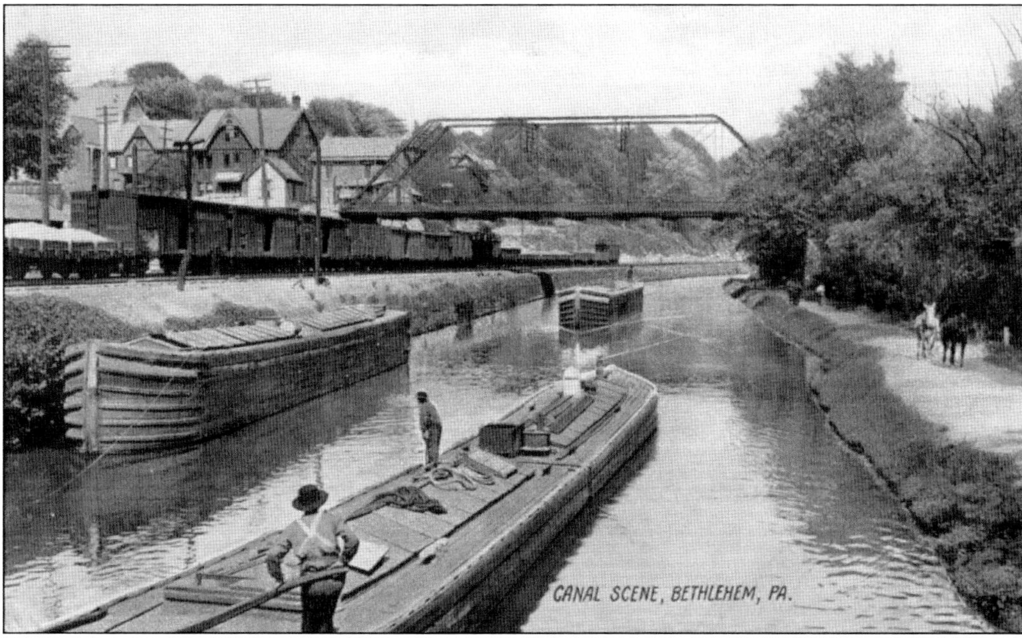

Here is a busy scene on the Lehigh Canal as one canal boat makes way for another on this narrow waterway. By the time this photograph was taken in the early 1900s, the tonnage of anthracite coal had fallen to less than a quarter of its 1855 peak of more than one million tons. An eight-mile segment of the canal towpath has been converted into a multiuse trail that runs from Freemansburg through Bethlehem to Allentown.

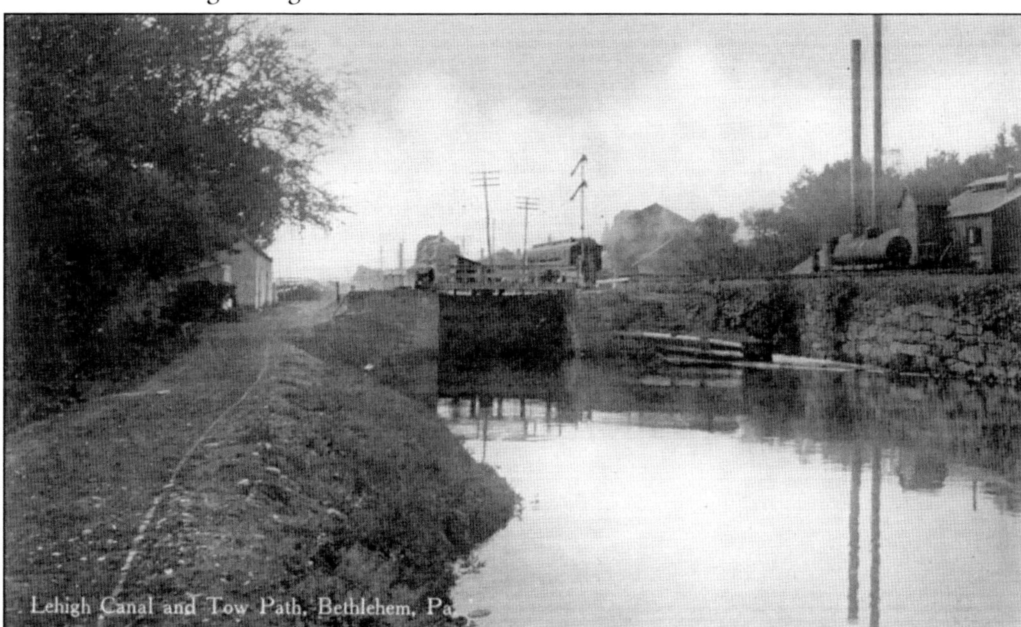

Here is another view of the Lehigh Canal and towpath. Lock No. 42 is in the center of the photograph with the lock keeper's house on the left and the Central Railroad of New Jersey on the right. The railroad proved a mighty competitor, and eventually, it put the canal out of business. This canal was used until the 1940s, longer than other similar canals.

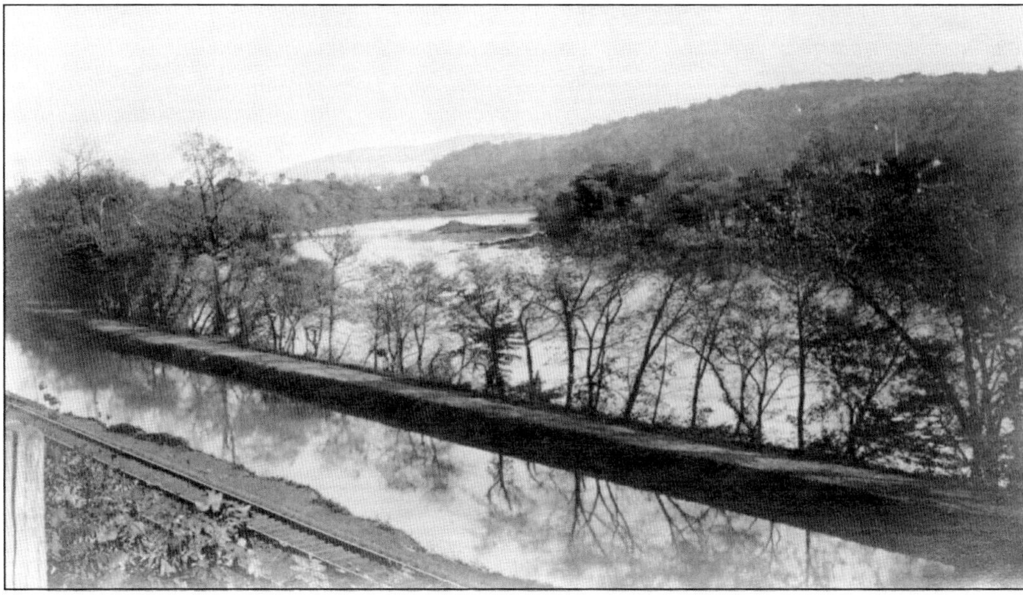

Here is a scene that captures the Lehigh Canal, towpath, Central Railroad of New Jersey rail line, and South Mountain. Canvass White, who was an engineer on the Erie Canal, designed the Lehigh Canal. It was constructed between 1827 and 1829 and ran over 46 miles in length between Mauch Chunk (present Jim Thorpe) and Easton.

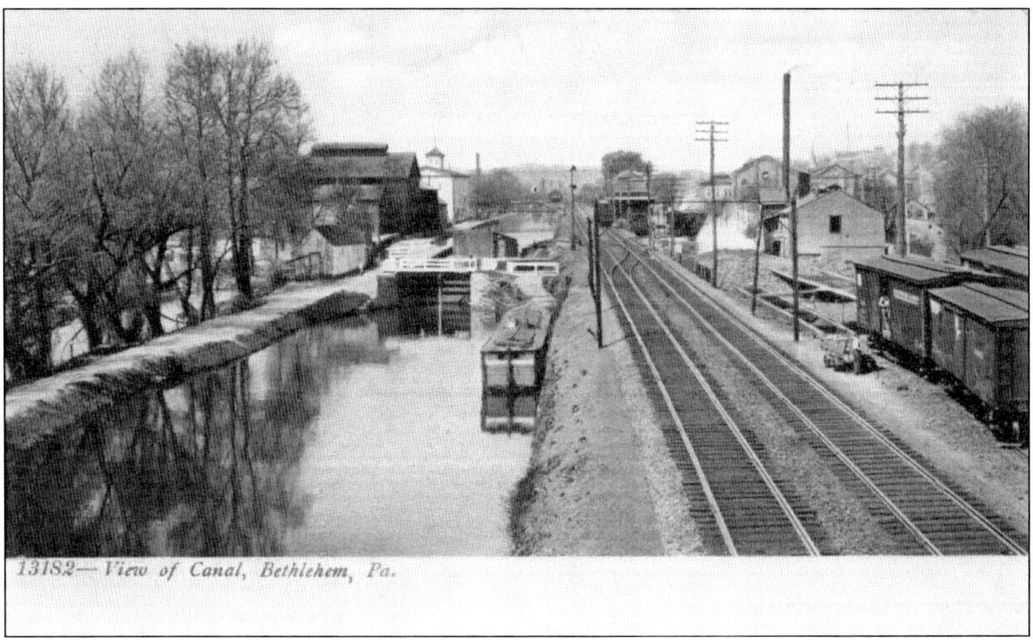

13182—*View of Canal, Bethlehem, Pa.*

The Lehigh River is on the far left, the Lehigh Canal at center, and the Central Railroad of New Jersey at the far right. This image was taken at canal lock No. 42. A canal boat is docked on the canal waiting for the lock to open.

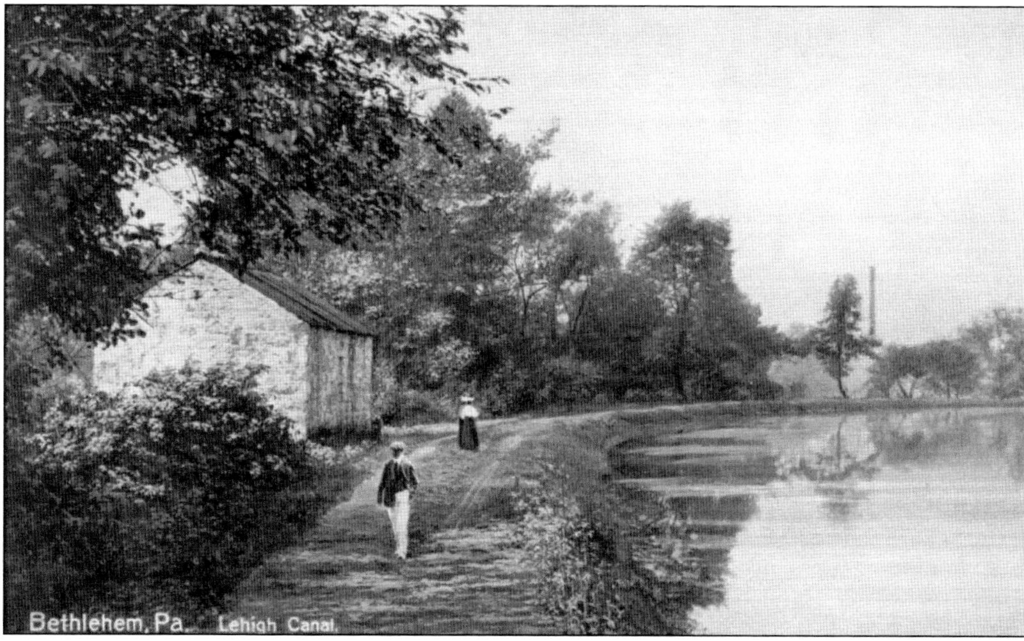

The people pictured here are enjoying a summer's day walk along the towpath of the Lehigh Canal. In the distance on the right, one can make out one of the smoke stacks of Bethlehem Steel Corporation. On the left is a lock tender's home, which was supplied to him rent-free by the Lehigh Coal and Navigation Company's canal, plus an acre of land and a salary of $150 a year.

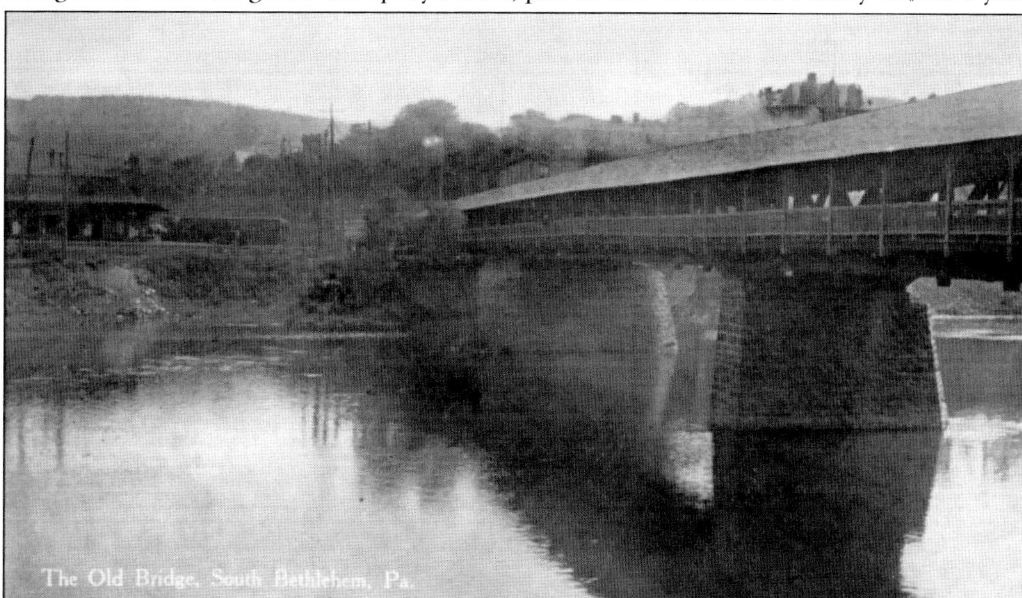

In 1841, the Bethlehem Bridge Company built the third bridge to cross the Lehigh River immediately to the west of the current Hill-to-Hill Bridge. It was a covered wooden bridge, 400 feet long and only 23 feet above Lehigh's low watermark. The Lehigh River caused damage to Bethlehem's bridges every time its waters rose. A flood in 1862 destroyed the northern half of the bridge. It was immediately rebuilt, but it was clear that a different type of bridge would be needed to counter the frequent rise in water.

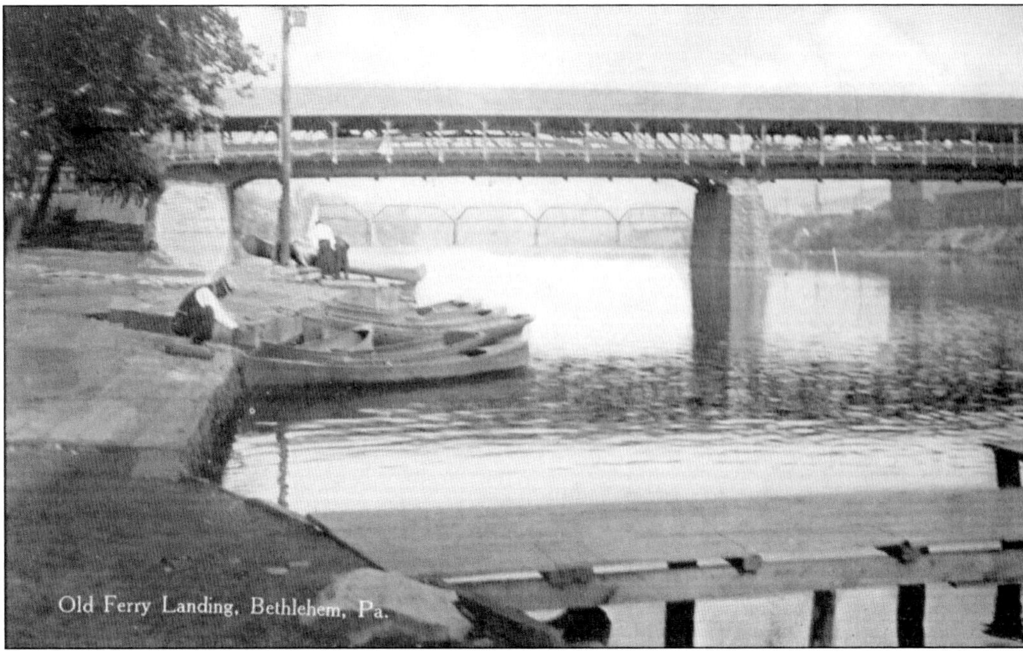

The old ferry landing played an important role in Bethlehem history. Before there were bridges, the service, run by the Moravians, transported people, horses, and wagons across the Lehigh River. Travelers arrived at the ferry from points south by the Bethlehem Pike, which opened in 1734 and served as one of the earliest transportation routes between Bethlehem and Philadelphia.

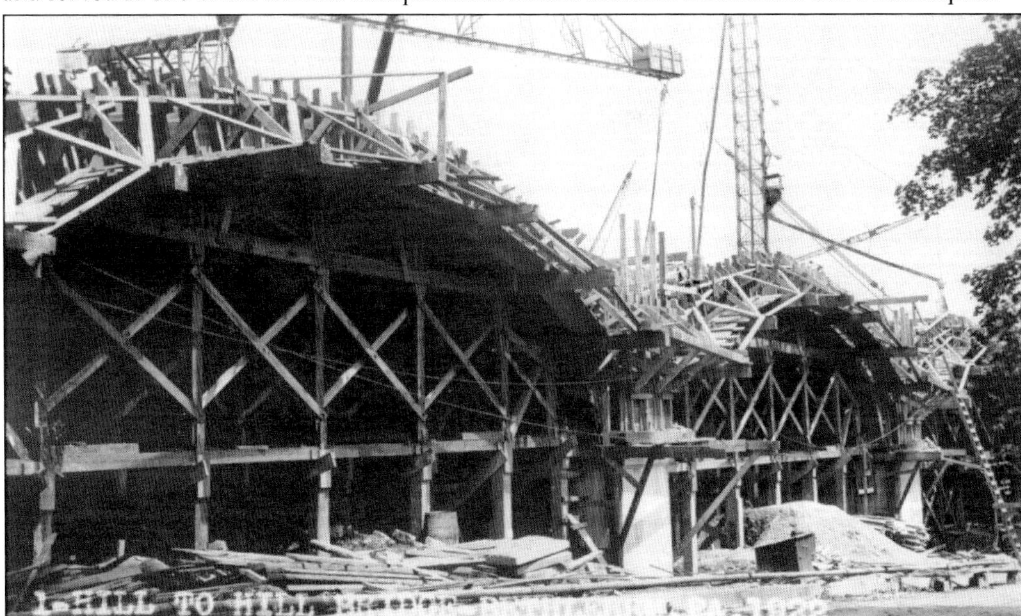

World War I interrupted the building of the Hill-to-Hill Bridge. Work finally began on August 1, 1921. This postcard shows the progress on the bridge a year later. The wooden bracing holds the concrete in place as it sets and was later removed. During the summer of 1922, a thousand cubic yards of concrete were poured in a 24-hour day. Over 400 men were employed to build this engineering marvel.

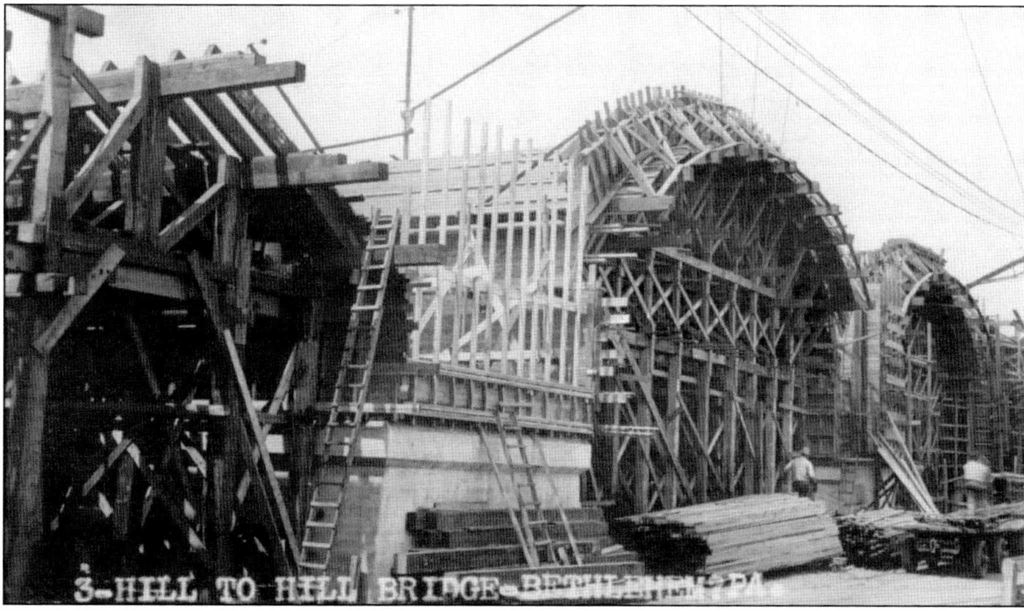

The wooden temporary structure shown here for the building of the Hill-to-Hill Bridge was put in place to support the pouring of 107,000 cubic yards of concrete. The cement was purchased from the Pennsylvania Cement Company then mixed into concrete onsite. The bridge was constructed almost entirely of reinforced concrete. The Construction Lumber Company of Pittsburgh and Trexler Lumber Company of Allentown supplied the lumber.

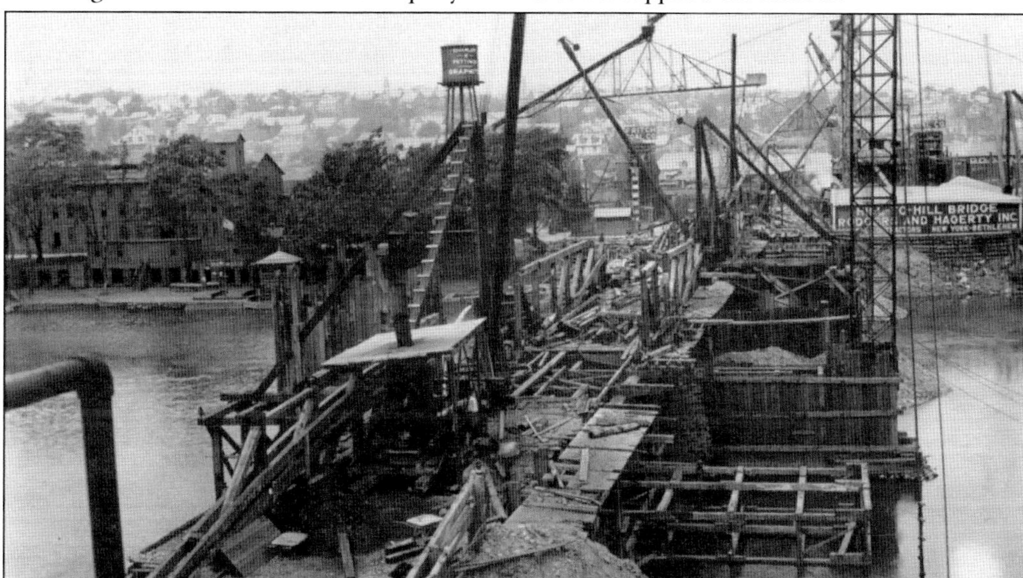

Here is a photograph, looking north, of the razing of the old covered bridge, built in 1841. It would take two more years before the Hill-to-Hill Bridge was completed in 1924 at the same site as the old bridge. The bridge would span between Fountain Hill and Nisky Hill, which resulted in the name "Hill-to-Hill." There is a large sign along the bank for the builders of the bridge, Rogers and Hagerty, Inc., of New York. At the height of construction, over 400 men were employed.

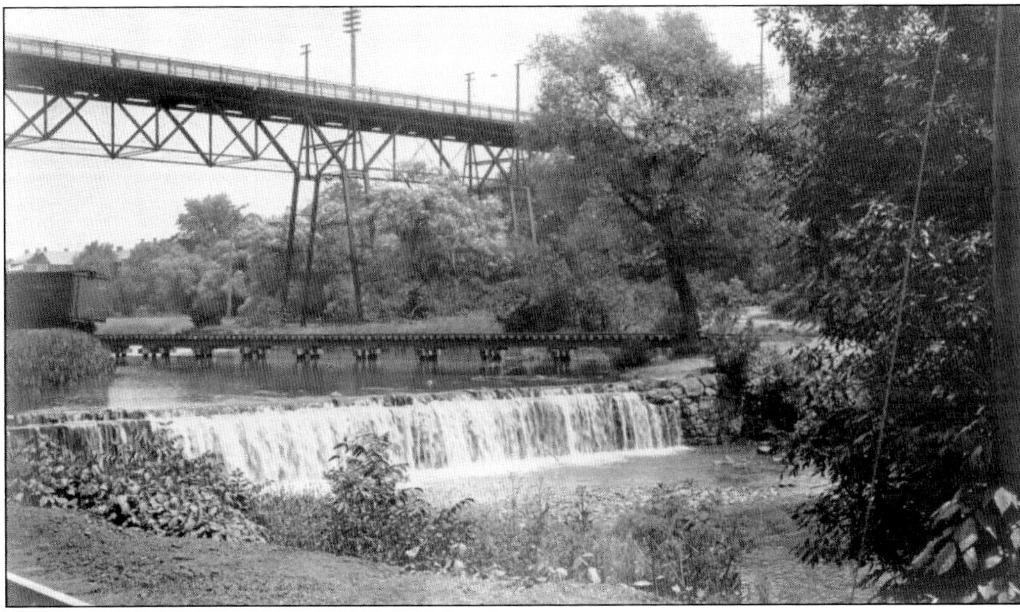

Here is a view looking northeast from Conestoga Street of the Monocacy Creek. The old Broad Street Bridge is in the background. It was an iron-and-wood bridge used from 1871 to 1909. In 1936, the Works Progress Administration enlarged an existing 50-foot dam across the Monocacy Creek. At that time, residents of the city could dive and swim in the lake that formed upstream of the dam. The dam was removed in 2013 to improve water flow.

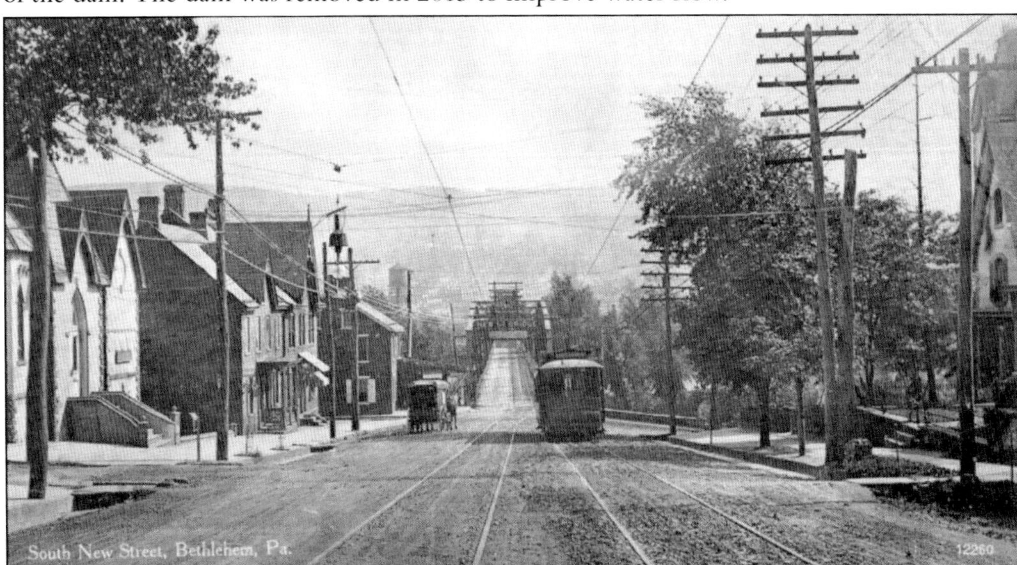

This photograph is looking south down New Street toward the New Street Bridge. Note the trolley and horse and wagon. The last structure on the left before the bridge is the old toll taker's house. The New Street Bridge was opened on September 2, 1867. Pedestrians were charged a 1¢ toll, and vehicles were charged 5¢. Everyone called it "the Penny Bridge." The Lehigh Valley Transit Company leased the rights from the bridge company to lay trolley tracts over the New Street Bridge. On May 31, 1892, a southbound trolley car rode the rails over the bridge for the first time to Bethlehem's south side.

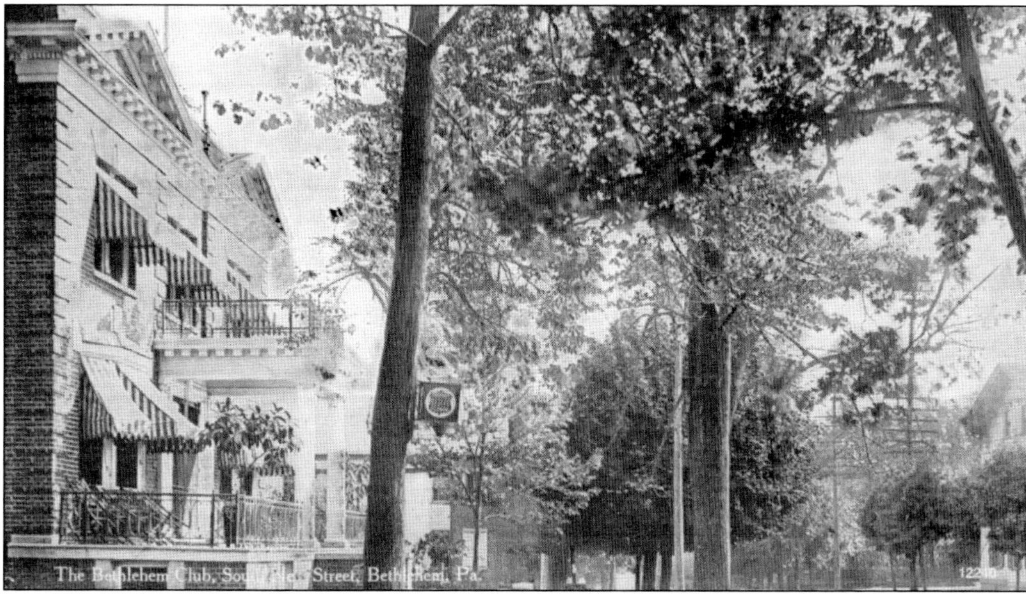

The Bethlehem Club on New Street opened in 1909 for Bethlehem Steel executives to socialize and unwind. The building also housed the Loopers, Bethlehem Steel's newest hires, who were trained by working through each department in a loop pattern. The three-story brick building was 18,000 square feet. There was a bowling alley in the basement and 12 dorm-style rooms on the second floor. The club closed in 2007 but was restored by Glemser Technologies in 2011 as headquarters for its consulting and software business for life sciences companies.

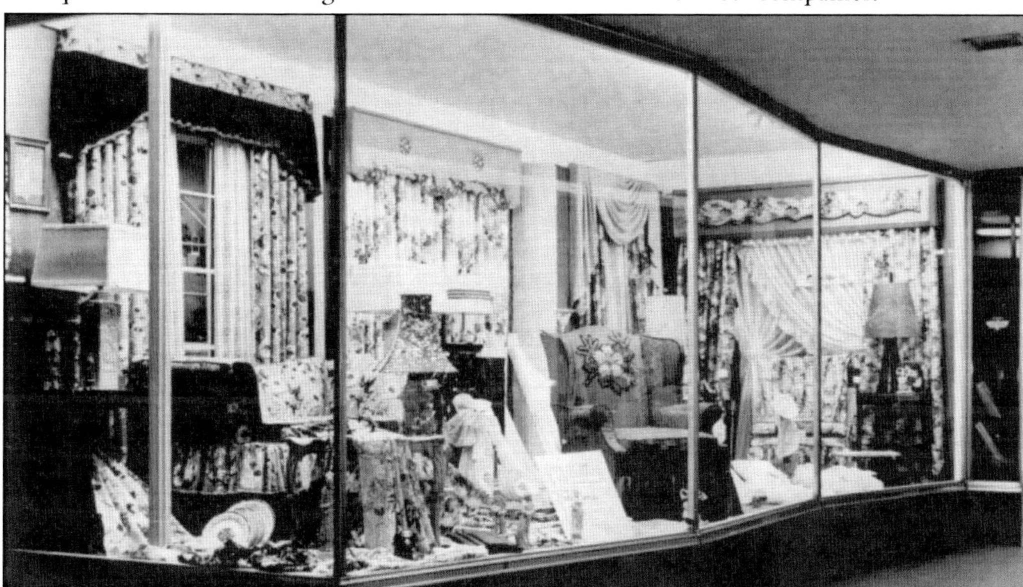

Fontaine's Decorators at 33 West Broad Street offered fabrics in a wide variety of patterns and colors. A customer could order slipcovers, drapes, and bedspreads made to his or her specifications. The display window presented examples of rich fabrics arranged as one would expect to find in the most elegant homes. Making slipcovers was a cornerstone of Fontaine's business because, before air-conditioning was available, they were considered essential to protect upholstered furniture from sweat during summer months.

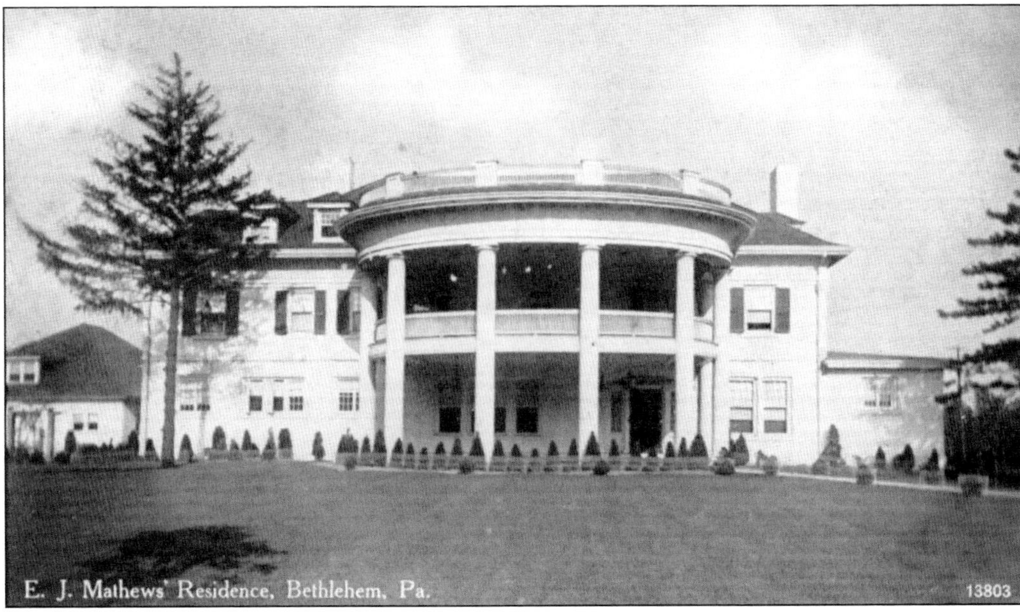

E.J. Mathews lived with his family in their mansion, built in 1915. The mansion was known by locals as "the White House" and was located on Linden Street. Mathews was an executive with Bethlehem Steel Corporation. This Neoclassical Revival home with richly detailed wood moldings, elegant stained glass, and overall grandeur is beautifully preserved to this day. In 1964, the Long Funeral Home purchased the building for its business, which for several years was Styer Convalescent Home.

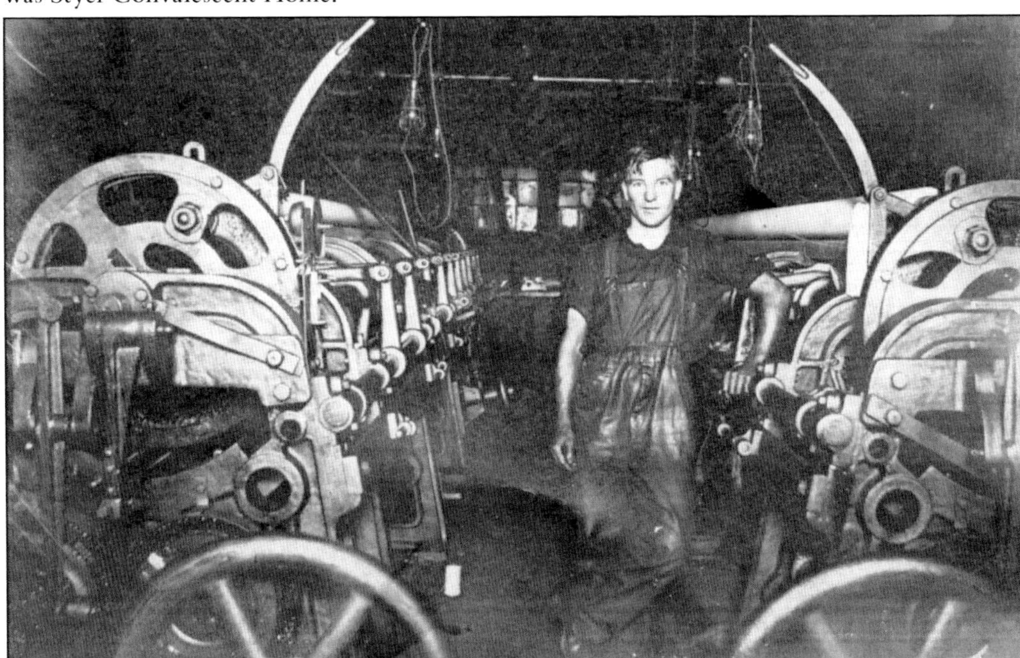

Written on the back of this postcard is the notation, "Picture of Dad when he was 24 years old." From looking at dad's clothes, one can tell that working at a Bethlehem silk mill was a hot, grimy job. He seems at home with the wheels and gears that surround him.

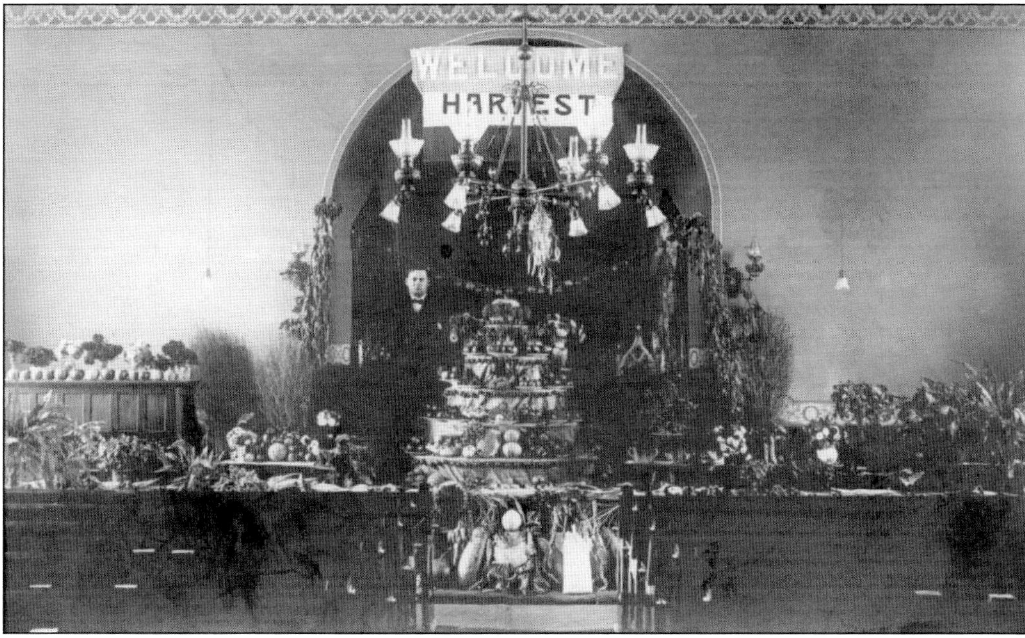

Here is a photograph of an artistically arranged assortment of fruit, vegetables, and flowers around the altar of a church to celebrate Harvest Festival. The black-and-white photograph does not do justice to the spectacular array of colors of the apples, squash, and chrysanthemums. Members of the congregation donated produce from their own gardens. The collection of the harvest would then usually be given to St. Luke's Hospital. It was an annual tradition in Bethlehem's churches in the early 1900s. The man in the photograph is most likely the reverend of the church.

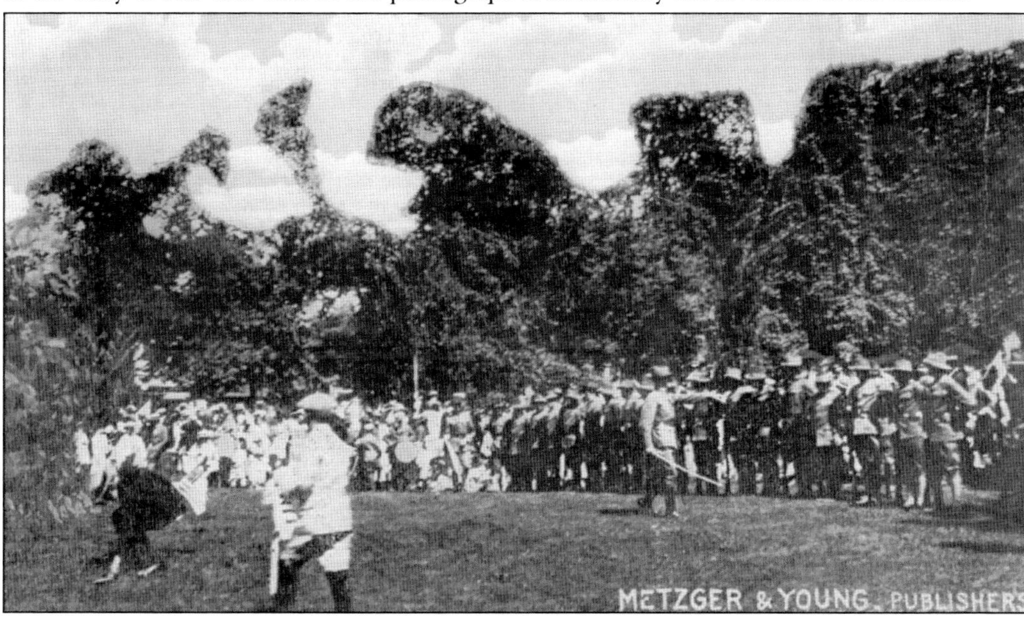

The 4th Regiment of Pennsylvania was the first regiment mustered in to fight in the Spanish-American War. It reported for duty in 1898 as a volunteer unit in the war against Spain. Company M, shown here parading in Bethlehem, was from Pottstown. They are celebrating Memorial Day, a day of remembrance of those who have died in the nation's service.

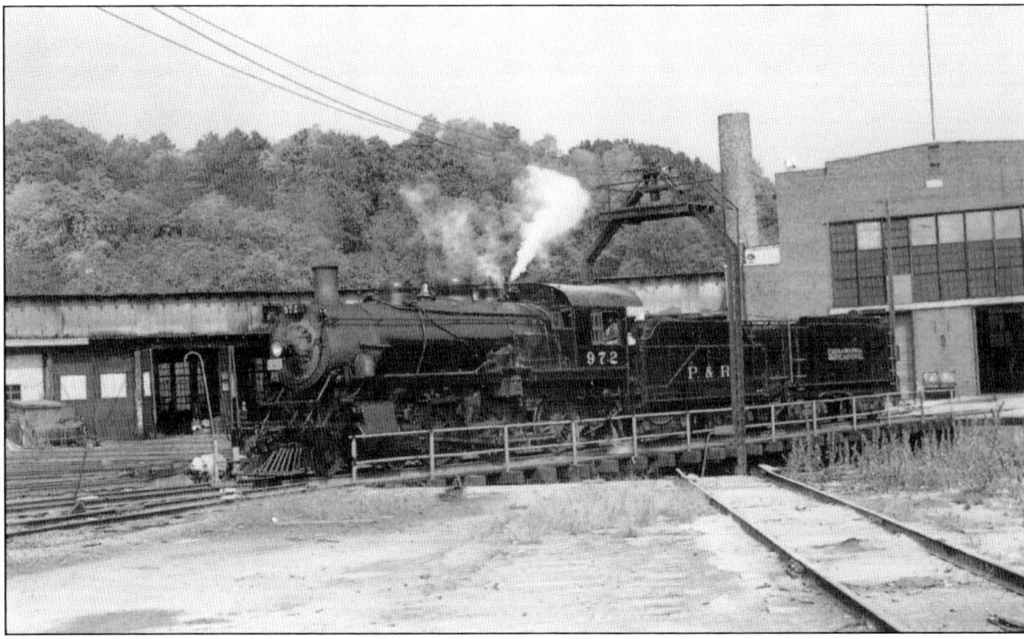

This former Canadian No. 972 engine, built by the Montreal Locomotive Works in 1912, shows lettering of the Philadelphia & Reading Railroad. This photograph was taken on October 10, 1983, at the turntable yard of the Conrail Railroad, originally Central Railroad of New Jersey, in Bethlehem.

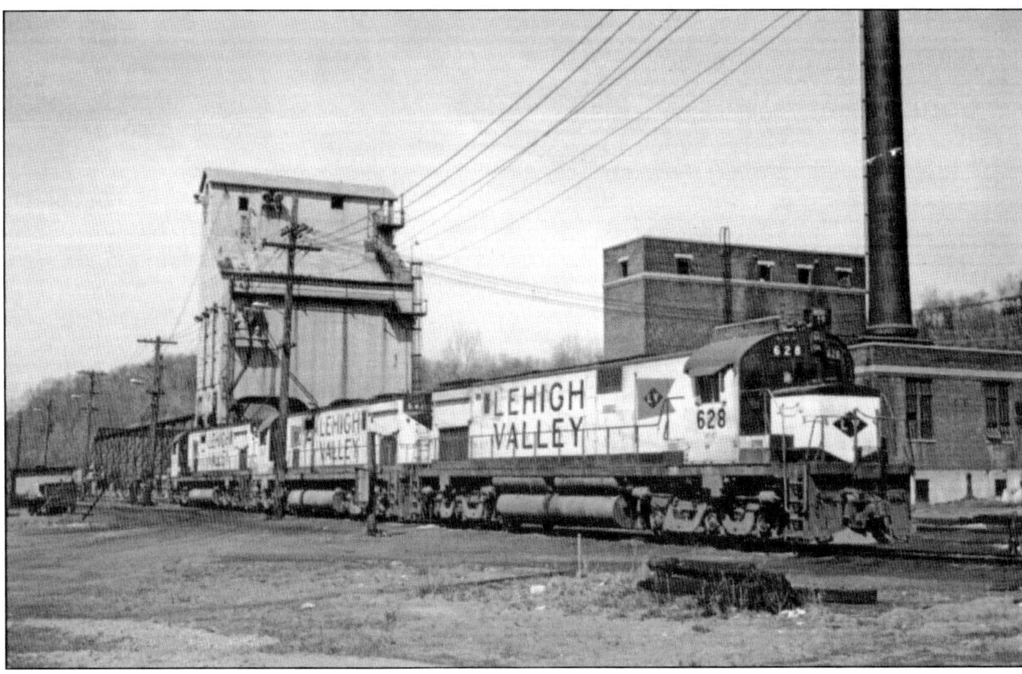

Lehigh Valley No. 628 passes the Lehigh Valley Railroad Engine Terminal in South Bethlehem. The cars are painted in the black-and-white snowbird scheme. The photograph was taken in April 1972, a few weeks after Lehigh Valley took over the Jersey Central terminal.

Two

SOUTH SIDE REVISITED

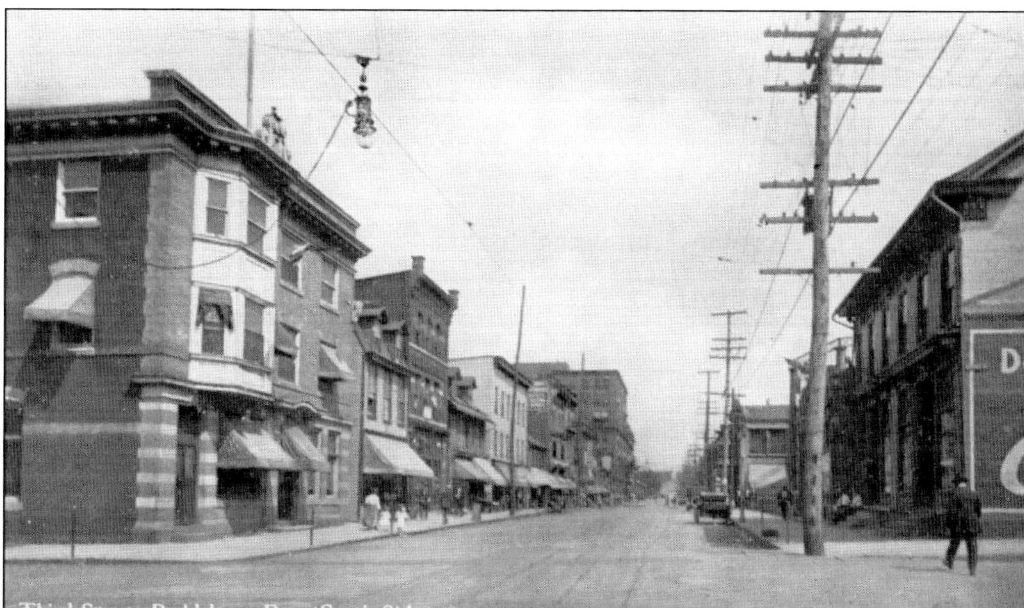

Here is the view looking east down Third Street at what is now Fillmore Street in the early 1900s. The trolley tracks are embedded in the dirt street. The telegraph poles and electric streetlamps fill the sky with wires. This was a main shopping district in South Bethlehem, with a great variety of shops mixed in with residences. Bethlehem Steel Corporation was located a few blocks from here, and it was the largest employer in Bethlehem. During World War I, the corporation employed over 8,000 men. This created a demand for housing and goods.

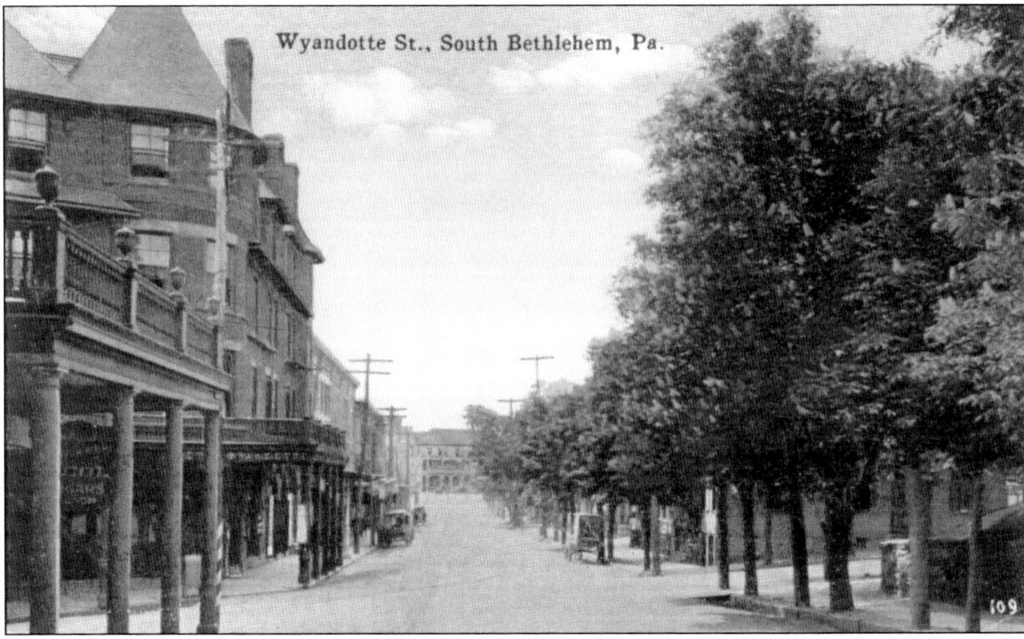

Here is a view from Fourth Street, looking west to Wyandotte Street. The Wyandotte Hotel is on the right. Just to the south is the public entrance to the Fountain Hill Opera House (later known as the Globe Theater). The hotel and opera house were razed, and a parking lot is now located on this corner.

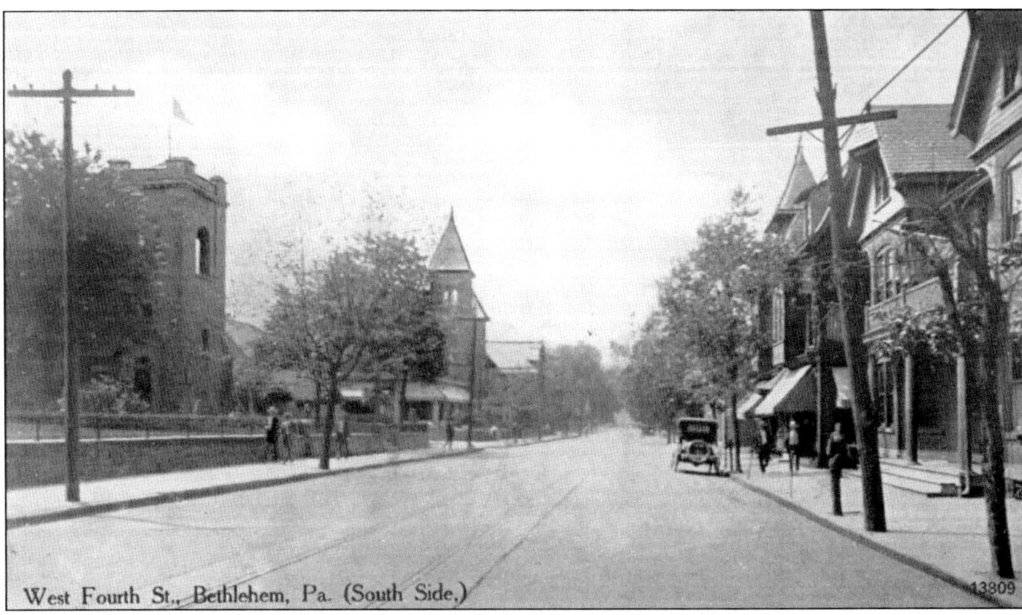

Fourth Street, a main thoroughfare through South Bethlehem, has more churches than any other street in Bethlehem. The image is looking west on Fourth Street, near the intersection of Martel Street. The stone church on the left with a flat, square tower was the First Presbyterian Church. The Presbyterian church was designed by Benjamin Price of Philadelphia and no longer stands. The next steeple on the left was St. Mark's Evangelical Lutheran Church, designed by A.W. Leh.

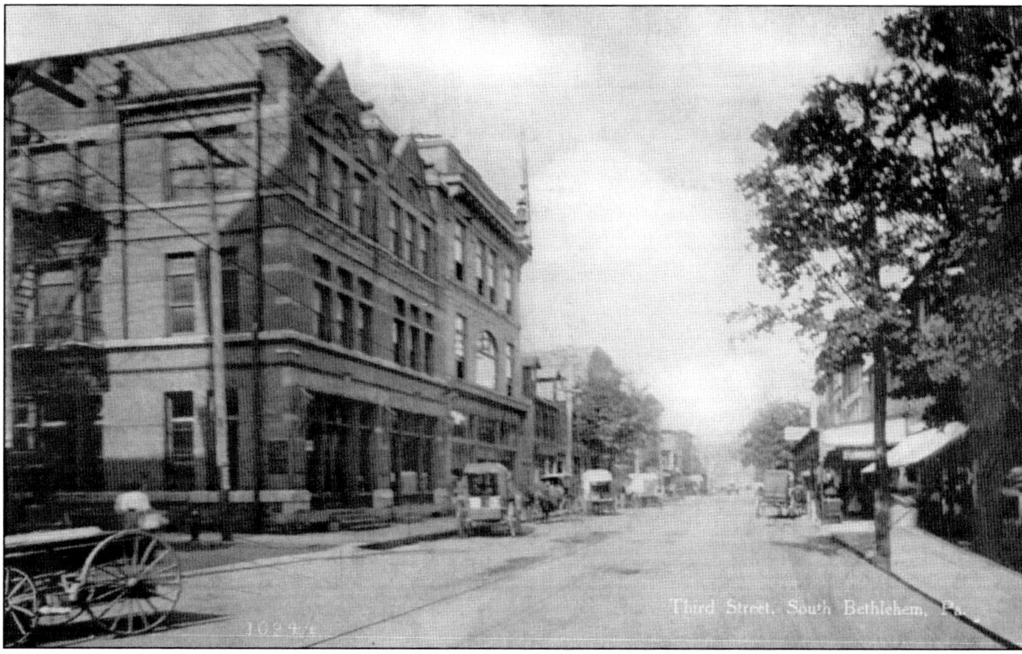

Here is an early-1900s view of Third Street in South Bethlehem, looking west. Trolley tracks are installed on the dirt road. The pedestrians and horse carts show it was a center of commerce. On the far left is the South Bethlehem National Bank, located at the intersection of Third and Adams Streets.

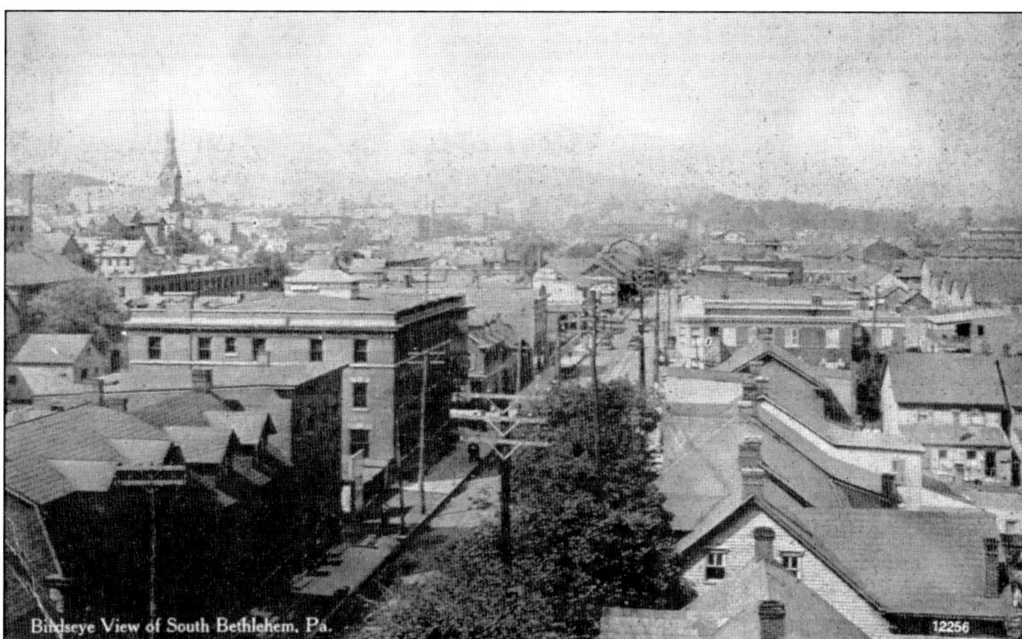

This aerial view of South Bethlehem is looking west on Columbia Street toward Fountain Hill. The steeple in the distance on the left is the Holy Infancy Church on Fourth Street at Taylor Street. The photograph appears to have been taken in the area of the Bethlehem Steel headquarters at Third Street.

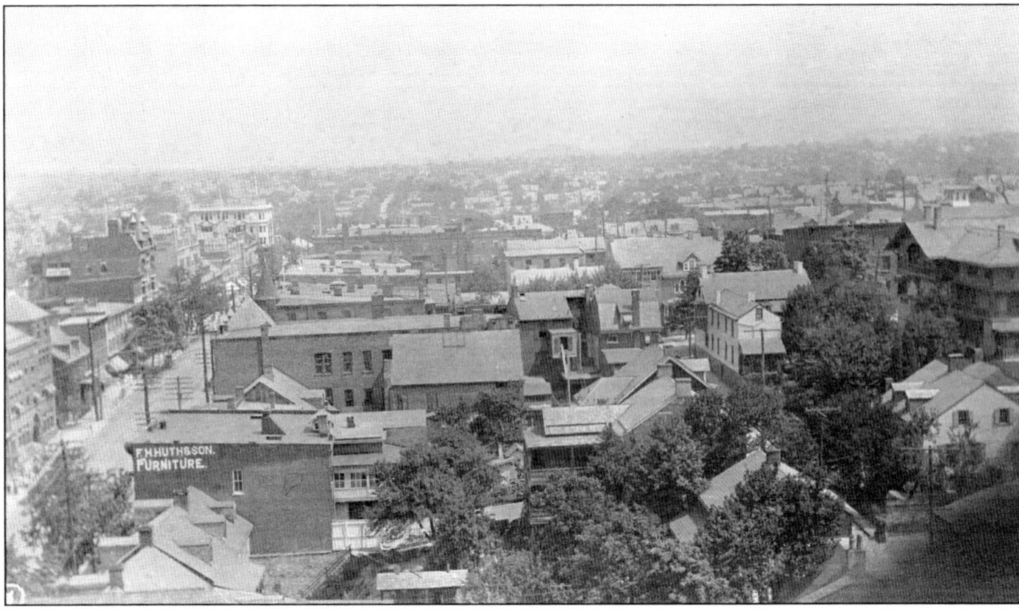

This is an early photograph of industry located north on Main Street. On the left is South Main Street; the first building on the left (west) side of the street is the Lehigh Valley National Bank at the intersection of Market Street, with the Goundie House next door; further up the street on the same side one can see the turreted Myers Building; even further up is the Bethlehem Trust Company at Broad and Main Streets. The alley to the right in the photograph is Heckwelder Place. At far right bottom is the John Heckwelder House (now the headquarters of the Bach Choir of Bethlehem) with two dormer windows in the top floor.

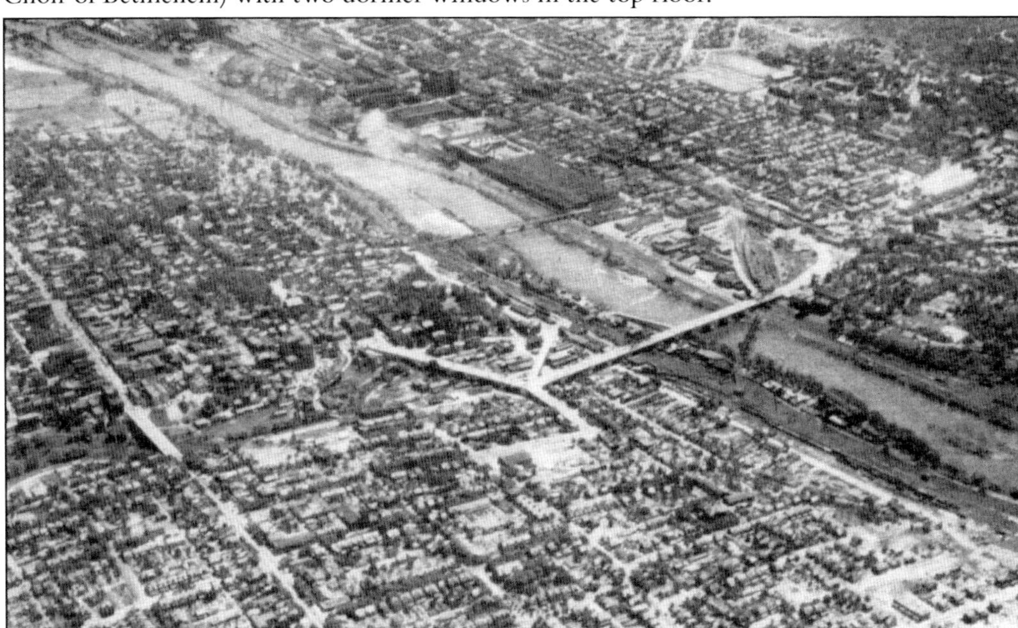

This is an aerial view of the Hill-to-Hill Bridge before Route 378 was connected to the bridge in 1967. The plaza is still there, with the Second Street and Water Street ramps. The eight original ramps allowed travelers to avoid numerous railroad tracks.

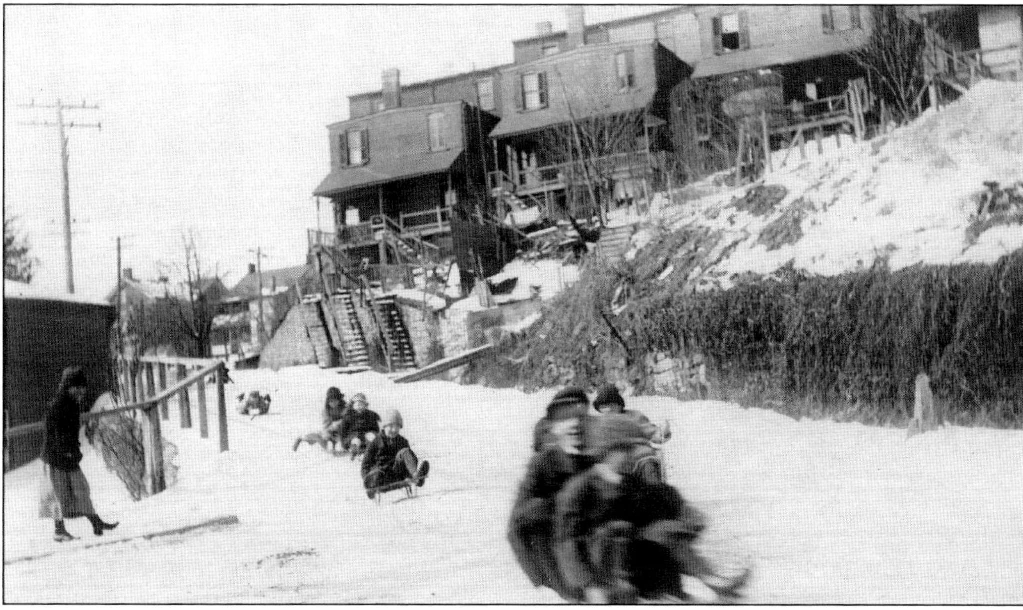

The steep hills of South Bethlehem were great for sledding down in winter but were exhausting to walk up. A day like this could be hazardous for automobiles or horse-drawn wagons, which may be why the children had the streets to themselves. The exact location of this photograph is not known, but it is a familiar scene in South Bethlehem.

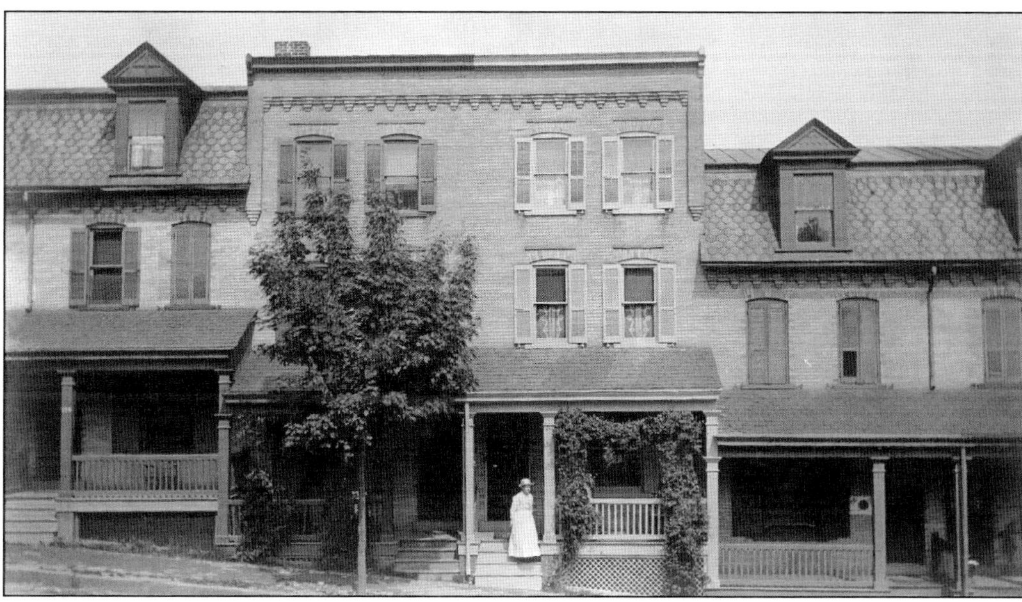

Almost every square inch of South Bethlehem was used for building housing for the employees of Bethlehem Steel and other manufacturers. The builders managed to erect buildings on the steepest hills. Surprisingly, many of the residents found ways to fit in small gardens to grow vegetables in these crowded neighborhoods. In the center of this photograph, the woman in white on her front steps is dressed in her Sunday best. She may have been on her way to church services or shopping downtown.

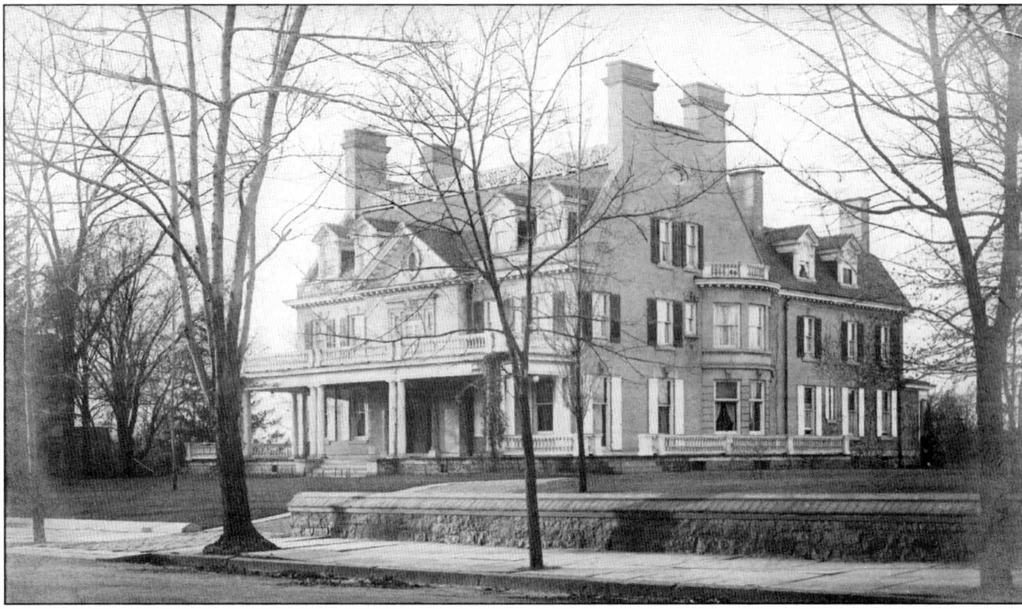

At the turn of the 20th century, the president of the E.P. Wilbur Trust Company, Warren A. Wilbur, built his Colonial Revival mansion on West Third Street, where he lived with his wife, Kate Brodhead Wilbur. Wilbur's married son, Robert, lived on the corner of West Third and Cherokee Streets and from his proximity fondly called the mansion "the big house." After Warren's death in 1932, the mansion eventually went into the ownership of the Illick family, who turned it into apartments.

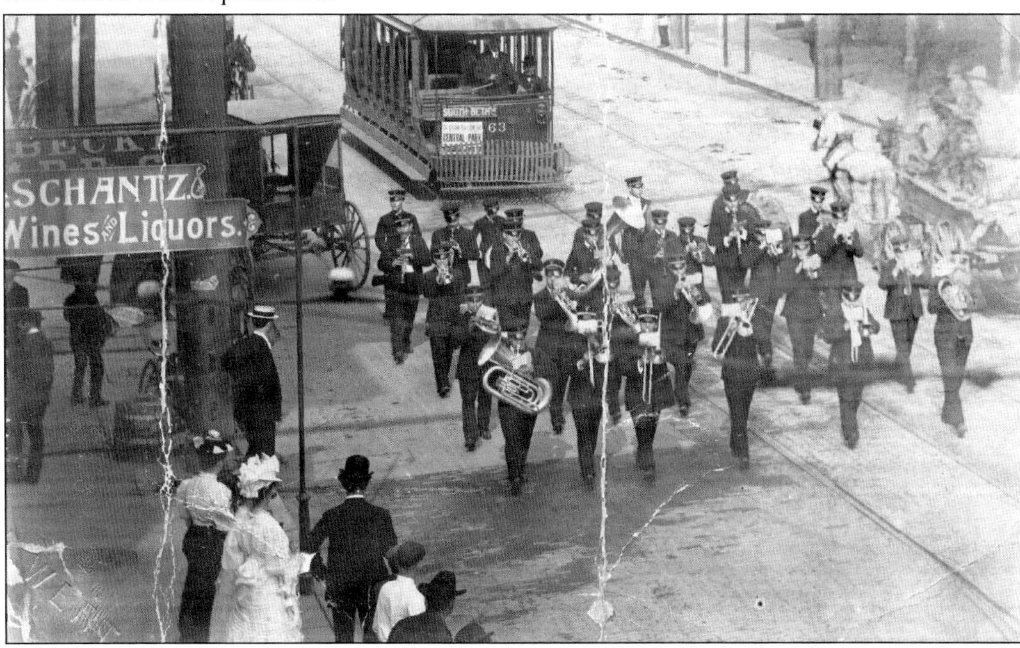

A brass band is seen marching in a parade in Bethlehem with trolley car No. 63 following close behind. The trolley is marked South Bethlehem and has a sign advertising Central Park. The band is also passing a sign for Schantz Wines and Liquors. A carriage and wagon make way for the parade. Wertz Photography of Allentown, Pennsylvania, published this card.

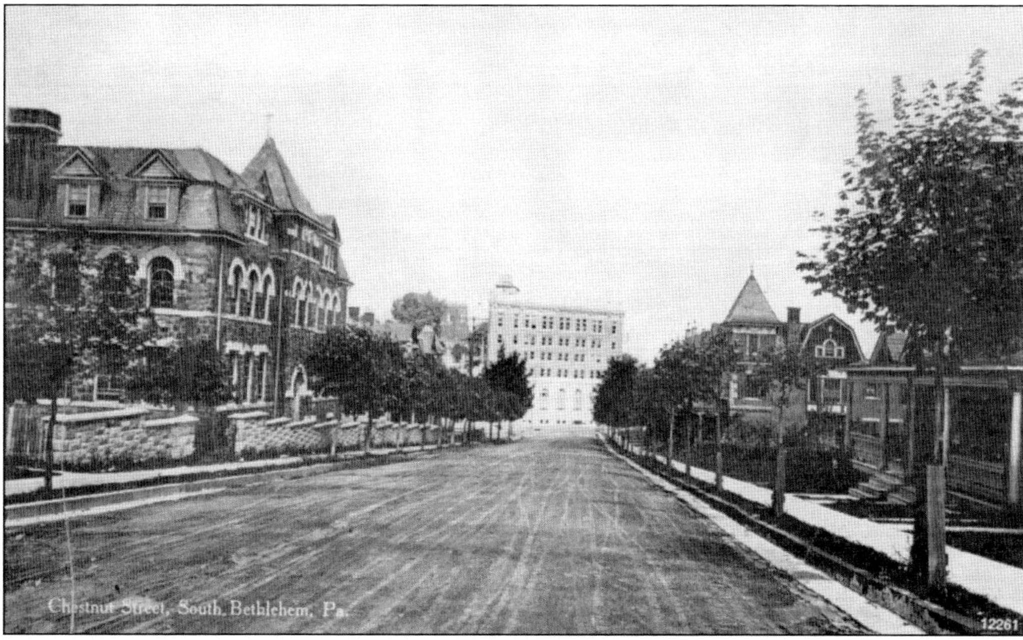

Looking north on Chestnut Street, now known as Montclair Avenue, the Flatiron or the E.P. Wilbur Trust Company Building is seen in the distance. On the far left is the Holy Ghost Parochial School. Also on the left, hidden at the end of the block, is the Colosseum Skating Rink. This view has not changed much today except the road is now paved.

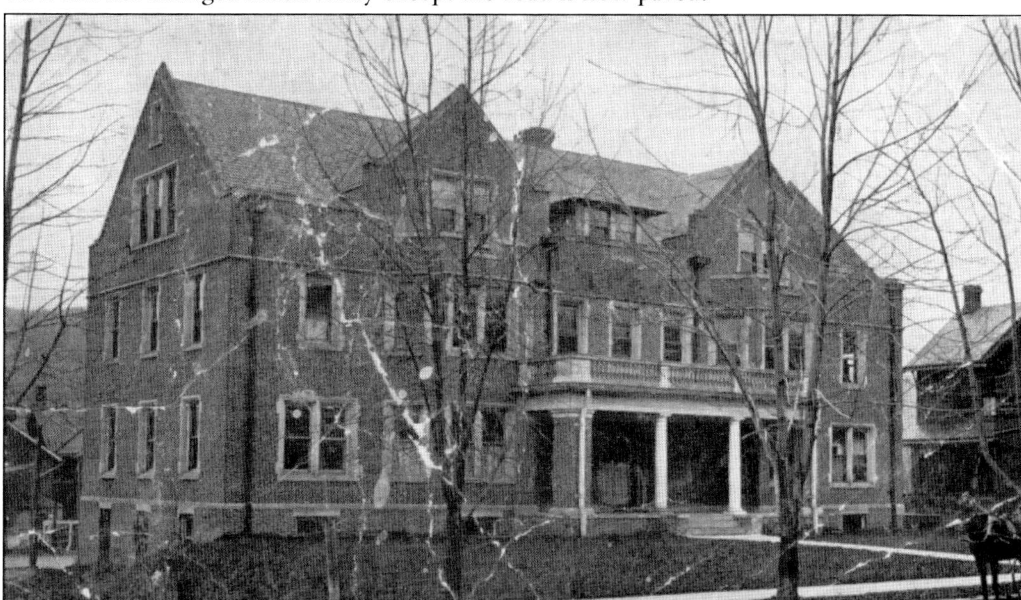

Here is Leonard Hall, founded in 1907 by the Rt. Rev. Ethelbert Talbot, in the 800 block of Delaware Avenue, Fountain Hill. It was originally built as a home for pretheological students who were pursuing undergraduate studies at Lehigh University in preparation for the ministry of the Episcopal Church. Talbot opened the home to Bethlehem Steel employees during a housing shortage due to World War I armament orders. The building was remodeled in 1960 and housed the offices of the Episcopal Diocese of Bethlehem. St. Luke's Hospital now owns the property.

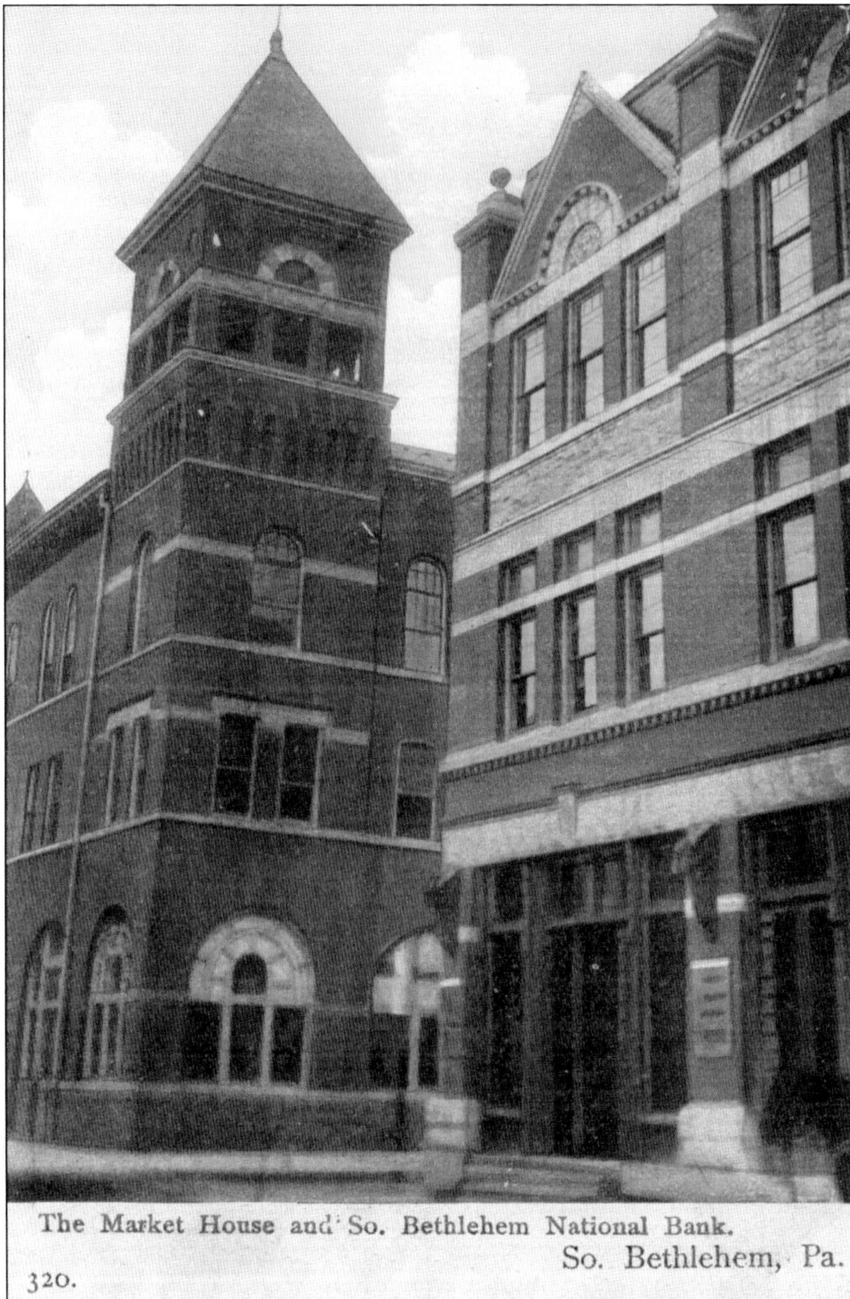

In this view, one can see the Market House and the South Bethlehem National Bank at Third and Adams Street. The Market House, built in 1875, was a three-story brick building with a tower. It was designed by A.W. Leh to serve as a market on the first floor, the second floor for borough offices, and the third floor as an auditorium. The South Bethlehem National Bank opened in 1889. The bank served South Bethlehem until 1934. During those years, the bank also printed $1,140,110 worth of national currency. The bank became known as Bethlehem National Bank in 1920 and moved across the street.

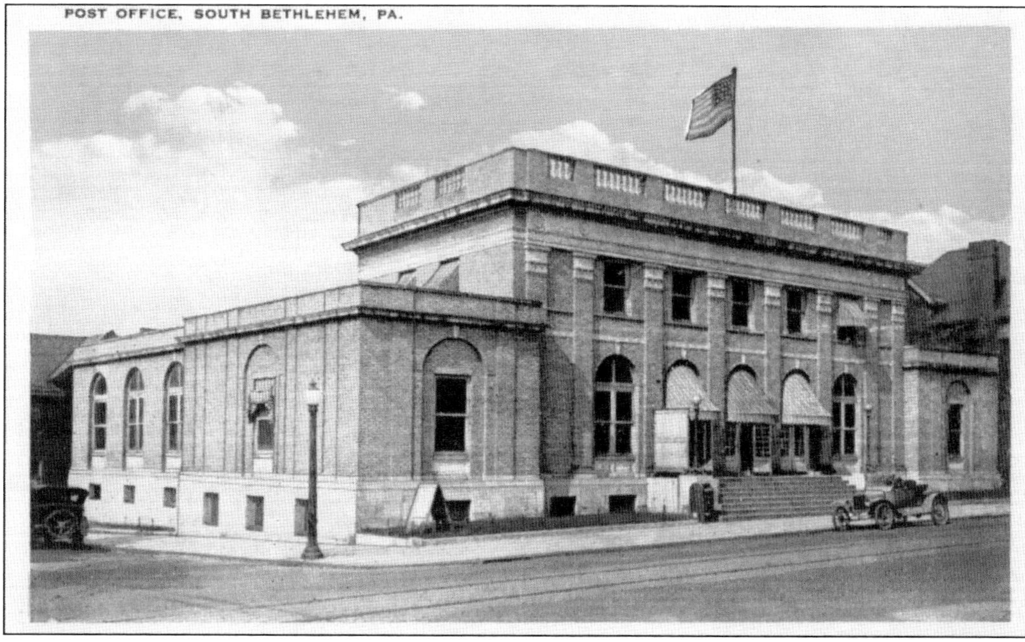

The post office for South Bethlehem is at the intersection of West Fourth Street and Brodhead Avenue. The Beaux Arts–style building was erected in 1916. Architect A.W. Leh had offices in this building. In 2011, the US Postal Service selected the post office for closure, but after public outcry, it was kept in service. The building is included in the South Bethlehem Historic District.

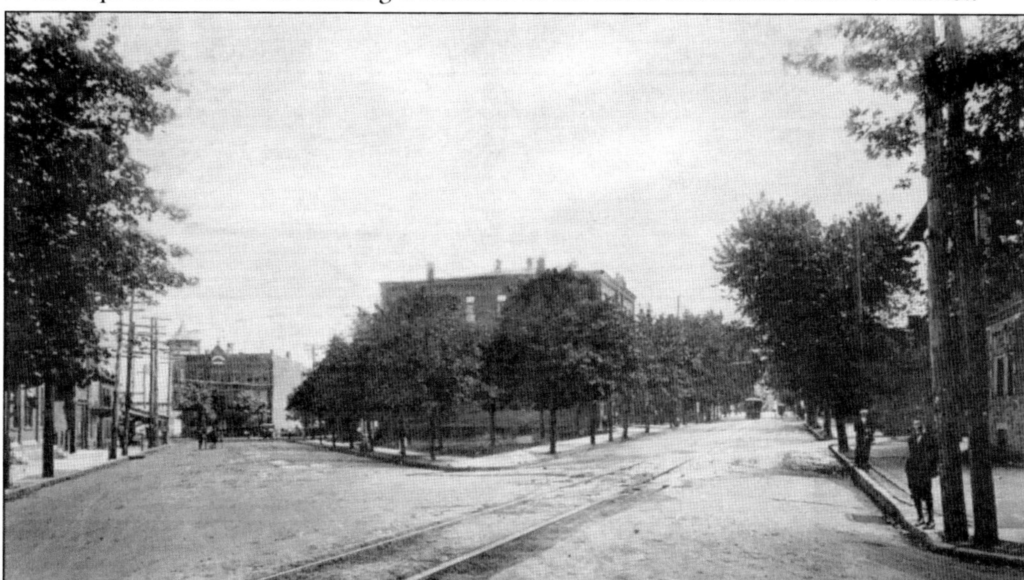

At the intersection of Fourth Street (on right) and Broadway is a trolley. Broadway ends at New Street where Broadway Hotel is located. On the right, where the gentleman is standing on the corner of Birkel Street was the Northampton Club, complete with a bowling alley. The executives of the Lehigh Valley Railroad founded this club. Bethlehem community leaders sought to belong to the club at the time, such as Archibald Johnston, the Wilbur men, and Lehigh University faculty. One could enjoy a good-quality beer and "Pennsylvania Dutch" meals.

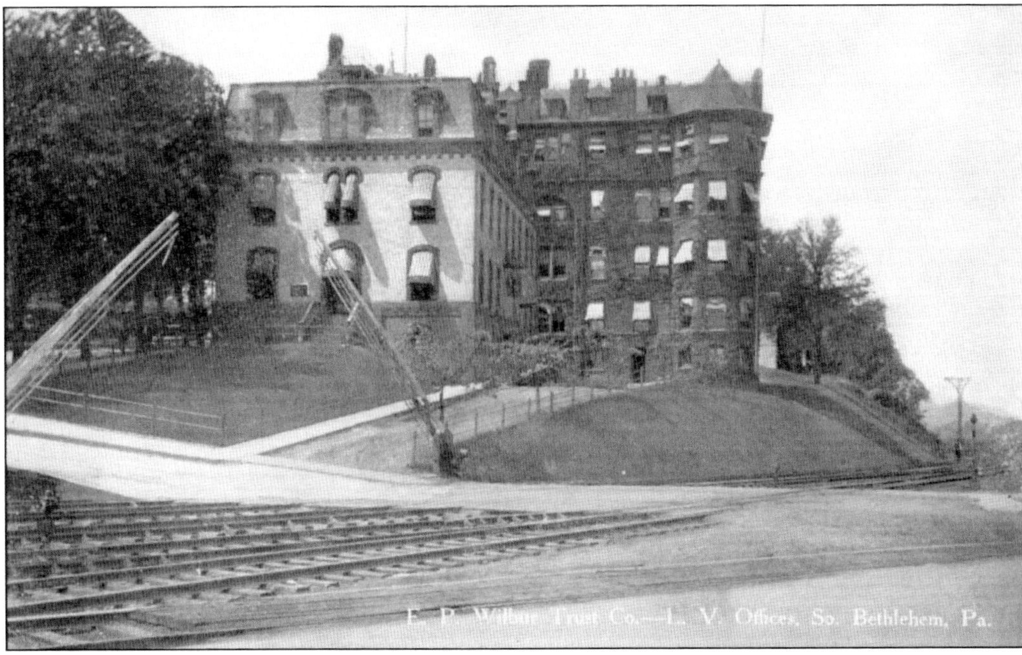

Here is a view of Elisha Packer Wilbur Trust Company (chartered in 1870) and the Lehigh Valley Railroad headquarters with railroad tracks and crossing gates in foreground. Wilbur, nephew of Asa Packer, was an ex-president of the Lehigh Valley Railroad and lived in a beautiful mansion one block away on Wyandotte Street. These buildings are a part of the Fountain Hill Historic District and are used as apartment buildings today.

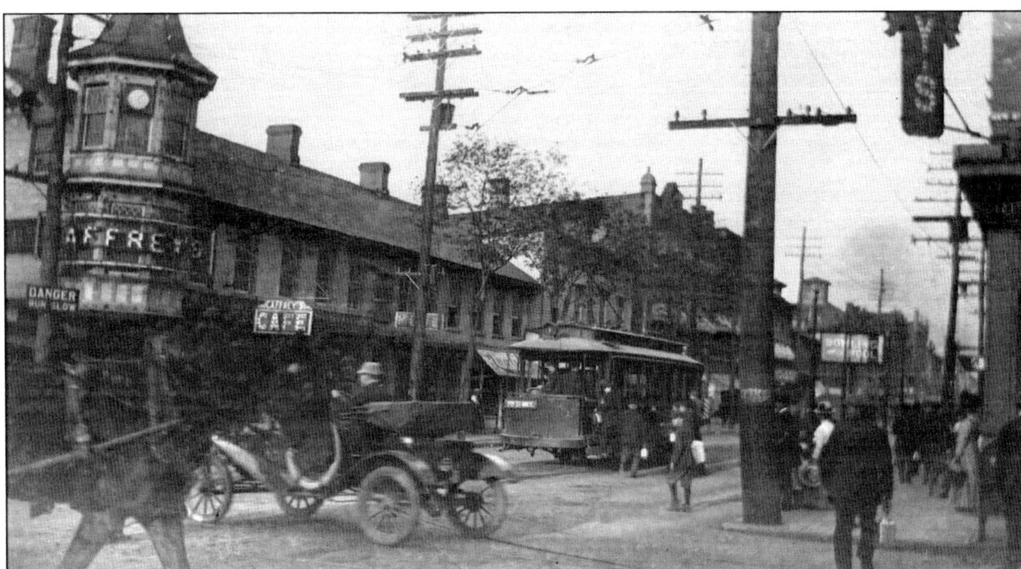

Here is the busy intersection of Third and New Streets. The sidewalks are full of pedestrians, and the automobile needs to cross the intersection quickly before the trolley arrives. On the far left is Caffrey's Hotel. Terrence C. Caffrey built the hotel, which included a restaurant and bar room, in 1887. Caffrey arrived in Bethlehem in 1878 to work for the Bethlehem Iron Company. He saved his earnings to invest in real estate in South Bethlehem.

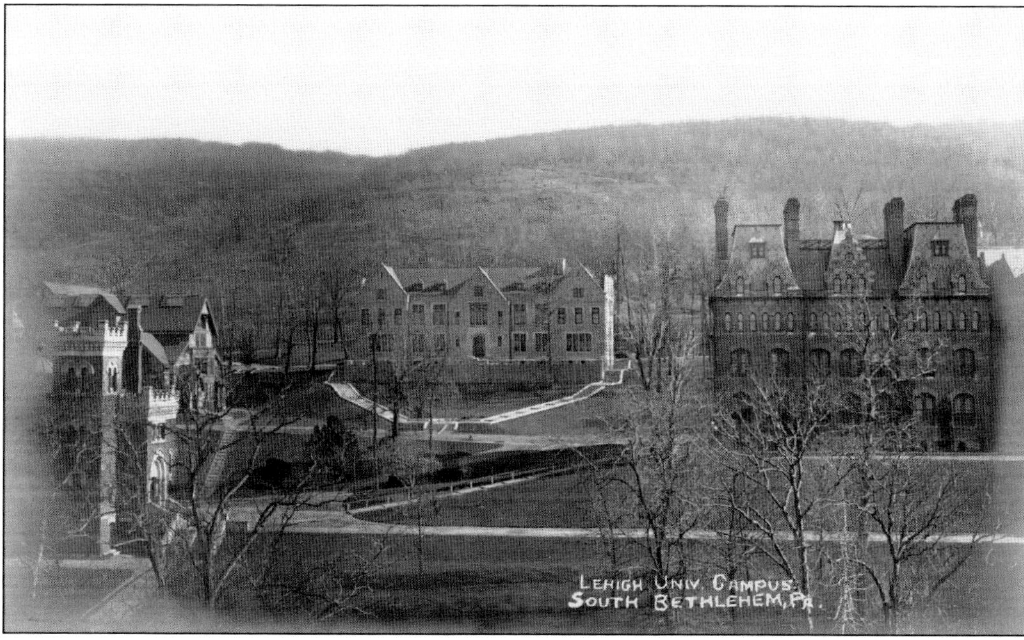

This is an early-1900s view of the Lehigh University campus. On the left is Lucy Packer Linderman Library. Asa Packer endowed $500,000 to build a library and purchase books in memory of his daughter. The library was completed in 1877. In the center is Richards House, a dormitory, and on the right is the University Center.

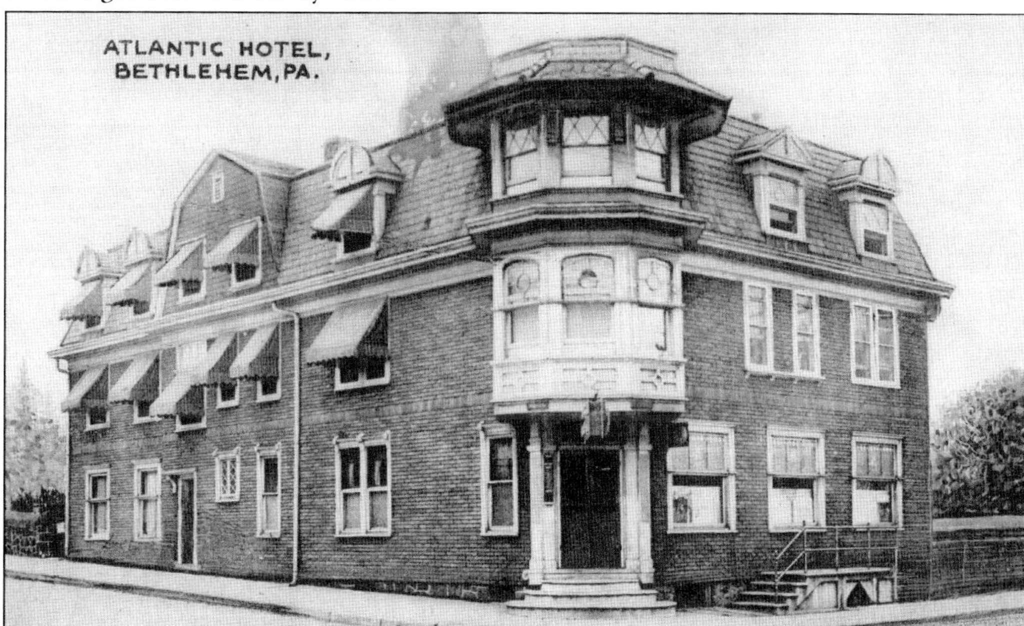

This is the Atlantic Hotel, which is located at Atlantic and East Fourth Streets. The hotel still stands within the Four Blocks International, a neighborhood in South Bethlehem, and operates as a rooming house. Louis Katona operated the hotel until the 1950s, and then Ernest Shinko became the proprietor. It was a Hungarian neighborhood hotel that offered rooms by the day or week.

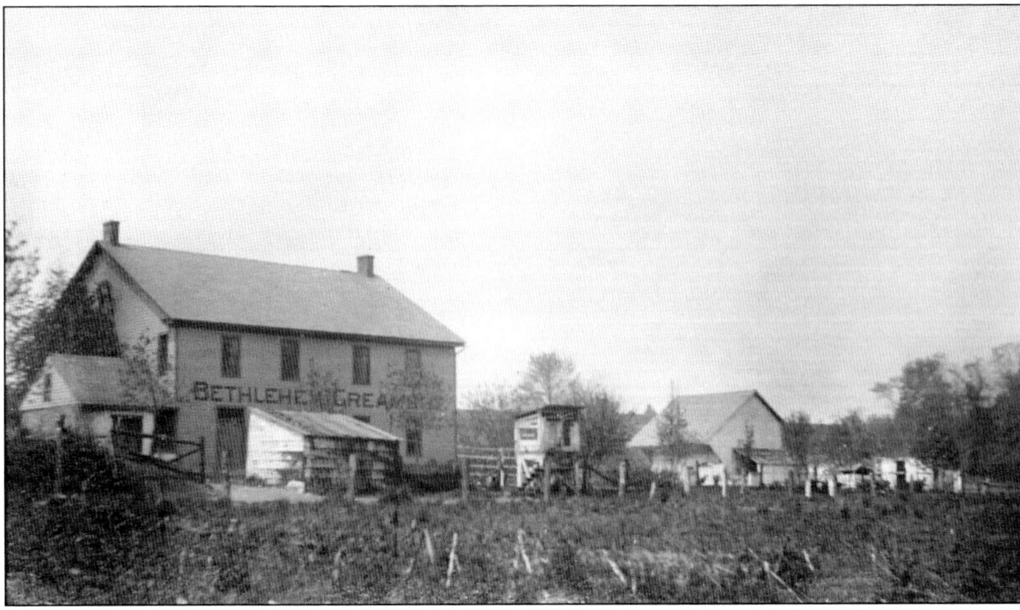

Bethlehem Creamery was a small dairy farm that operated in the early 1900s and was a member of the Pennsylvania Dairy Union. Its specialties were butter, cheese, and condensed milk. Located south of Bethlehem, it was a single-owner business. In 1918, the Bethlehem Creamery placed an ad in the *American Produce Review* to sell its dairy processing equipment. As no more information could be found on this enterprise, one can assume it went out of business.

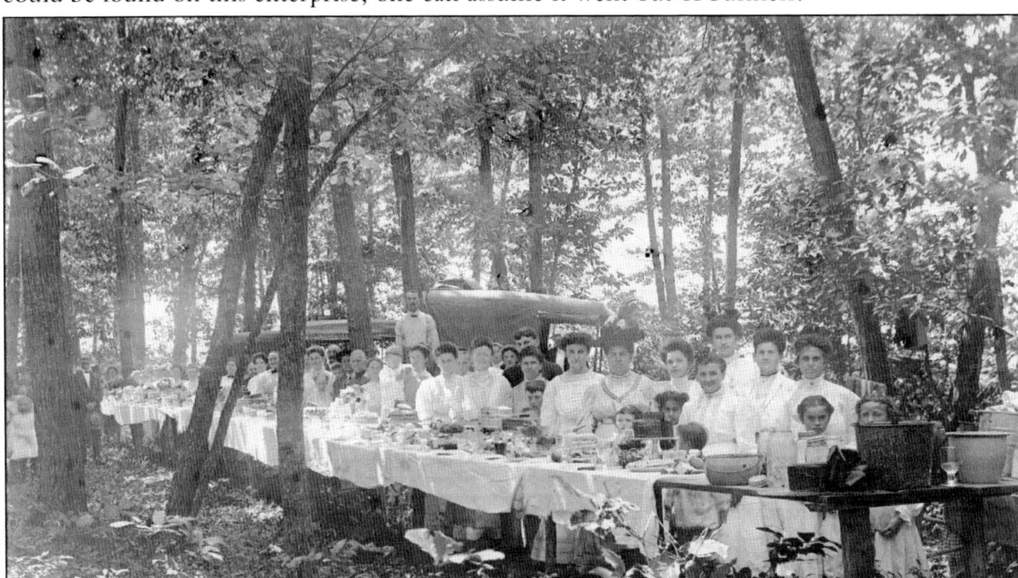

On a hot August day, this church Sunday school group gathered for a picnic in a shady grove along the Lehigh River. The families are dressed in their best Sunday clothes for their annual picnic. A few members of the group owned automobiles to help transport the food, dishes, pots, and cups. For many of the churches in Bethlehem, Sunday schools were organized years before the church buildings were constructed. Sunday schools were an effective way to assimilate young people through a moral and social education.

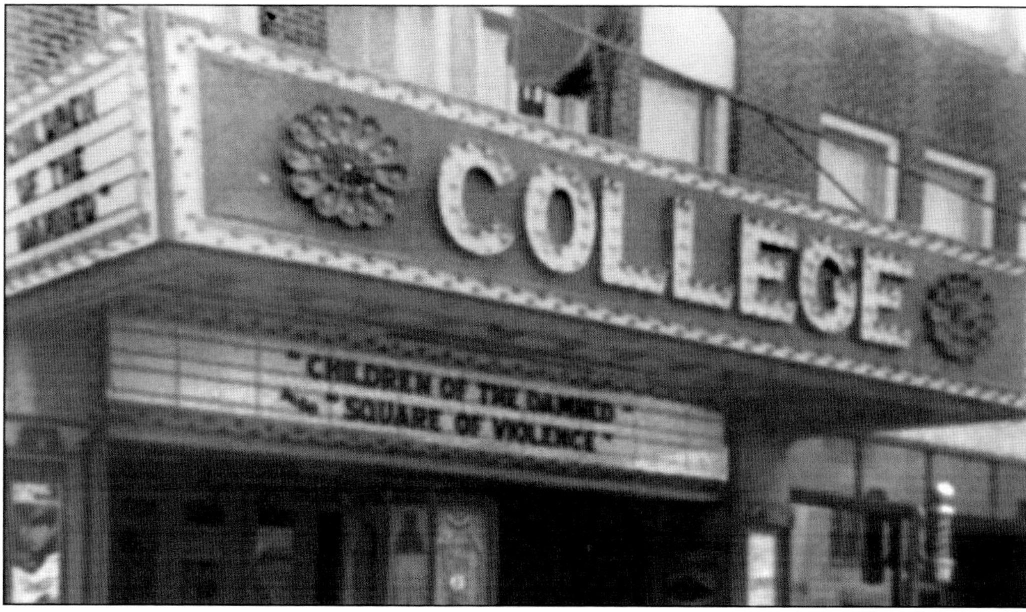

College Theater was located on Fourth Street and was built in the 1930s. It was designed by architect William Harold Lee to have 1,381 seats. The Cities Theaters Corporation owned the theater from 1935 to 1940. Leggett-Florin Booking Service became the owner in 1950. From 1961 to 1969, the Boyd Theater Circuit owned it. Adult movies were shown there in the 1970s. The block was torn down in the 1990s. The Goosey Gander restaurant is now located on the site.

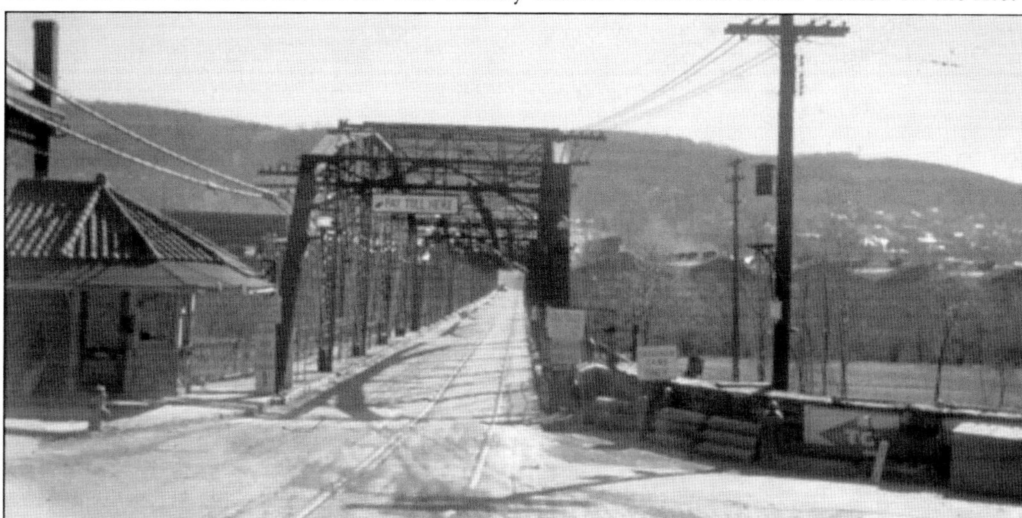

With the expansion of Bethlehem Steel in the early 1900s, an additional bridge was needed to serve Bethlehem. A site was selected from Front and Anthracite Streets in Northampton Heights on the south side to the eastern end of Broad Street on the north. It was in the area known as Minsi Trail, an old Native American fording site. R.E. Newmeyer, an engineer, designed the iron bridge to carry traffic through the Bethlehem Steel property. Structural failures plagued the bridge in the 1970s. The pedestrian walkways were the first to go. In 1979, the Pennsylvania Department of Transportation closed the bridge. The new concrete Minsi Trail Bridge opened in 1984.

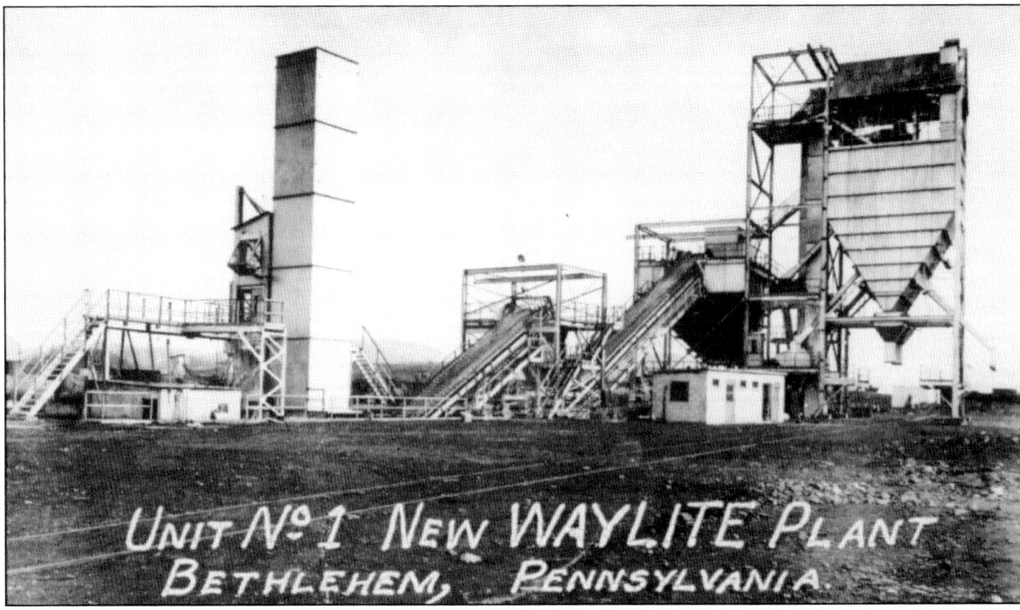

Here is a photograph of the Unit No. 1 of the Waylite plant, located on Easton Road. The plant, a subsidiary of Bethlehem Steel, used a process that combined blast furnace slag with water to make pellets used in the manufacture of concrete building blocks. Roy McMindes bought the company from Bethlehem Steel in 1985.

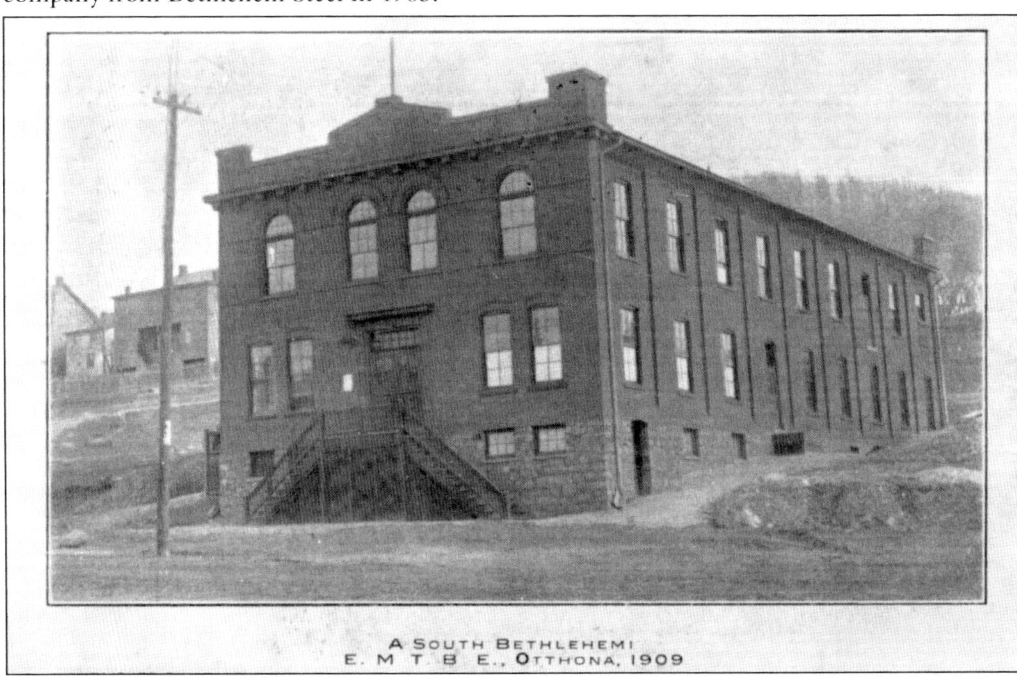

The Hungarian community in South Bethlehem built this hall on Evans Street. The Hungarian word for home is *otthona*. Frank Biro, a popular photographer on the south side, took this photograph in 1909. At the time, the building housed a large dance hall with a stage, a kitchen and bar, a bowling alley, and offices for insurance policies. Today, the Panthers Athletic Association Bowling League uses the building. The building has 10 lanes, a bar, jukebox, and a restaurant.

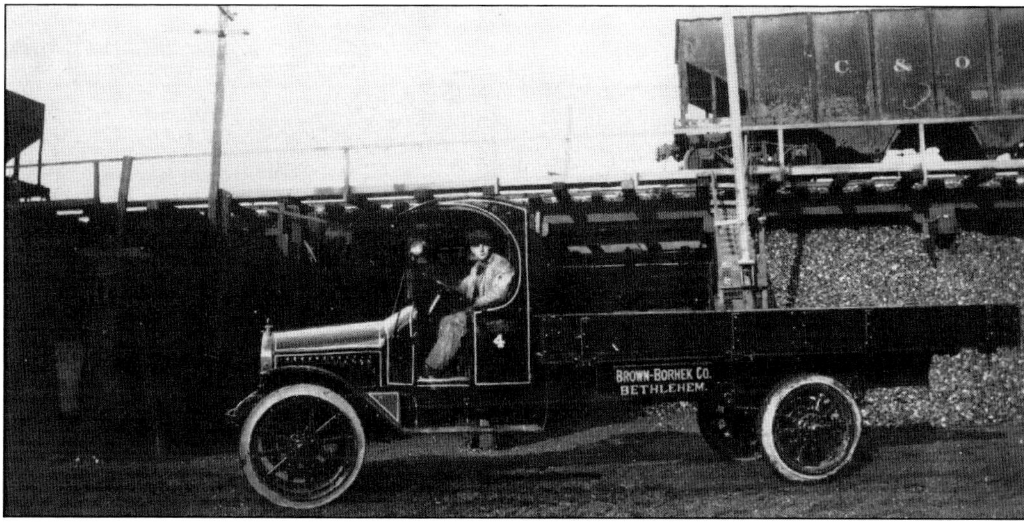

Here is a coal delivery truck of Brown-Borhek Company, owned by Charles Brown and Ashton C. Borhek. The company was founded in 1849 by Ashton's grandfather Frederick Borhek. The company was comprised of a wood planing mill on West Third Street and Brodhead Avenue and a lumber and coal yard at Main Street and Lehigh Avenue. In 1853, Frederick Borhek built the first three houses in South Bethlehem when it was still primarily farmland. This was a few years before the Lehigh Valley Railroad began running trains to Bethlehem. Brown-Borhek supplied building materials for the early Bethlehem Iron Company and then Bethlehem Steel Corporation.

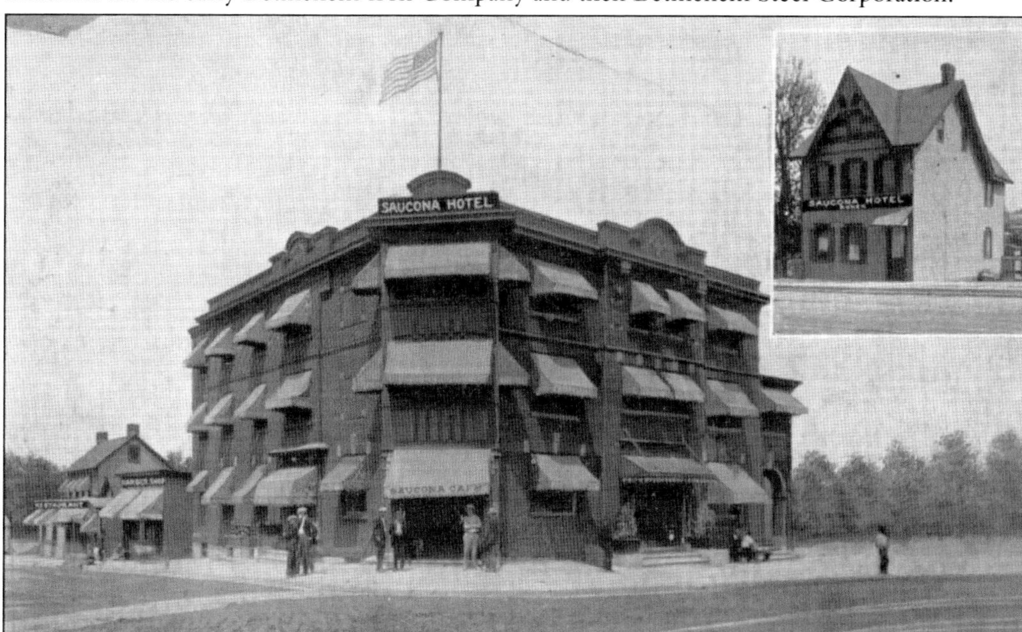

The Saucona Hotel was located at Fourth and Anthracite Streets in the Northampton Heights. The hotel offered its guests a restaurant, steam bar, café, barbershop, and garage. This was a favorite place in the early 1900s to go for dinner for a special occasion. Owner Charles Boyd hired A.W. Leh to design alterations to the hotel in 1918. Frank and Theresa Ortwein Keller and their daughter Catherine and son-in-law Andrew were the last owners of the hotel until it was demolished in 1967 to make way for Bethlehem Steel Corporation's new basic oxygen furnace.

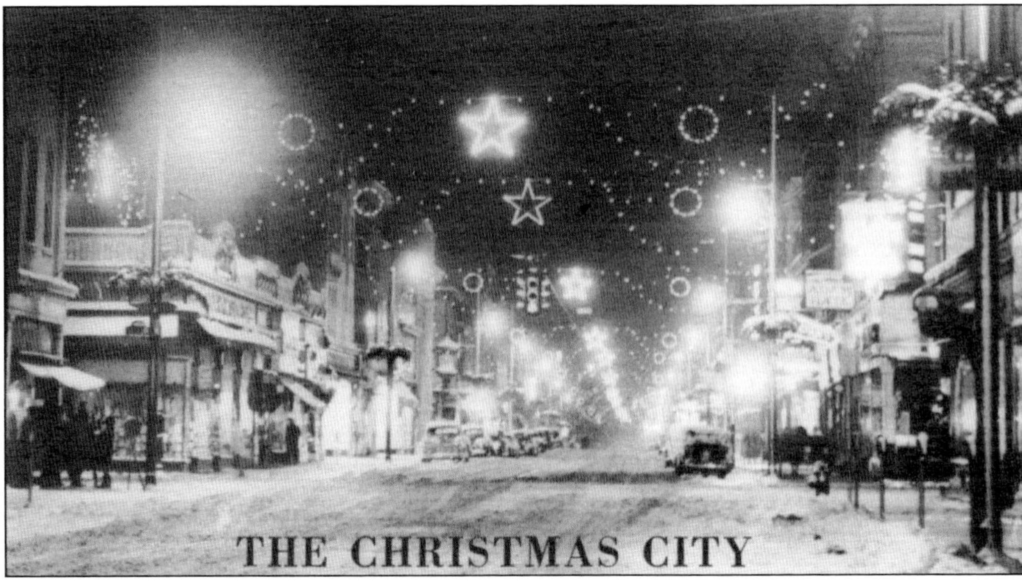

Here is a photograph of Third Street, lit for the holidays. Bethlehem is famous for its lovely decorations during the Christmas holidays. Vernon K. Melhado, president of the Bethlehem Chamber of Commerce, was the guiding force in establishing the Christmas City Program in 1931. The country was suffering through the Great Depression, and the 100-foot electric Christmas star and extensive street and bridge lights were just what people needed. Thousands of tourists visit the city to take in the spectacle and continue the tradition today.

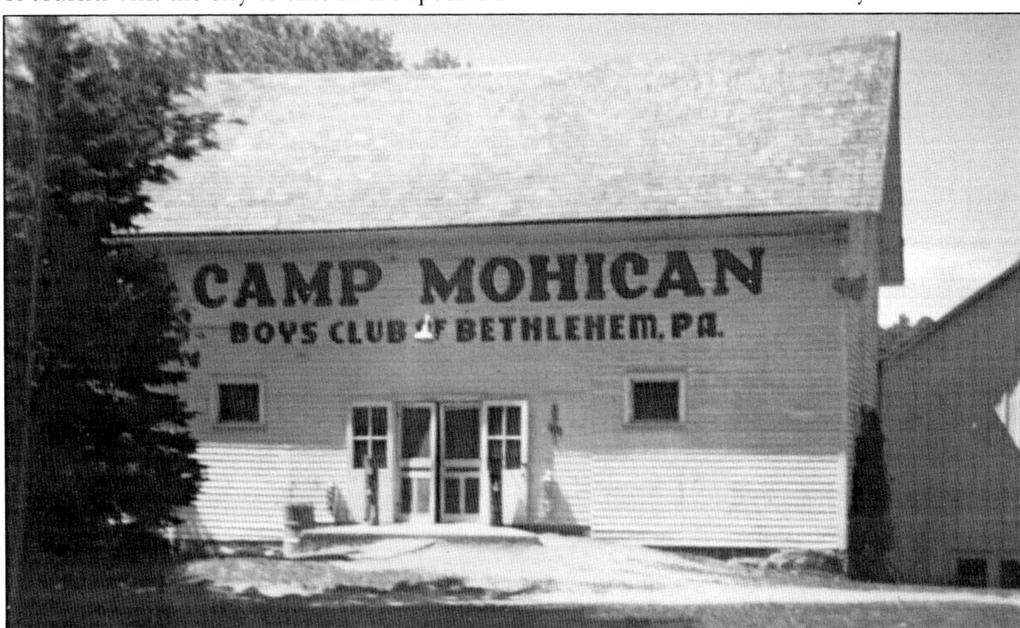

The Boys Club of Bethlehem organized a camping program every summer for four weeks at Camp Mohican. The camp was located in Delaware, New Jersey, near the Rattlesnake Swamp Loop Trail on the Appalachian Trail. It was started in the 1920s as a place for the boys to escape the heat of the summer in Bethlehem. The camp is now owned by the federal government and leased to the Appalachian Mountain Club.

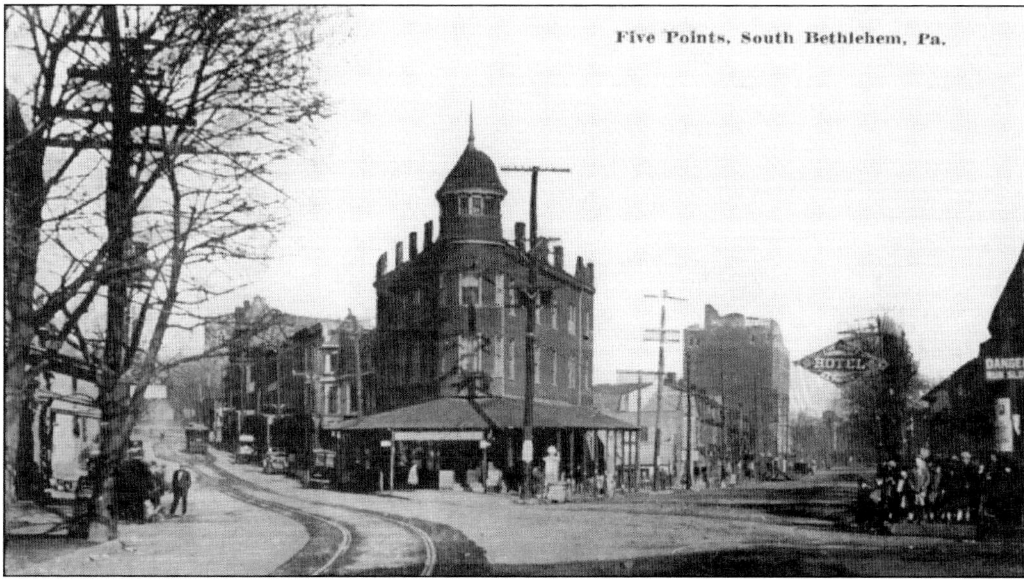

This is Five Points, an important business district in South Bethlehem. It includes Wyandotte Street, Broadway, and Dakotah Street. Directly center is a grocery store. On the far right is a sign for the Five Points Hotel. A trolley of the South Bethlehem & Saucon Street Railway Company makes its way up Wyandotte Street on the far left. The back of the E.P. Wilbur Trust Company building can be seen on the left on Broadway. It is a busy intersection with people on each corner navigating through the cars and trolleys.

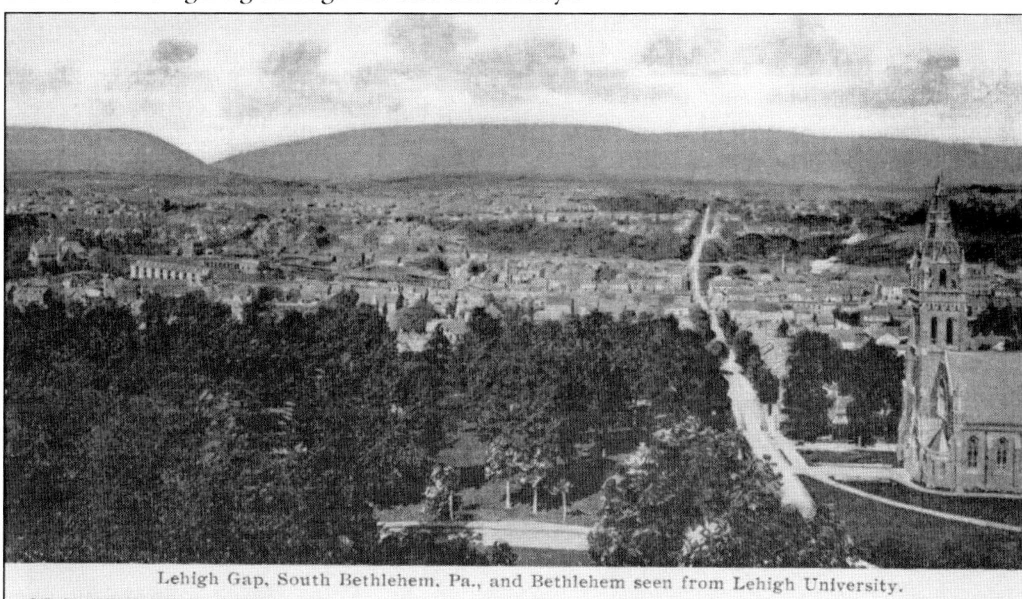

Here is a view of Bethlehem looking south from Lehigh University. On the far right is Packer Memorial Chapel, which was designed by architect Addison Hutton in memory of the founder of Lehigh University, Asa Packer. It was built in 1884. This early-1900s photograph of the Lehigh University campus looks empty without its current buildings. This is a view down New Street and over the New Street Bridge that connected South Bethlehem with Bethlehem. Far off in the distance is the Lehigh Gap.

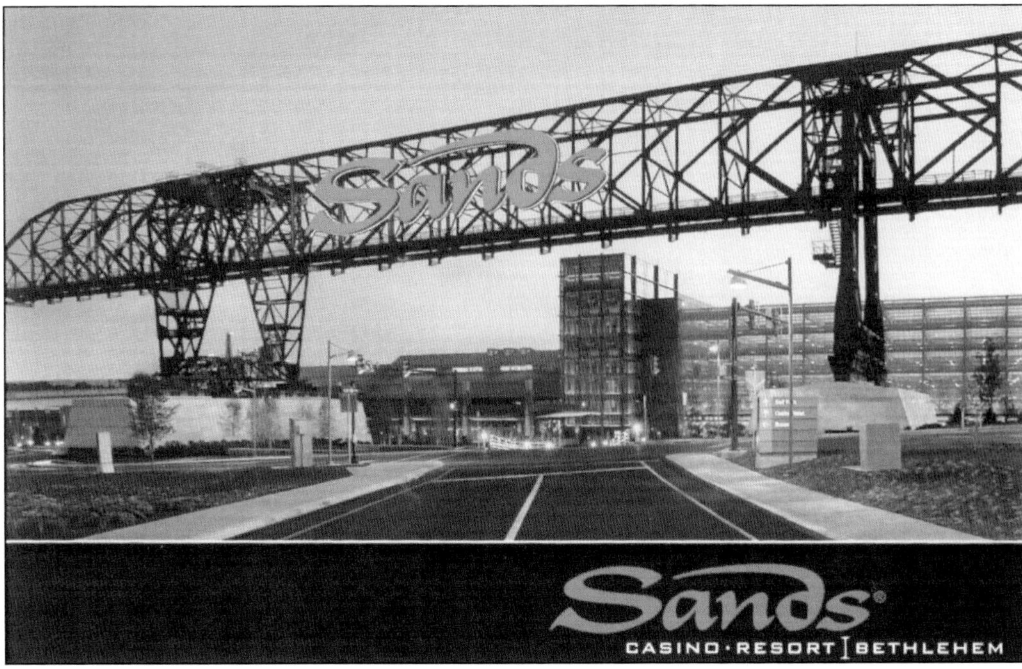

The 139,000-square-foot Sands Casino opened in 2009. It was designed with an industrial look to pay homage to the Bethlehem Steel Corporation, the previous owner of the site. The casino was built on the ore fields of the once-great steel manufacturer. Because of the economic recession of 2008, Sands has gradually added the hotel (2011), restaurants, and outlet shops. A massive ore bridge from the Bethlehem Steel days was saved for the entrance to the casino.

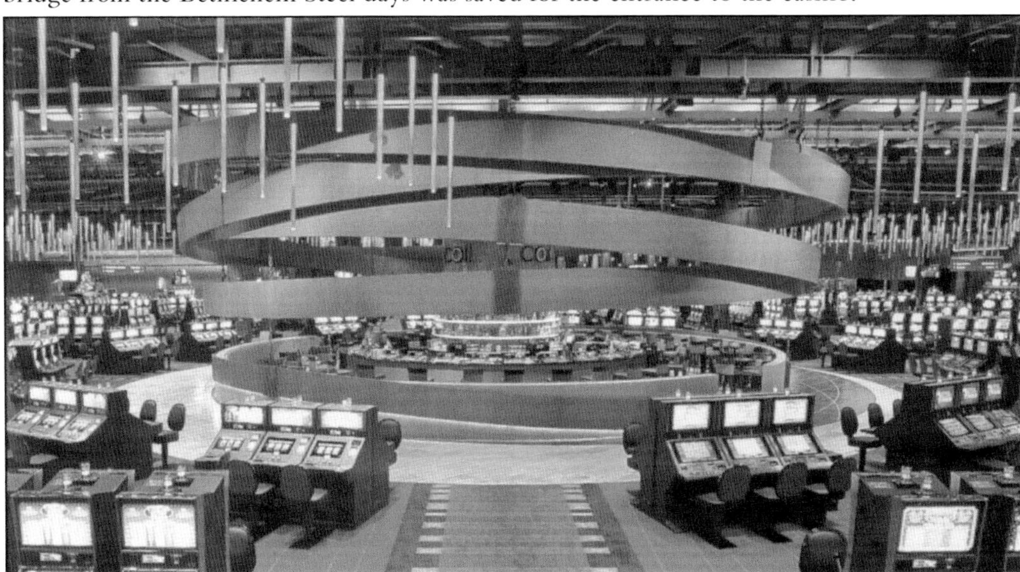

The Sands Casino is the most visited casino in Pennsylvania. The casino offers a variety of slot machines and tables for poker, blackjack, craps, roulette, baccarat, and pai gow tiles. Sands offers fine and casual dining through its 10 restaurants. The Sands Casino Resort Bethlehem Hotel has 300 rooms. The Shoppes at Sands, now the Outlets at Sands, provides luxury outlet stores like Coach, Chico's, DKNY, Izod, Lenox, Talbots, Van Heusen, and more.

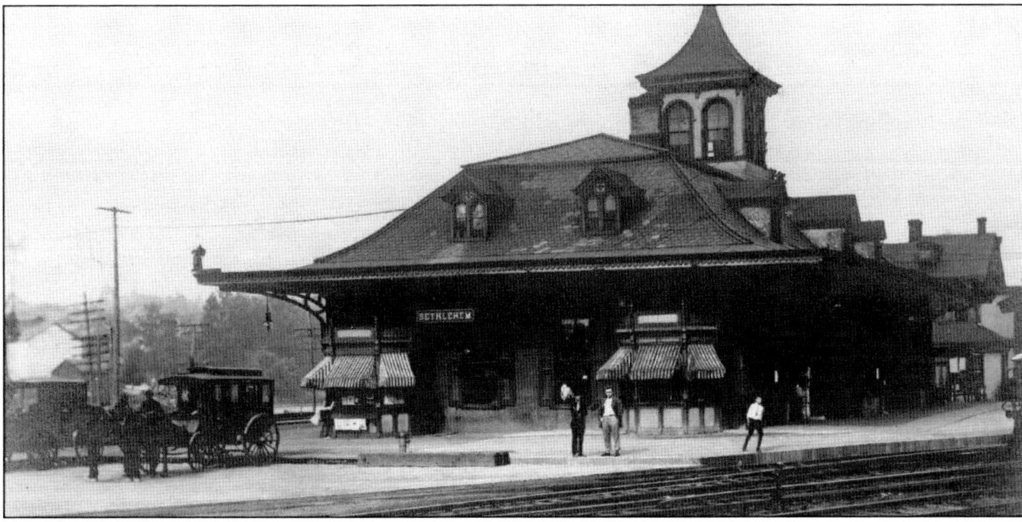

The Union Depot opened on November 18, 1867, to serve the passengers of the Lehigh Valley and North Pennsylvania Railroads. The businessmen of Bethlehem and employees of the two railroads lined the platform to welcome the first Lehigh Valley westbound train to arrive at the depot. Caleb Yohe, owner of the Eagle Hotel, arrived at the depot by a carriage drawn by four big gray horses and draped with American flags. The crowd was impressed with the new elegant Victorian-style wooden building. Sheriff Fetter bought the first ticket sold from each railroad company that morning.

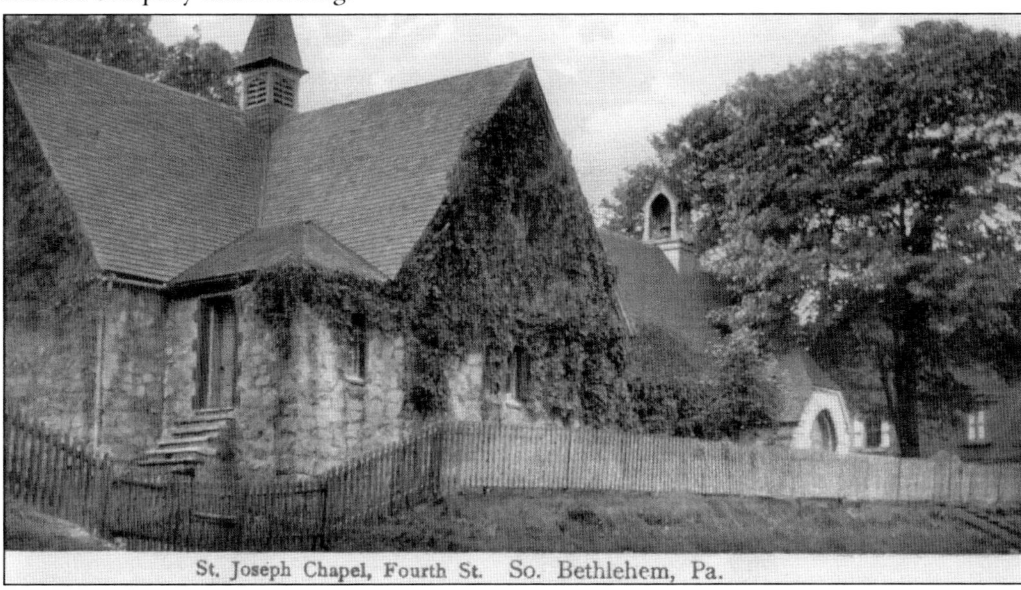

St. Joseph Chapel, Fourth St. So. Bethlehem, Pa.

Joseph and Anna Wharton, both Philadelphia Quakers, founded St. Joseph's Chapel in 1884 for the German immigrants working in the Lehigh Zinc Works. At the time St. Joseph's was built, its location at 1224 East Fourth Street in South Bethlehem was far from the center of town. St. Joseph's Chapel was built by J.S. Allam of South Bethlehem and completed by the winter of 1884. Ownership was transferred to the Church of Nativity in 1892. An addition to the building was constructed in 1897. Greek immigrants arriving in South Bethlehem in the early 1900s sought to establish an Orthodox church. In December 1917, this group purchased the building from Church of the Nativity. The Holy Bethel Pentecostal Church purchased the church in 1967.

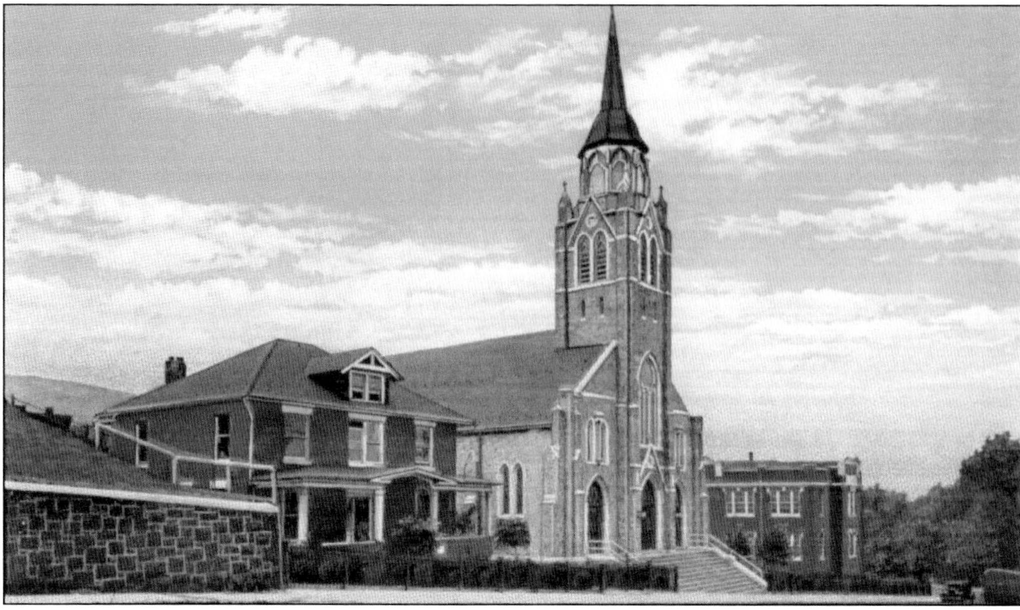

Twenty Hungarian Catholics in the South Bethlehem were interested in establishing their own church in 1903. They purchased property at the southeast corner of Fourth and Hayes Streets and built a stone basement structure. The church was named St. John's Capistrano Roman Catholic. The growth of the parish was rapid, and membership reached 2,000 in 1904. A new expanded church was built in 1910, with services held in the basement and a school and convent built above.

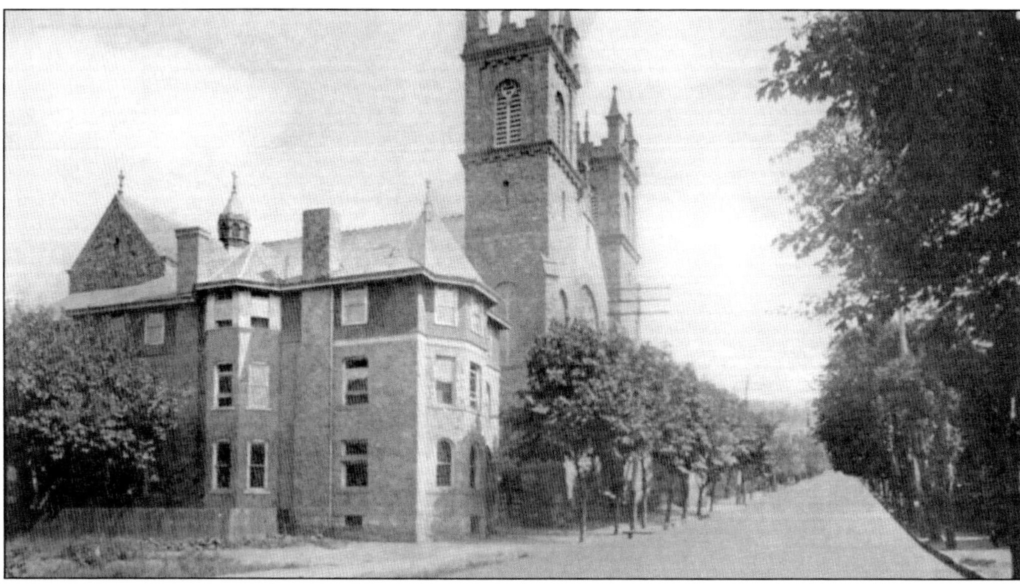

The German immigrants arriving in the second half of the 19th century were primarily of the Catholic faith. The group purchased a lot on Carlton Avenue and erected a 20-by-80-foot brick chapel in 1886, initially known as St. Bernard. Less than 10 years later, the congregation outgrew the church, and plans were made for a second, larger church. In 1906, the cornerstone of the second church, designed by A.W. Leh, was laid, and the church was completed and dedicated in 1910. In 2008, as part of the Diocese of Allentown's consolidation of parishes, the parish is now referred to as the University Parish of Holy Ghost.

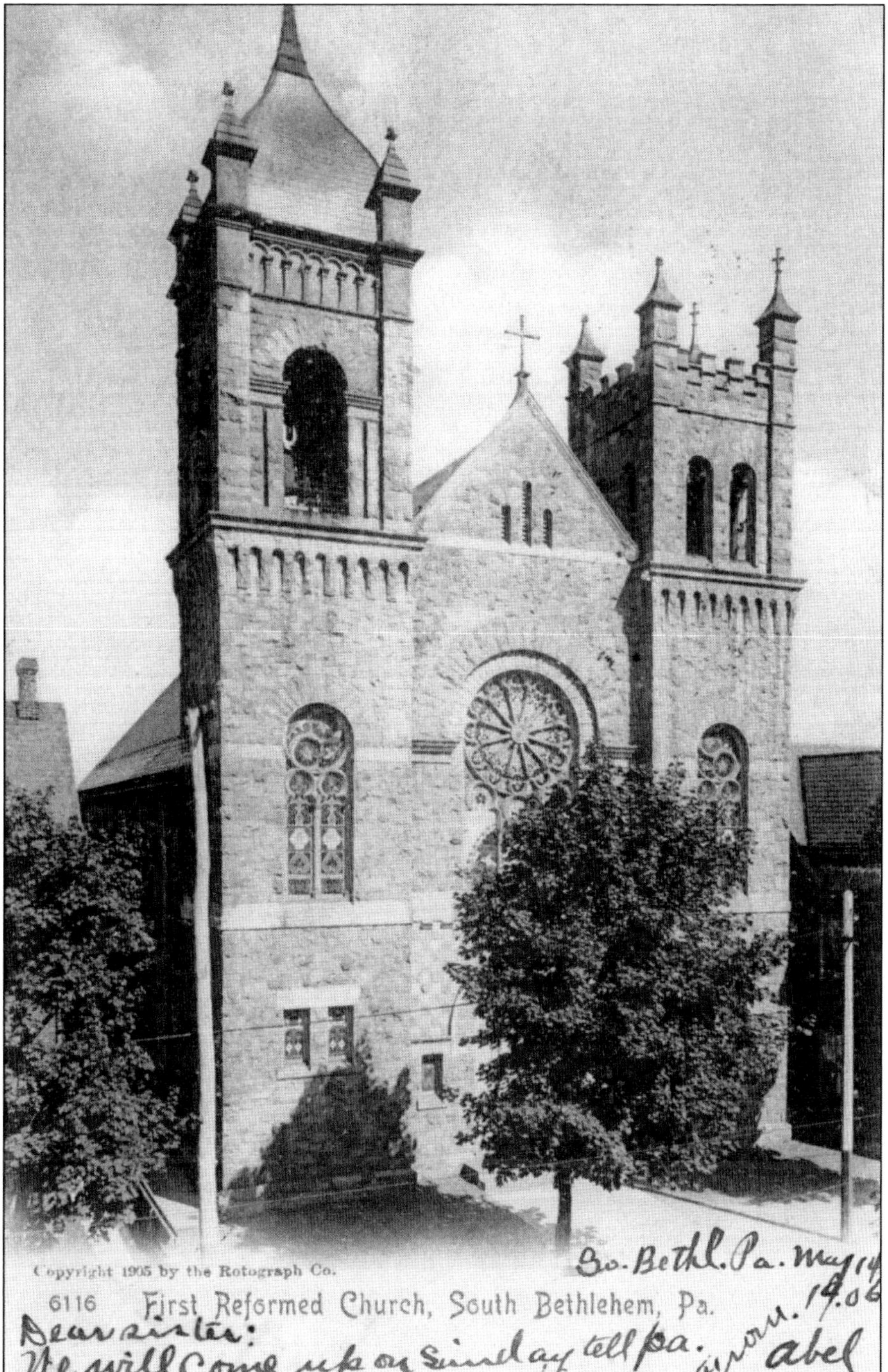

German immigrants in South Bethlehem organized the First Reformed Church in 1867. Shown here is their second church, built in 1896 and designed by A.W. Leh. The church sported double towers with battlements and elaborate arch work. Lightning damaged one tower, and it was never restored to look as it did originally. The facade of the brick structure was highlighted by a wheel window and opalescent stained glass.

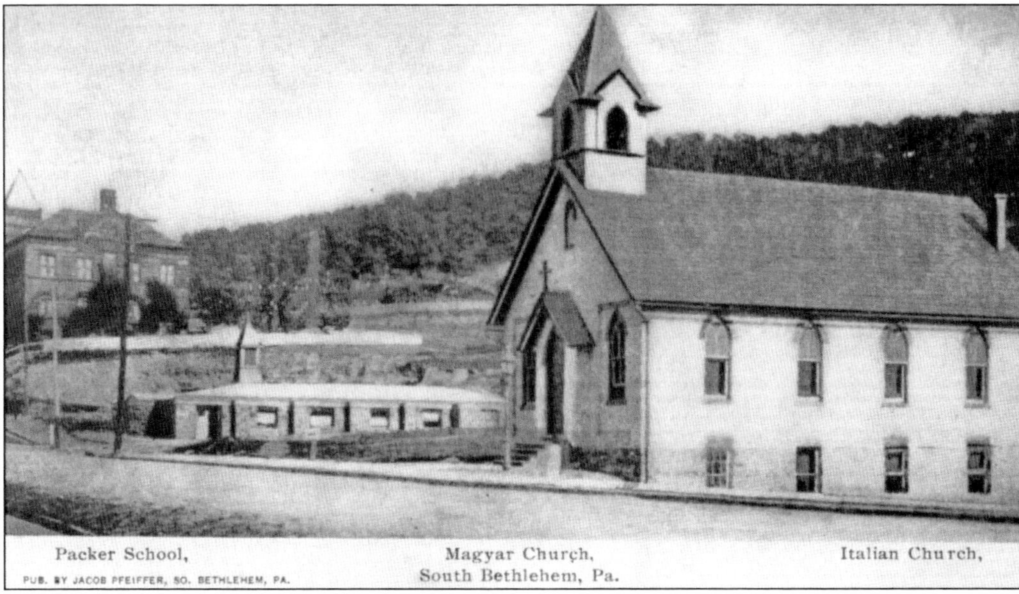

This postcard is unusual in that Jacob Pfeiffer, the publisher, used nicknames to identify the buildings instead of the official names. From left to right, the Packer School was built in 1890 at a cost of $15,473. It was located on the south side of Fourth Street, between Centre and Cemetery Streets. In 1903, St. John's Capistrano Hungarian Roman Catholic Church purchased property at the southeast corner of Fourth and Hayes Streets and built a stone basement structure for the church. The Church of the Holy Rosary was built at Fourth and Hayes Streets in 1902. This first church was of modest size and built of brick with belfry, spire, and cross. The builder was Benedict H. Birkel, the dominant church builder in South Bethlehem.

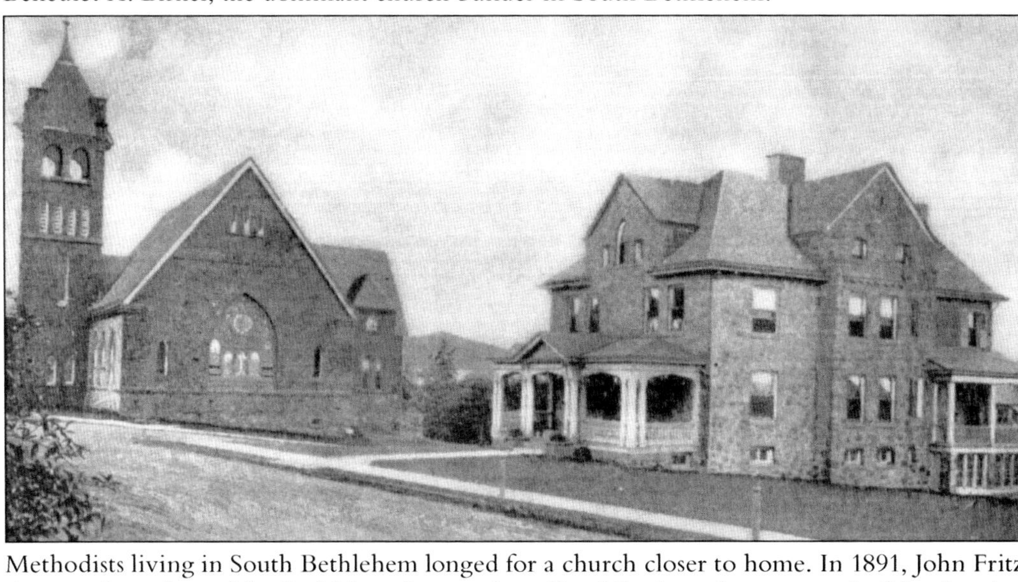

Methodists living in South Bethlehem longed for a church closer to home. In 1891, John Fritz, the superintendent of the Bethlehem Ironworks, offered funds to the group to build a church at the corner of Packer and Montclair Avenues. His donation covered the entire cost of the church and served to honor his parents, George and Mary Fritz. Architect A.W. Leh was hired to design the church in Gothic Revival style and to include an auditorium. It was the only church of its kind in South Bethlehem.

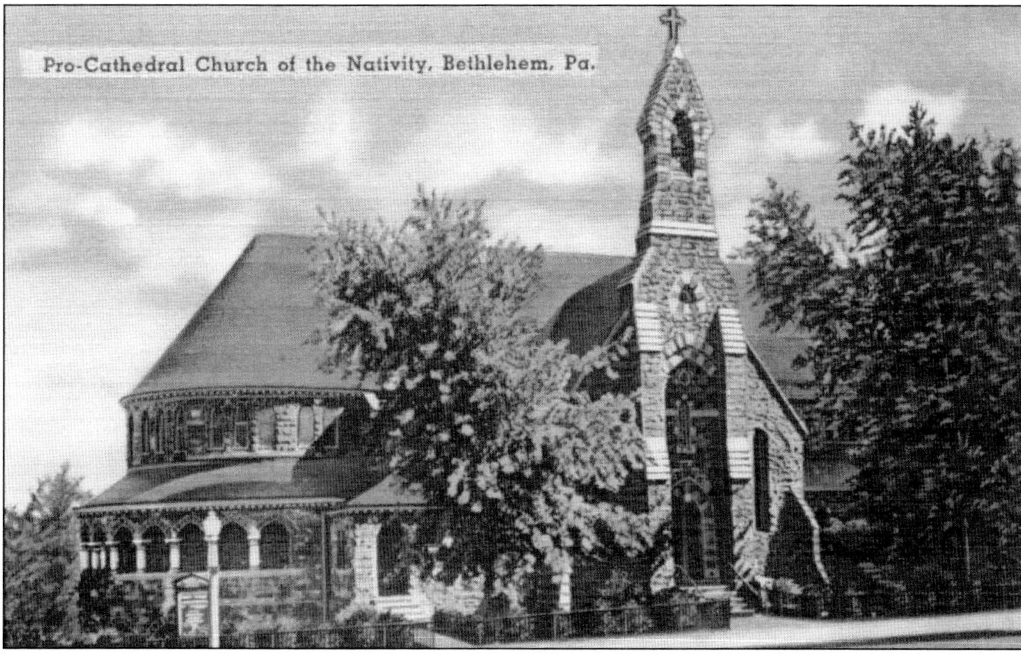

The Cathedral Church of the Nativity was erected in 1864–1865 and was in use by the congregation by December 1864. It was consecrated on the day of President Lincoln's funeral, April 19, 1865. The church was enlarged in 1888, and the parish house was added in 1897. The bell tower, which stands approximately 85 feet tall, was added in 1899. At night, the illuminated Cathedral Church of the Nativity makes a beautiful impression as one crosses the Hill-to-Hill Bridge to Bethlehem.

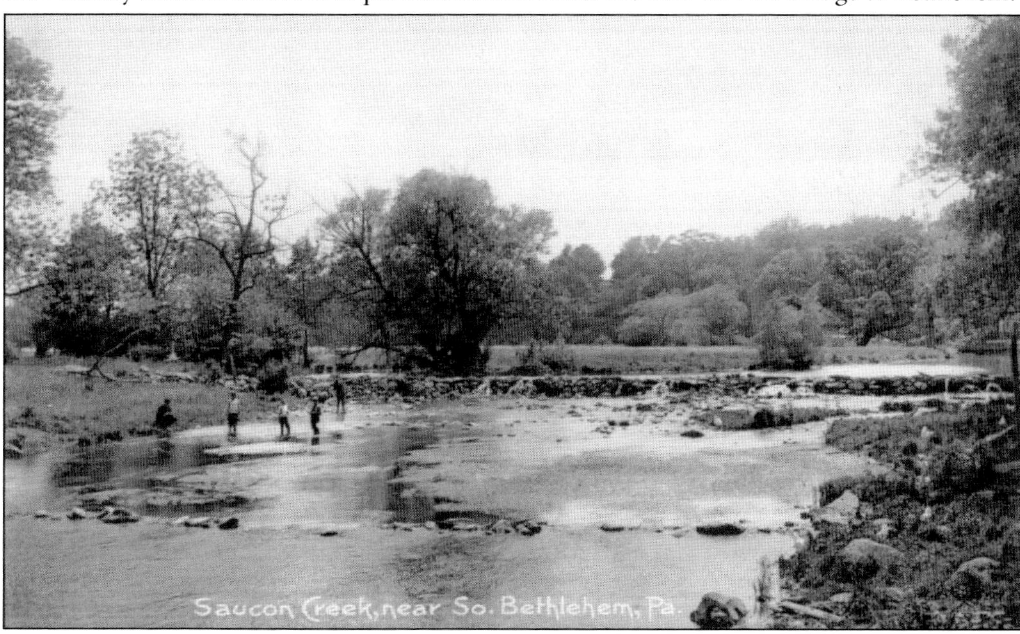

The Saucon Creek, a major tributary of the Lehigh River, drains into 58.2 square miles of the Lehigh basin for 16.5 miles. The course of the stream brings it in contact with forested lands, urbanized areas, residential property, and major roadways. The creek travels through Upper Saucon Township, Lower Saucon Township, Hellertown, and the city of Bethlehem.

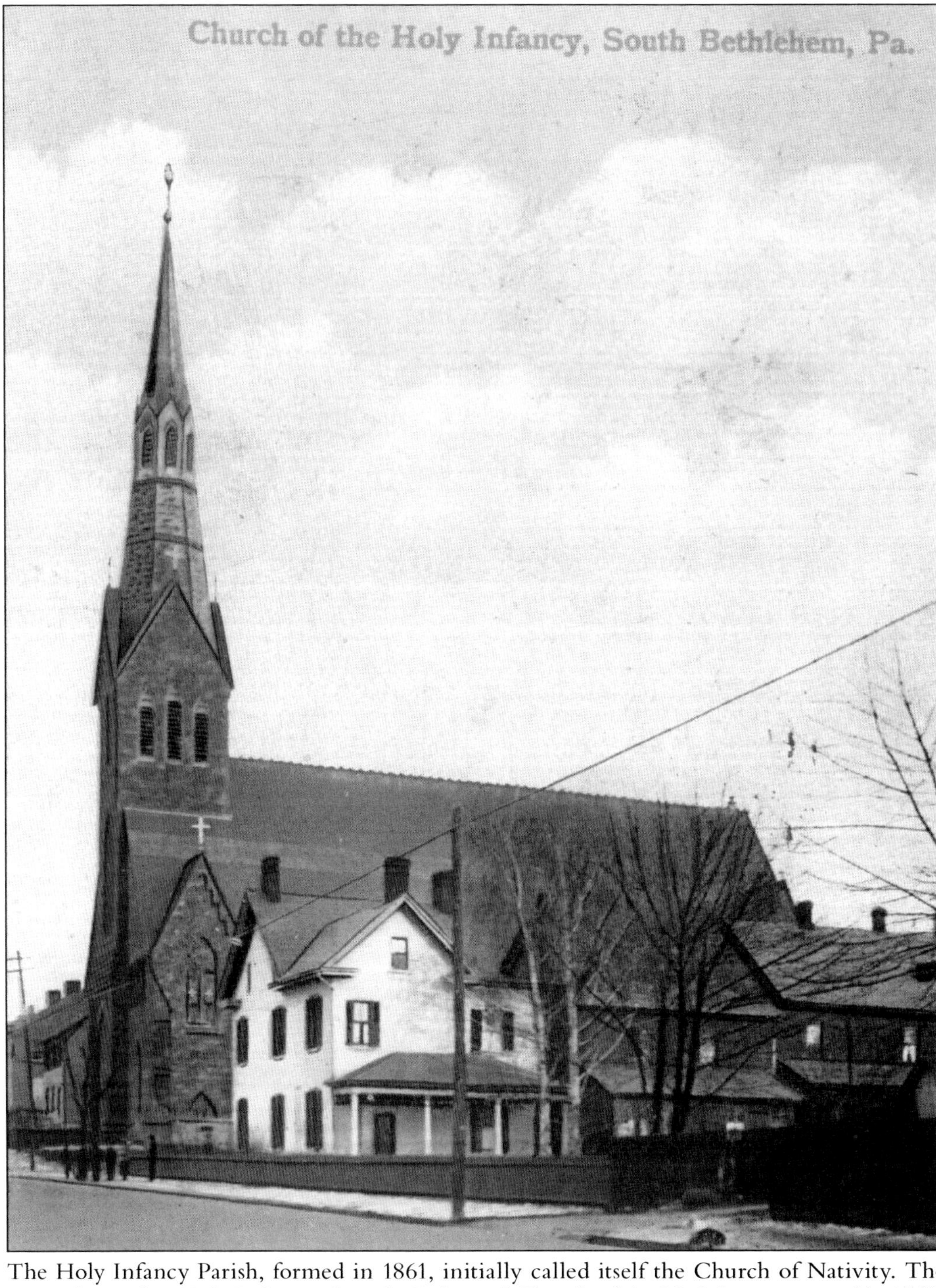

The Holy Infancy Parish, formed in 1861, initially called itself the Church of Nativity. The name changed to Holy Infancy when the Episcopal Church of the Nativity was started in 1862. Holy Infancy was established as South Bethlehem's first Roman Catholic church. A much larger church was needed, so the building of one was begun in 1882. It was a Gothic Revival design by the great ecclesiastical architect Edwin Forrest Durang, who also designed the Academy of Music in Philadelphia. The Moravians donated the bell in the belfry.

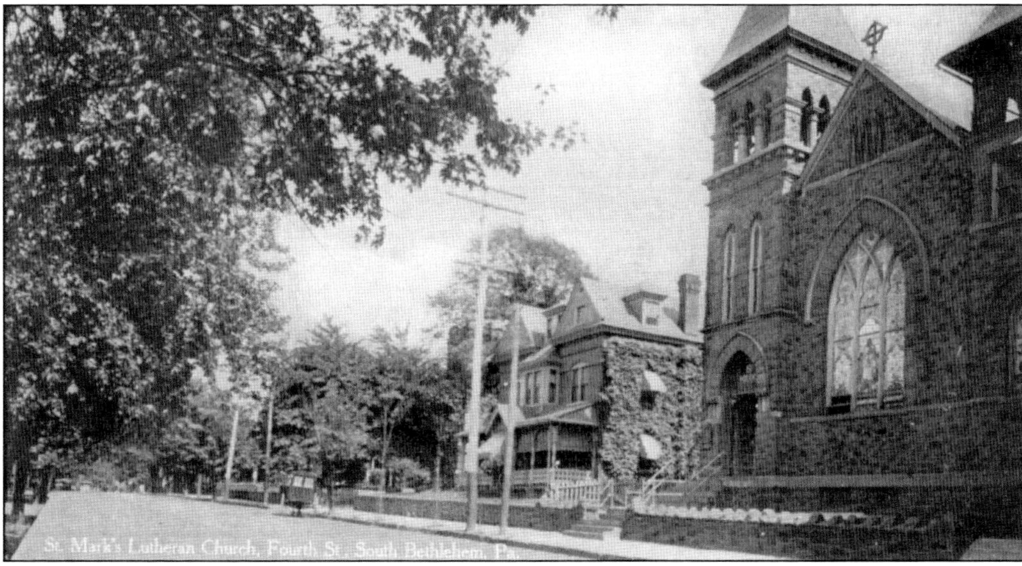

In 1888, a small group of Evangelical Lutherans desired a church where sermons were given in English. Their current church, St. Peter's, only offered sermons in German. The next year, the group built a small frame chapel on West Fourth Street and began holding services. A permanent building was designed in the Gothic style by A.W. Leh and built in 1895. The first chapel was moved to the rear of the lot and used for a Sunday school. The church was built of buff-colored sandstone. An annex was added in 1927. With the church members moving to the north of the city in the 1950s, the congregation purchased a lot on William Penn Highway. A new church was built there in 1972, and services were discontinued at the Fourth Street church.

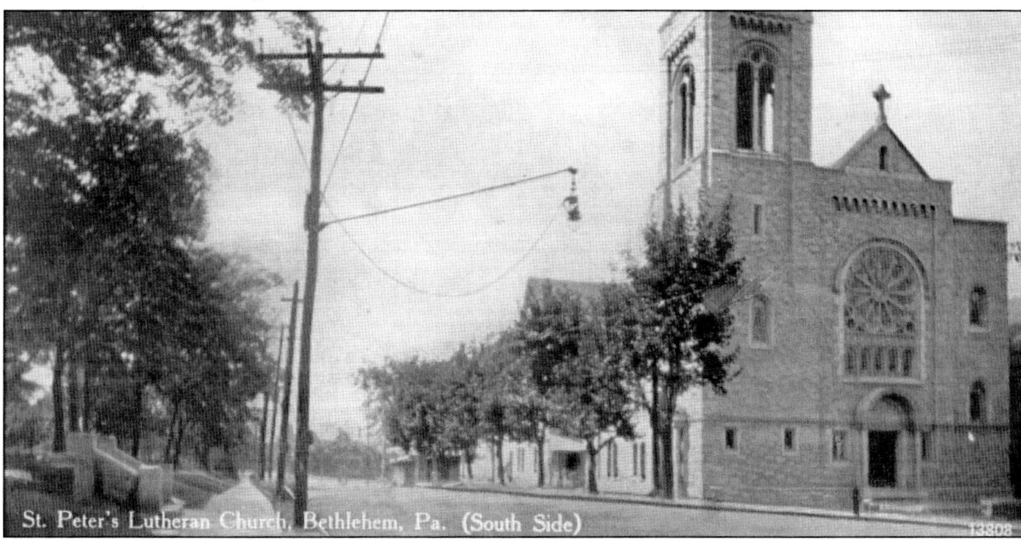

St. Peter's Evangelical Lutheran Church was founded in 1863 when Rev. A.T. Geissenhainer and a group of 20 German Lutherans worshipped in a private home. German was the primary language used in services well into the 20th century. St. Peter's was the first church built in South Bethlehem, in 1863–1864. The growth of the membership of St. Peter's corresponded with the rise in population of South Bethlehem. By the 1870s, the membership had grown to 400, and the need for a larger facility became paramount. The new church, 42 by 71 feet and two stories high, was built next to the first church in 1879.

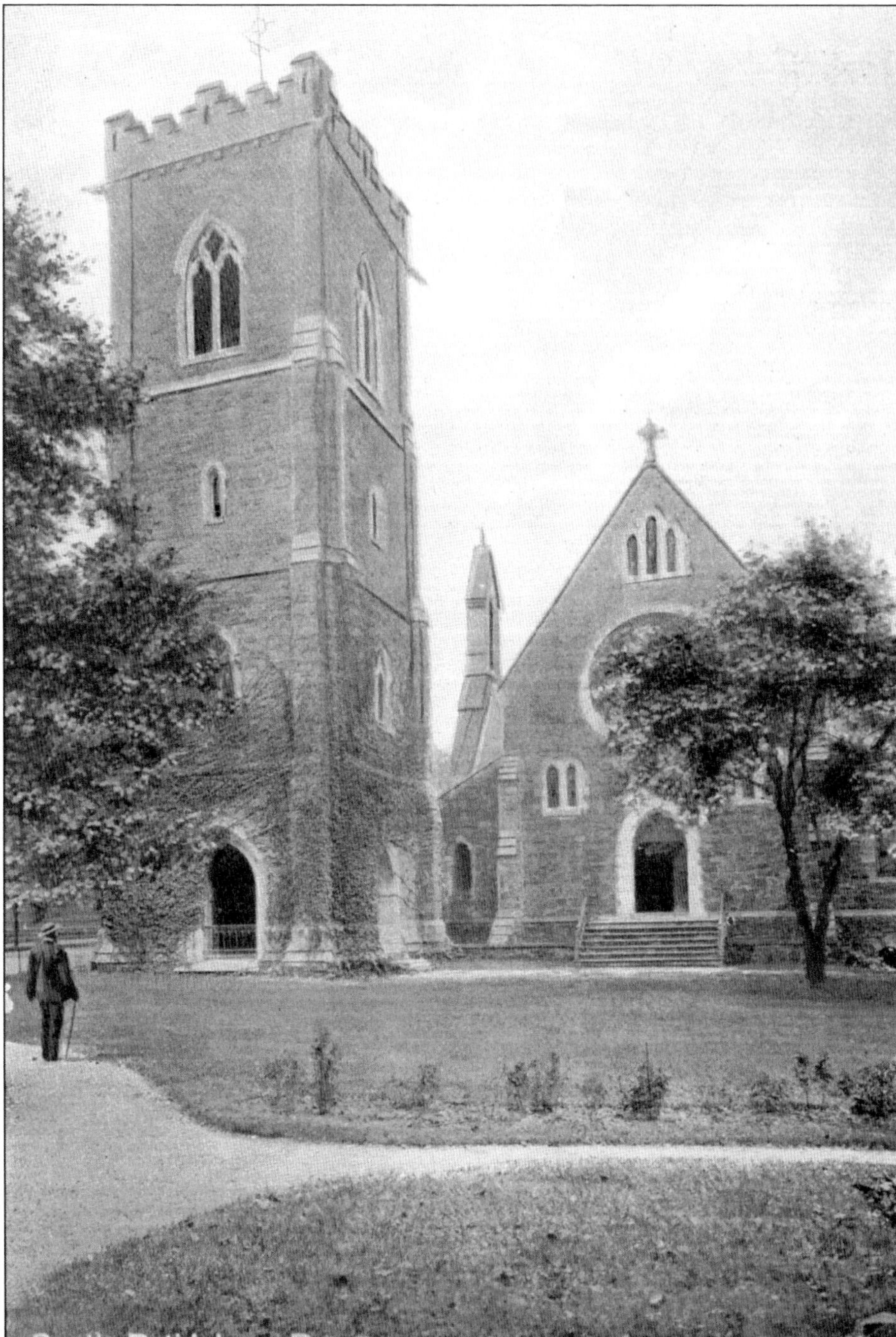

In June 1863, the Protestant Episcopal Church of the Diocese of Pennsylvania recognized the efforts of a small group of Episcopalians to form a parish in South Bethlehem. In 1862, in a meeting at Robert H. Sayre's home, eight people decided it was the right time to start a parish and build a church. They selected an administrative committee to organize the church; the Cathedral Church of the Nativity is shown here.

Three

North Side Revisited

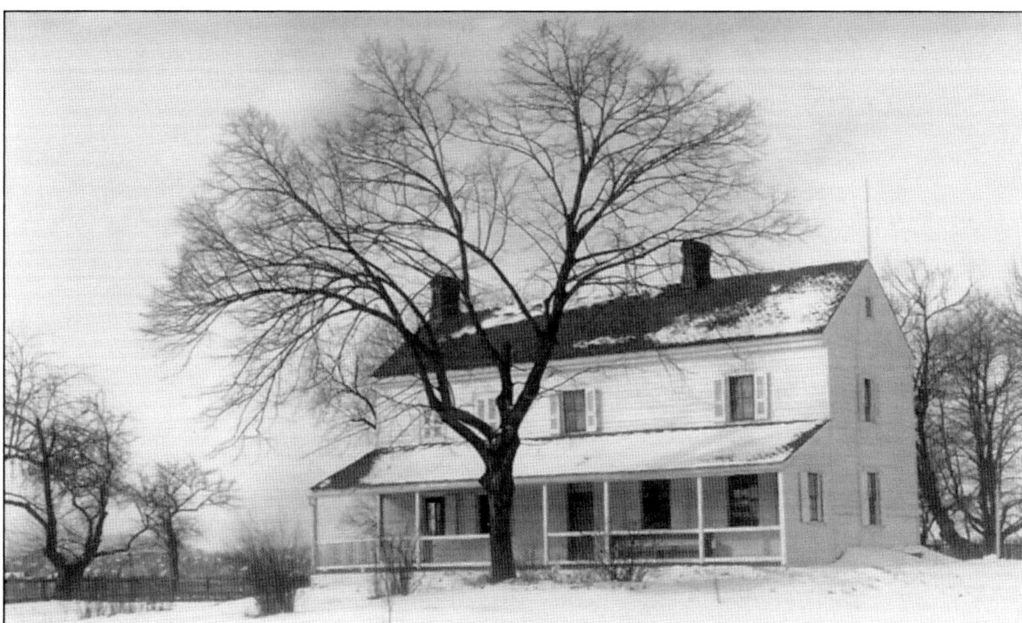

Shown here is the old Daniel Desh farmhouse, which is the location of Liberty High School today. The Bethlehem School Board purchased the 16-acre farm for $105,000 in 1915. Daniel Desh was a butcher and a Lutheran whose marriage to Antoinette Bishop, a Moravian, was considered a mixed marriage at the time. His butcher shop was located on Fairview Street near the intersection of Main Street.

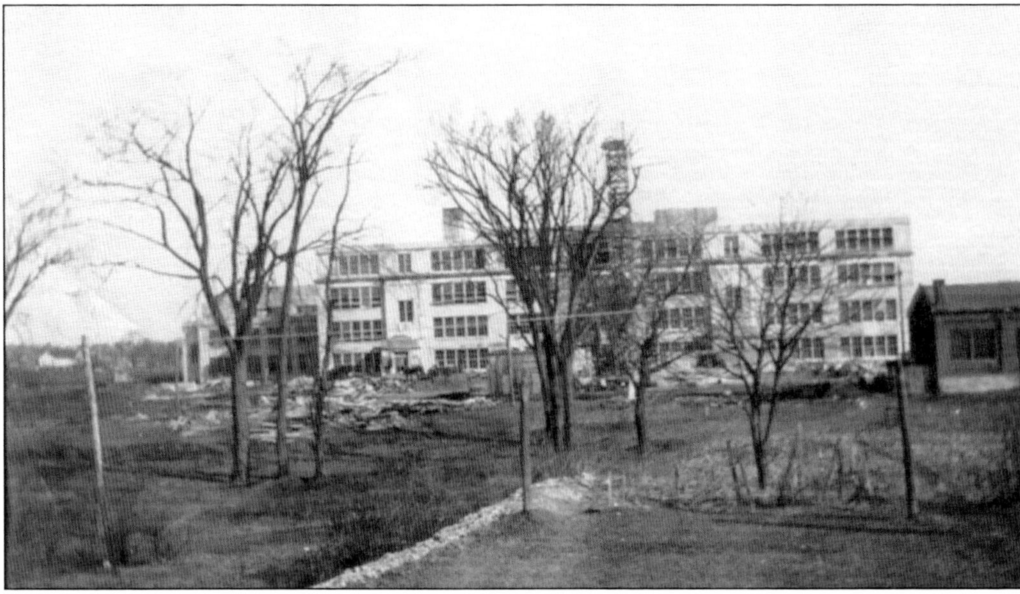

Liberty High School was built in 1918 and opened in 1922. The school was named as a memorial for World War I soldiers. This photograph shows the southern elevation of the school. When it opened, newspapers described it as the most beautiful school in the state. Besides the superior academic facilities, there was now room for athletic fields. The Liberty High School football team would produce several professional football players. (Courtesy of Jason Rehm.)

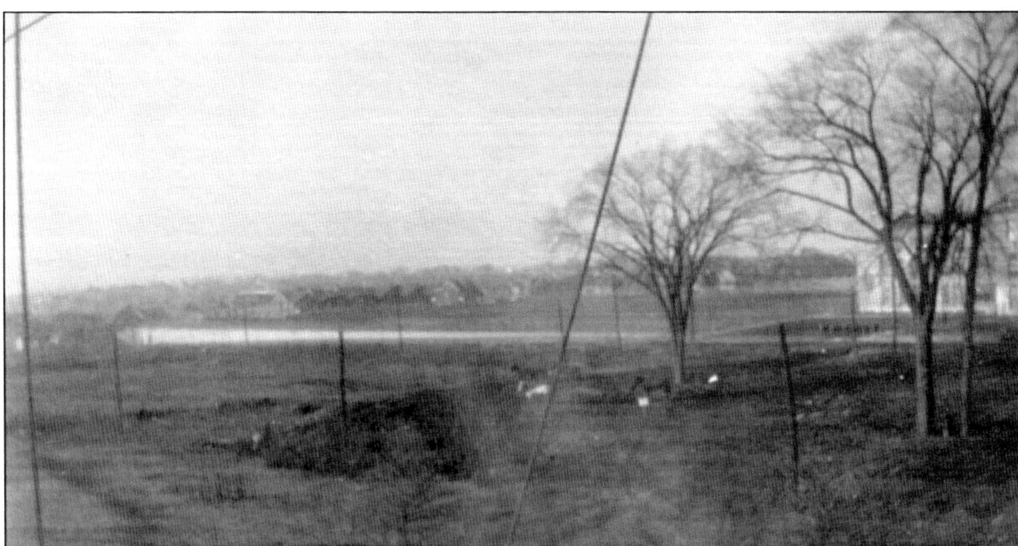

The site chosen for Liberty was the Desh homestead, a small farm property at Linden and Elizabeth Streets. Although it was built in the geographic center of Bethlehem, in the early years it seemed far away from the most densely populated areas of the city. Most students took the trolley to school. The site is seen looking to the northwest, where the stadium would later be built. The modern cafeteria made it easy for the students to stay at school for lunch. (Courtesy of Jason Rehm.)

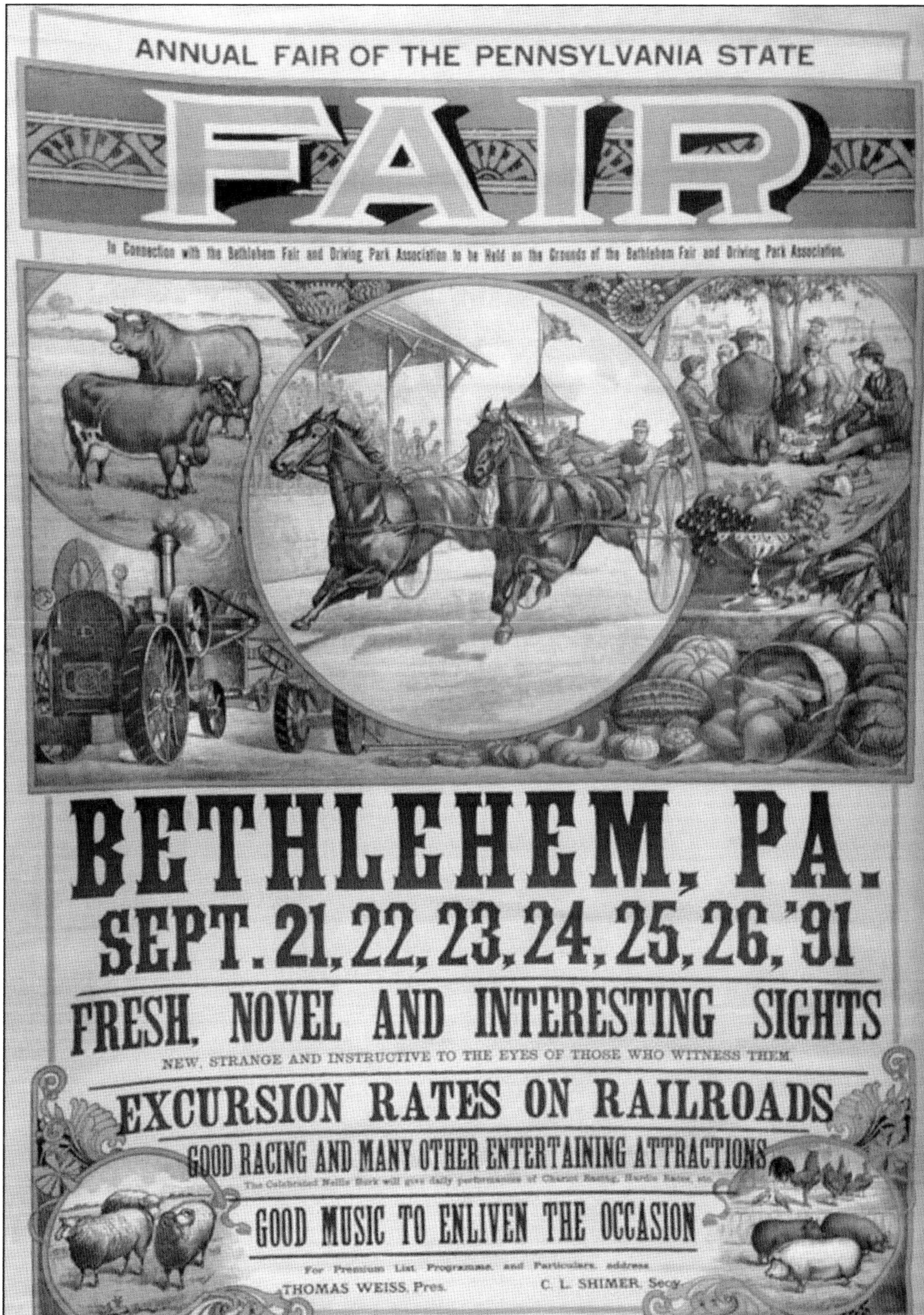

A new and exciting form of entertainment came to Bethlehem on the days of September 21–26, 1891. The Pennsylvania State Fair, which was a fair that traveled throughout Pennsylvania, opened at the new Bethlehem fairgrounds. The Bethlehem Fair and Driving Park Association purchased 35 acres in the area of Liberty High School, known as North Bethlehem. The association began work on the grounds in April 1891, and by September, the fairgrounds was ready to host the Pennsylvania State Fair.

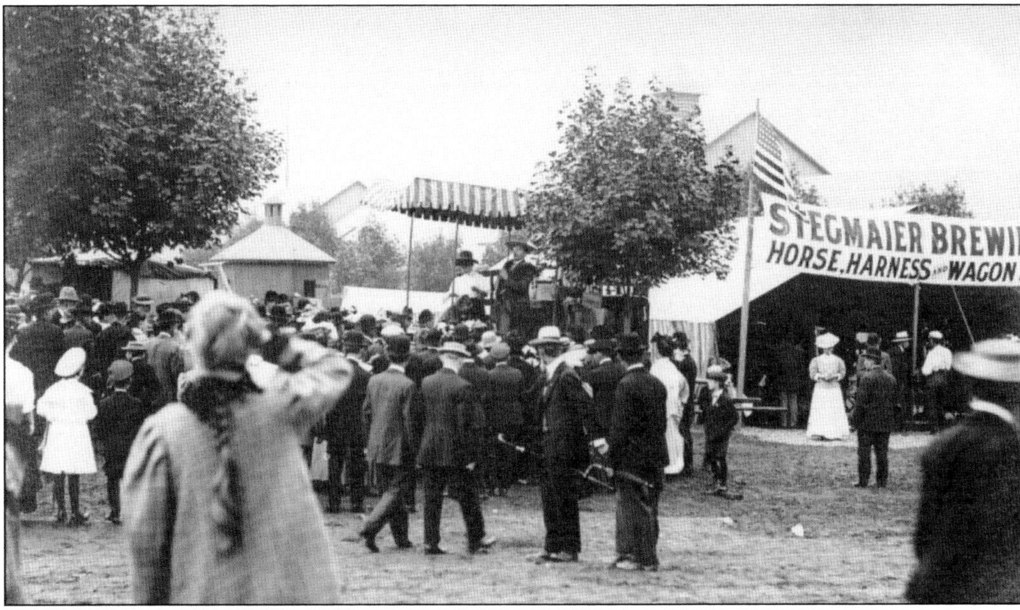

Most people attended the Bethlehem fair to watch the horse races. The grounds contained more than 200 horse stalls, a grandstand, and an excellent half-mile track. Many famous horses ran there, such as the legendary Dan Patch, who had set a world's record as a pacing horse in 1908. The sign to the right mentions the Stegmaier Brewery of Wilkes Barre, which sold very popular beers at the time.

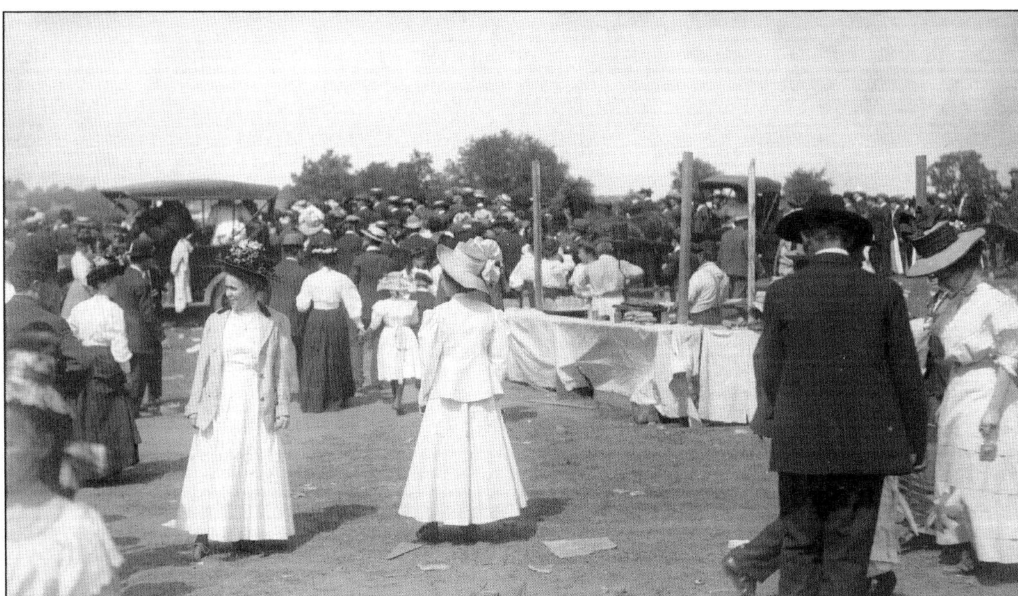

Many of the Bethlehem fairgoers appear preoccupied with action just out of view. Could it be a harness race? The women's large hats, tailored blouses, and trumpet-skirts and the men's homburg, straw, or bowler hats with stiff, high collars peeking out from their sack coats made for a more formal scene than how people dress for the fair today. Although two Model Ts are pictured, most of these fairgoers arrived by a trolley that traveled along unpaved Linden Street to the fairgrounds.

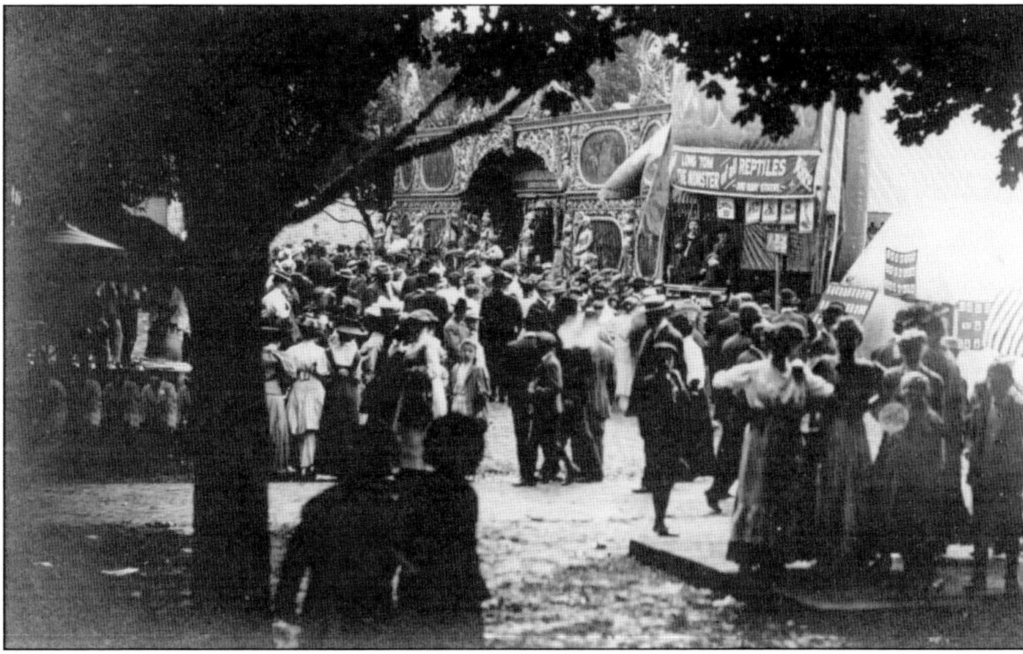

The Bethlehem fairgrounds were founded by a group of local businessmen. They organized in 1890 as the Bethlehem Fair and Driving Park Association. They later changed their name to Pennsylvania State Fair Association. Here is the always-flashy midway with exotic sideshows such as "Long Tom, the Monster of all Reptiles." In 1909, the high cost of maintaining the fairgrounds convinced the investors to sell the property off as lots.

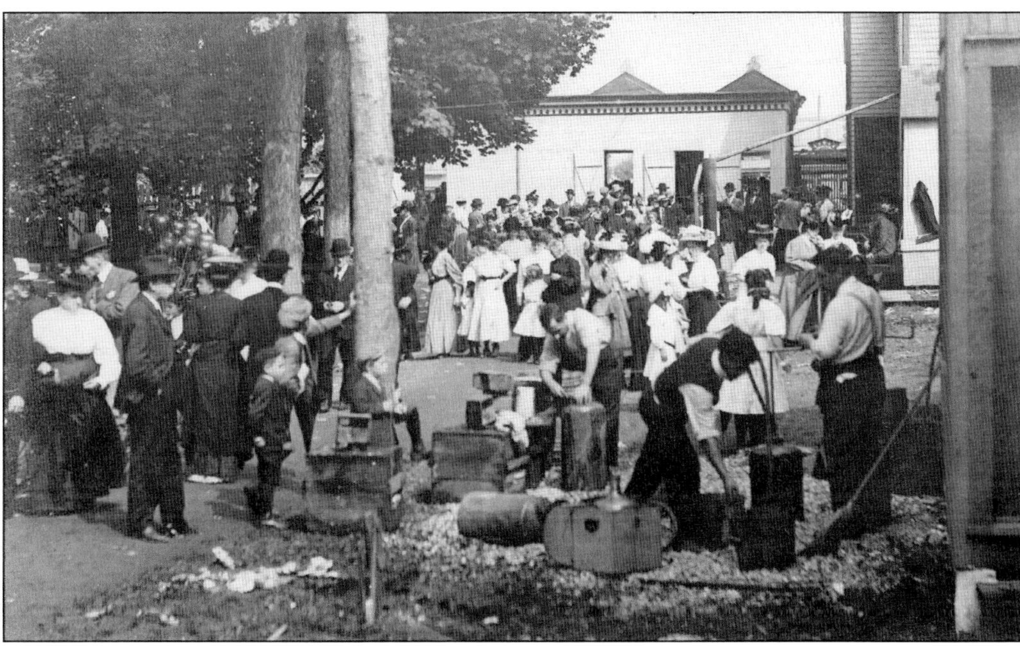

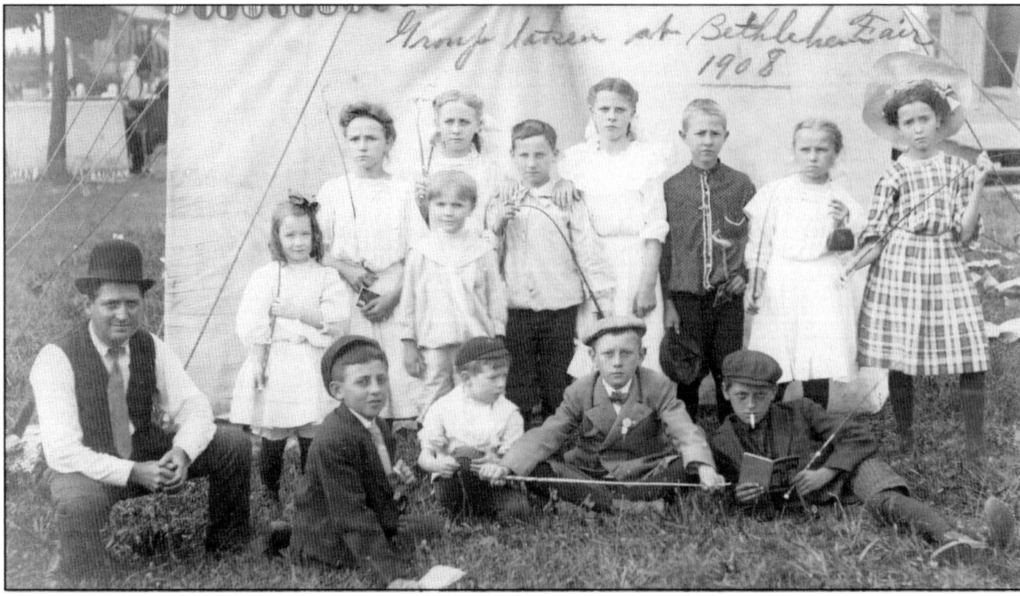

In 1908, this group of children posed for a photograph with their miniature driving whips. The young lad at bottom left assumes the look of a serious horse-racing fan. The whips might seem unusual toys today, but back in 1908, children were very familiar with handling horses.

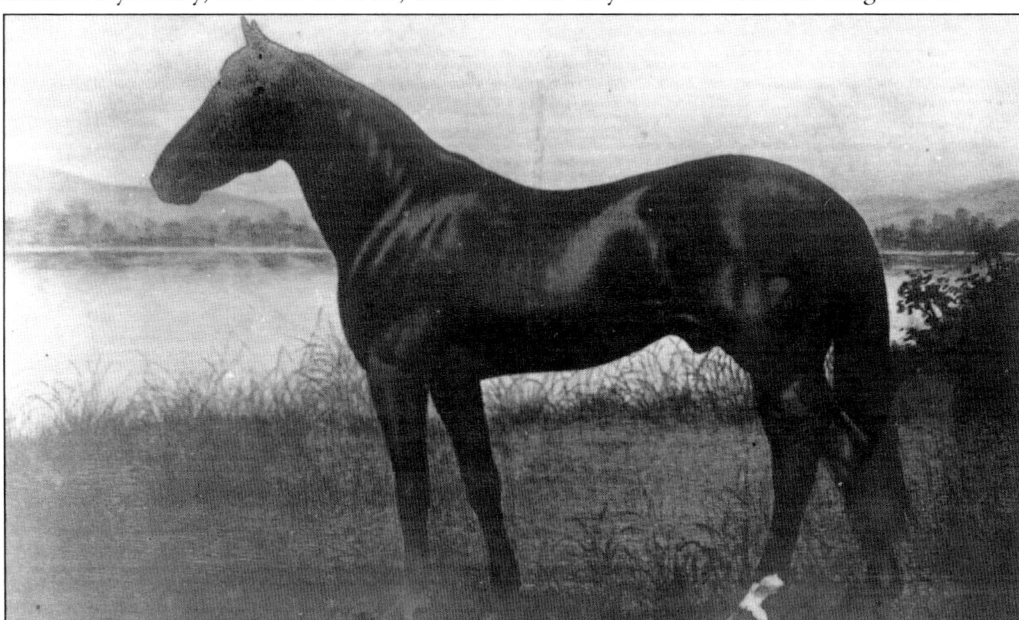

This is a promotional postcard of the famous harness racehorse George Wilkes. He was a rich seal-brown color, with a white pattern on his hind leg. Wilkes had a sturdy muscular build and was on the short side. He had the quickness of a much lighter horse. Wilkes ran in over 200 races in 12 years with exceptional speed. His foals became successful and were valued at the top of the market, going for as much as $150,000 each. Wilkes was one of the greatest of all champion progenitors during the late 1800s. Thomas Weiss of Bethlehem raised Wilkes descendants on his east end farm.

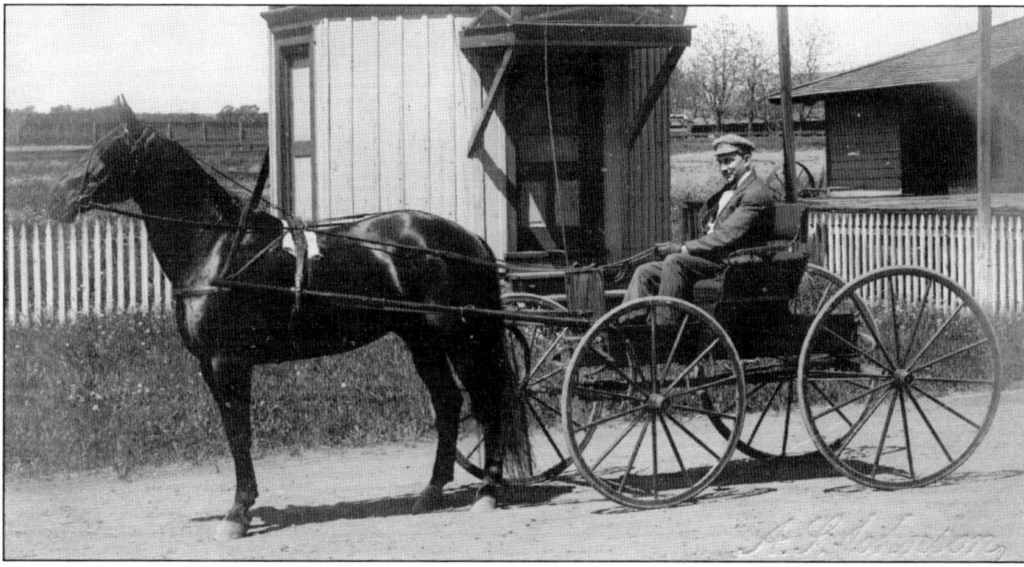

The harness racehorse shown here was undoubtedly a Wilkes breed and may have belonged to the president of the Bethlehem Fair and Driving Park Association, Thomas Weiss. Weiss became a horse breeder when he sold his business, Lehigh Shovel Works, a shovel manufacturing plant in South Bethlehem. In the background of the postcard, one sees the fairgrounds. This beautiful horse is attached to a passenger carriage and not a racing sulky.

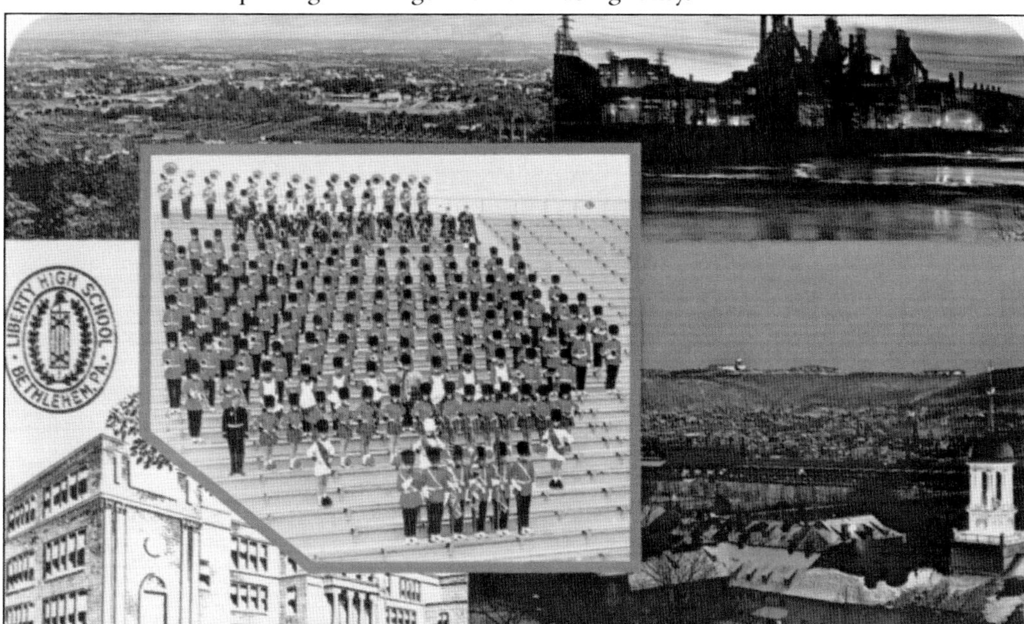

This postcard celebrates the many things that make Bethlehem a special place to live. In the upper left is a view of Bethlehem looking north from city hall. In the upper right is the Bethlehem Steel Corporation along the Lehigh River. In the lower left is Liberty High School, and in lower right is the Central Moravian Church belfry. In the center is the Liberty High School Grenadier Band. The postcard caption mentions that the band won the National Championship in 1967 and 1970.

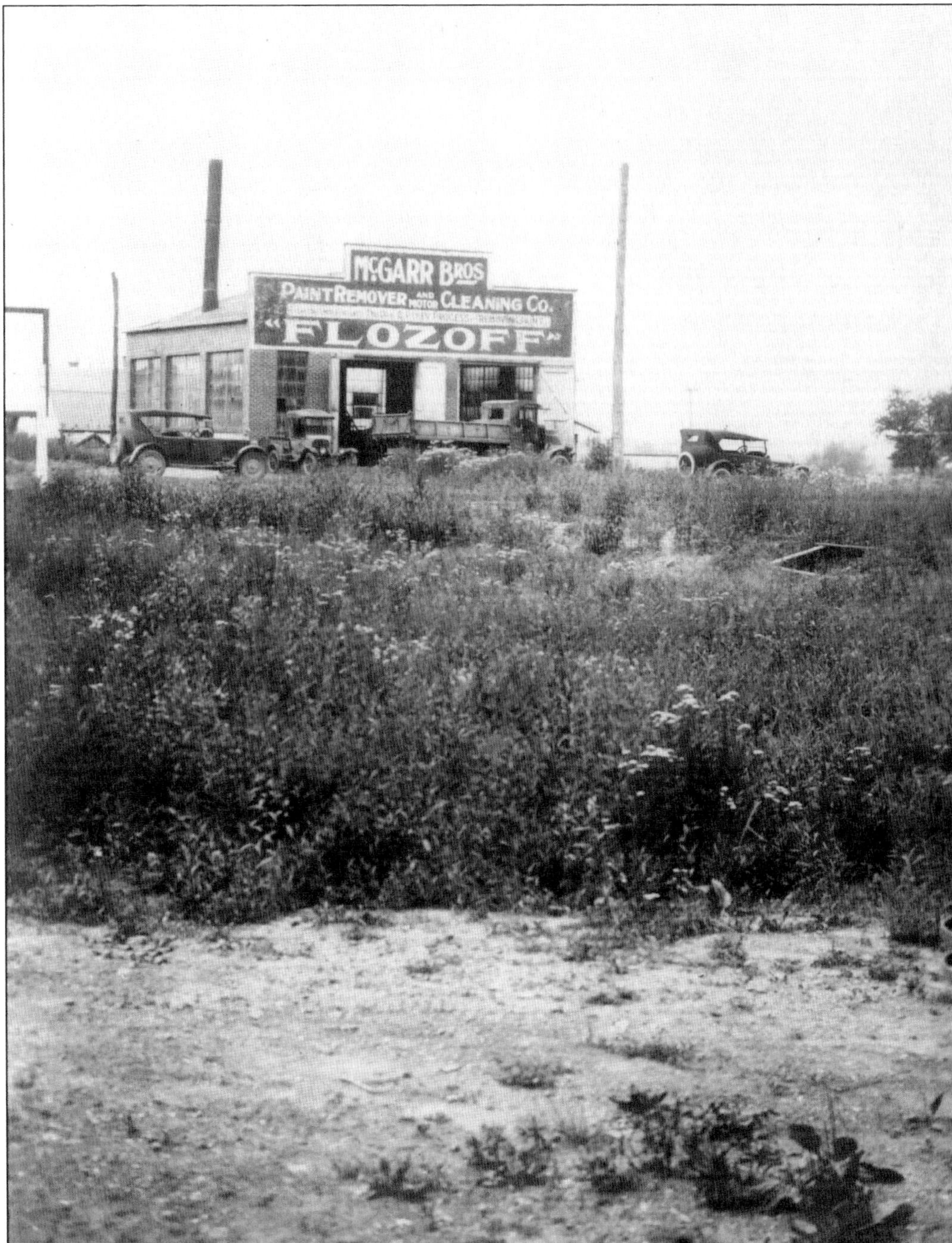

The McGarr Brothers Paint Remover & Motor Cleaning Company building was located at Woodlawn and Easton Avenues. "Flozoff" was a trademark (1919) for a compound that removed paint, varnish, and enamel from surfaces. Back in the 1920s, the garage was located in an isolated spot. In the late 1920s, the congregation of St. Anne's Church used the building. Next, it became the North End Wanderers Athletic Association Club. The club was established in 1934 and continues to operate in the building today.

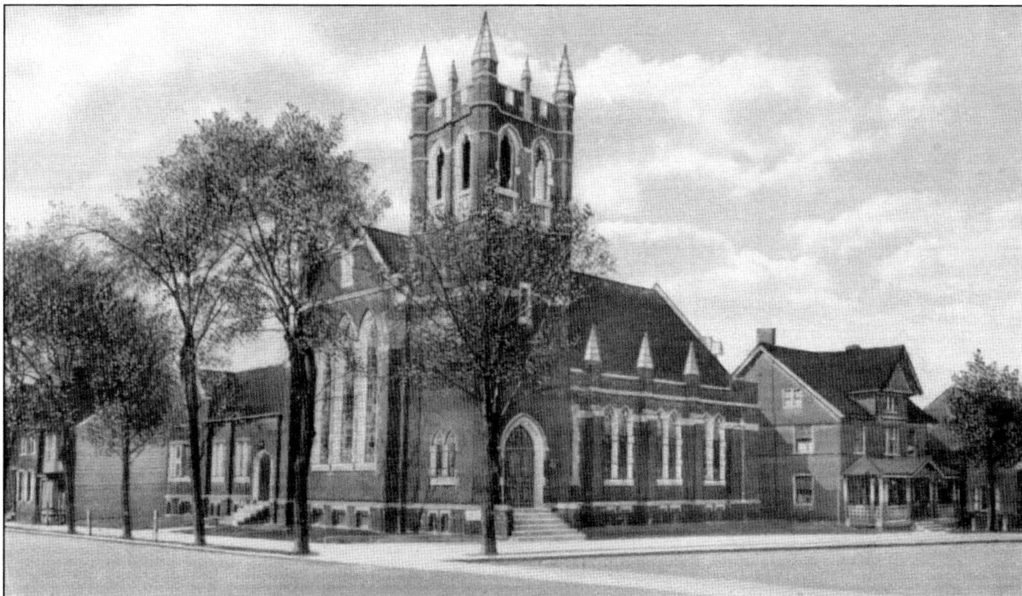

FIRST PRESBYTERIAN CHURCH, BETHLEHEM, PA.

In 1878, a visiting clergyman from Philadelphia, Rev. George Musgrave, gave the First Presbyterian congregation $2,000, more than one-fourth of the cost toward the construction of a chapel at Center and North Streets. The group was leasing a building and desired its own church. The new chapel was named "Musgrave Chapel" in appreciation. Rev. Alexander D. Moore served as minister during the years 1876 through 1891.

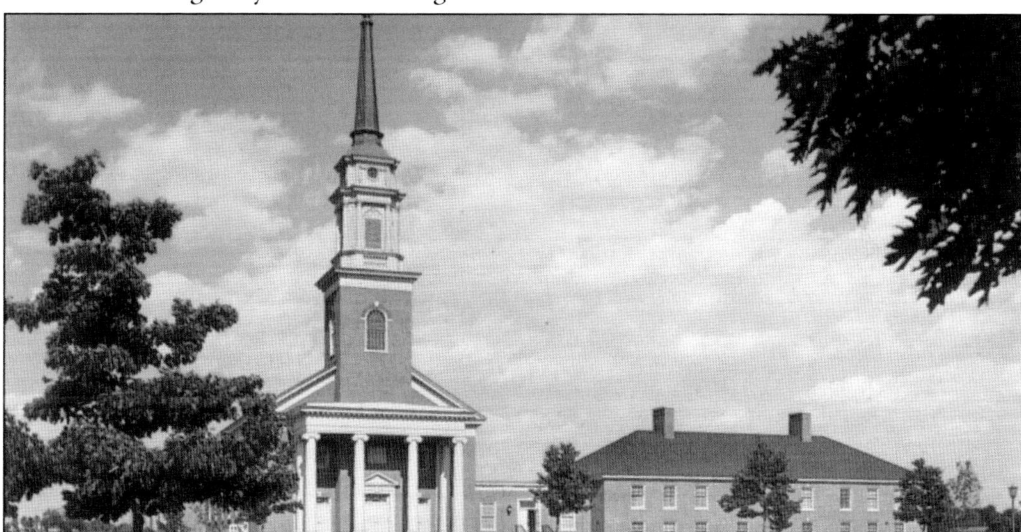

The First Presbyterian Church first organized in 1875, meeting on the second floor of the Young Men's Christian Association (YMCA). In the 1950s, the group purchased 52 acres of land on Center Street. In 1957, the new church was built. The prominent New York City architectural firm McKim, Mead & White designed it. The firm was responsible for Penn Station, the New York Public Library, and renovations to the west and east wings of the White House. This was the third church for the congregation, and three short years later, it would need to expand to add a north wing.

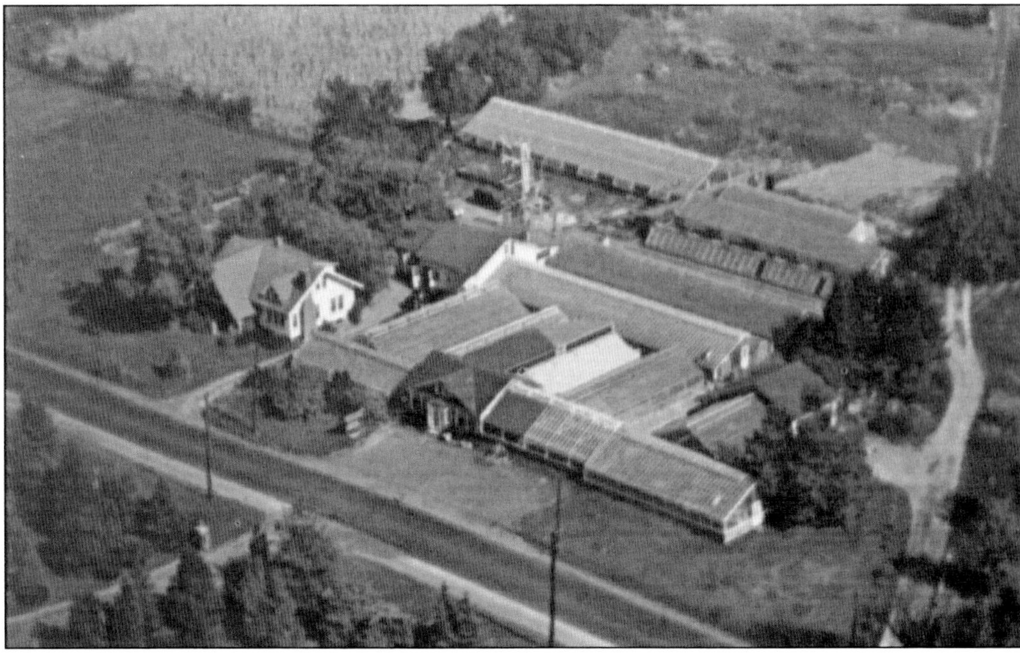

Here is an aerial view of Jamann's Greenhouse at 2612 Linden Street. Simon P. and Margaret R. Kramer Jamann established it 1928. They were known for their fresh flowers and were vendors in the South Side Market House for years.

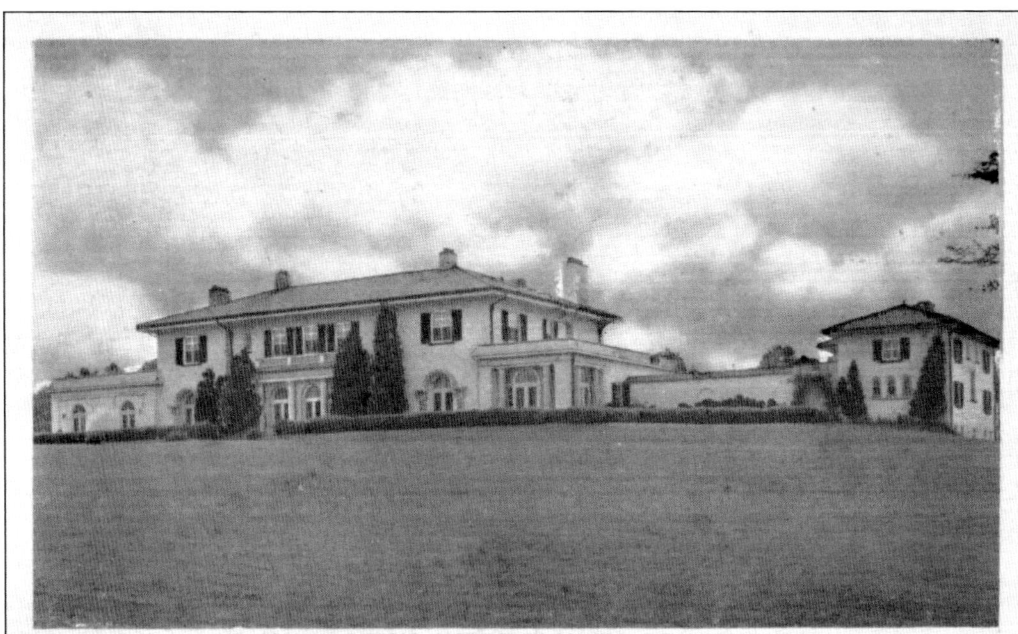

St. Francis Center for Renewal is located on 108 acres where the Monocacy Creek flows through rolling hills. The estate was opened in 1947 for the School Sisters of St. Francis. In this spacious building are 37 bedrooms, 4 conference rooms, and 2 chapels. The facility is used year-round as a spiritual retreat for a variety of groups.

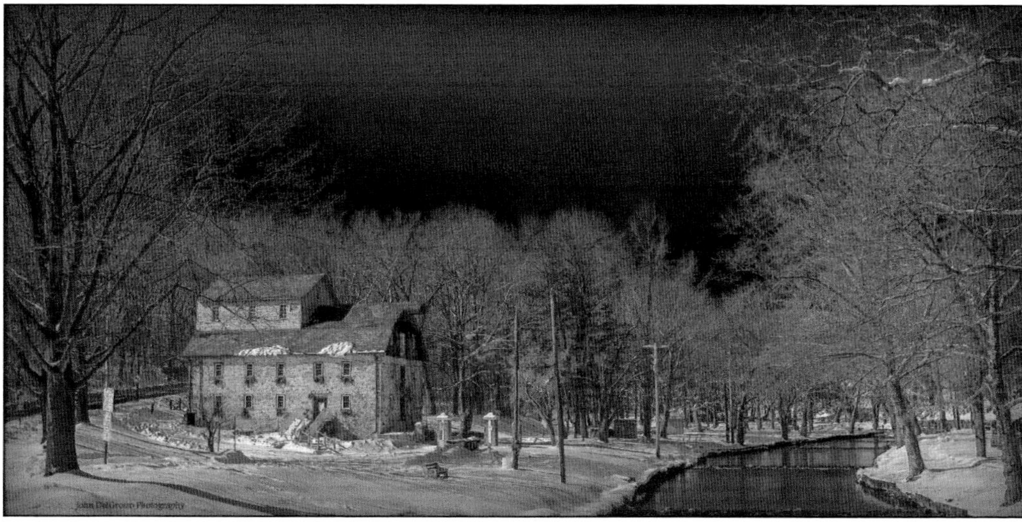

Waterwheels turned by the Monocacy Creek powered the equipment of Illick's Mill. Creek water was dammed and directed through a raceway where it entered the mill through a headrace, turned waterwheels, then exited through a tailrace. (Courtesy of John DelGrosso.)

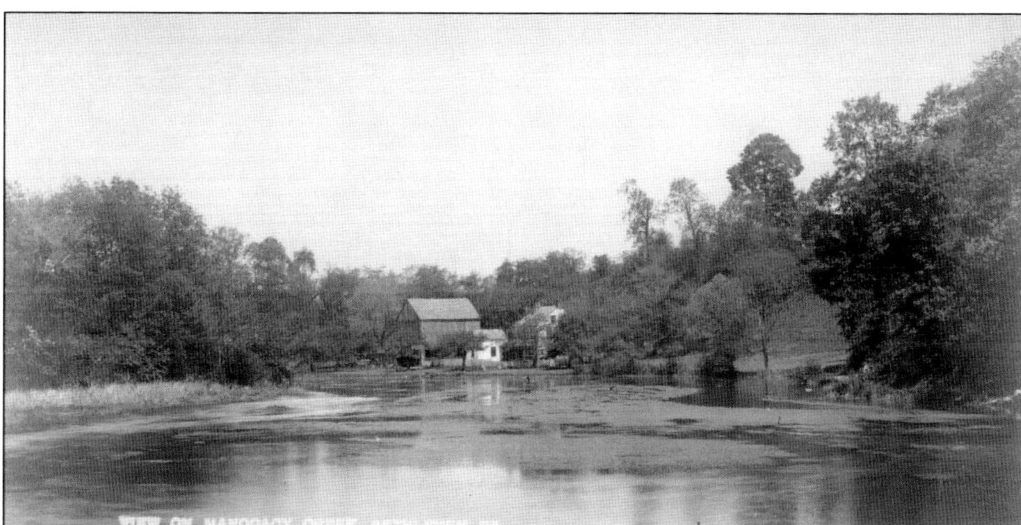

Here is the gristmill as seen from the Monocacy Creek. The first gristmill in Bethlehem was a log building constructed for the Moravians in 1743 by Gotthard Demuth. Henry Antes built the mill machinery and Adam Schaus became the first miller. This mill provided an essential industry not only for the small Moravian community but also for the neighboring farmers. From as far north as above the Blue Mountain, farmers traveled to the mill with their bushels of wheat, rye, barley, and corn for grinding into flour.

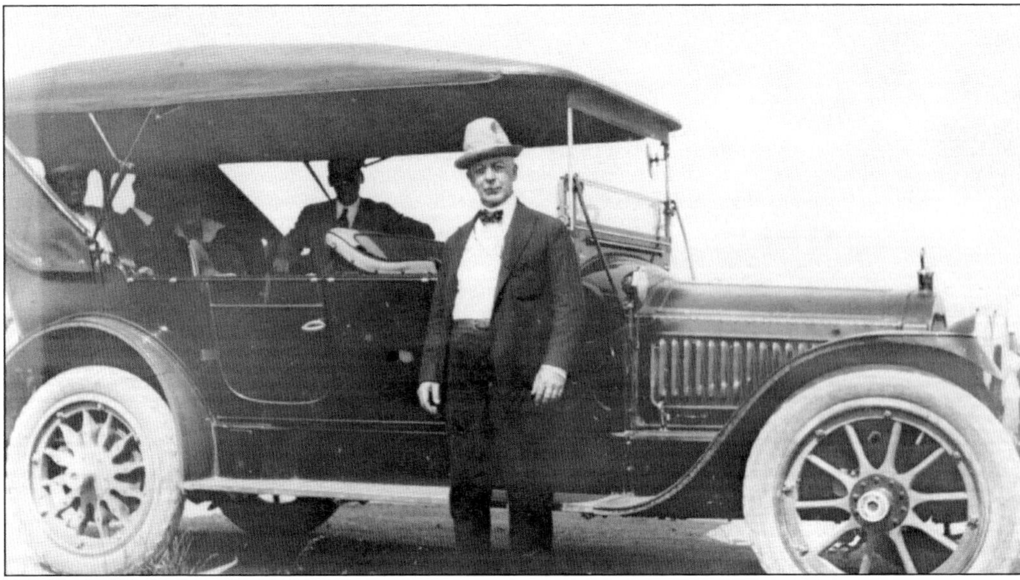

Archibald Johnston, the first mayor of the city of Bethlehem, Pennsylvania, and ex-president of Bethlehem Steel, stands in front of his 1927 Packard. He looks very fashionable in his fedora and bow tie. Johnston did much for the city, as he was credited with consolidating Bethlehem, South Bethlehem, and West Bethlehem in 1917. He was president of the Hill-to-Hill Bridge Committee, leading the effort to complete the bridge in 1924. Johnston's amazing estate in Bethlehem Township is currently in the process of being renovated.

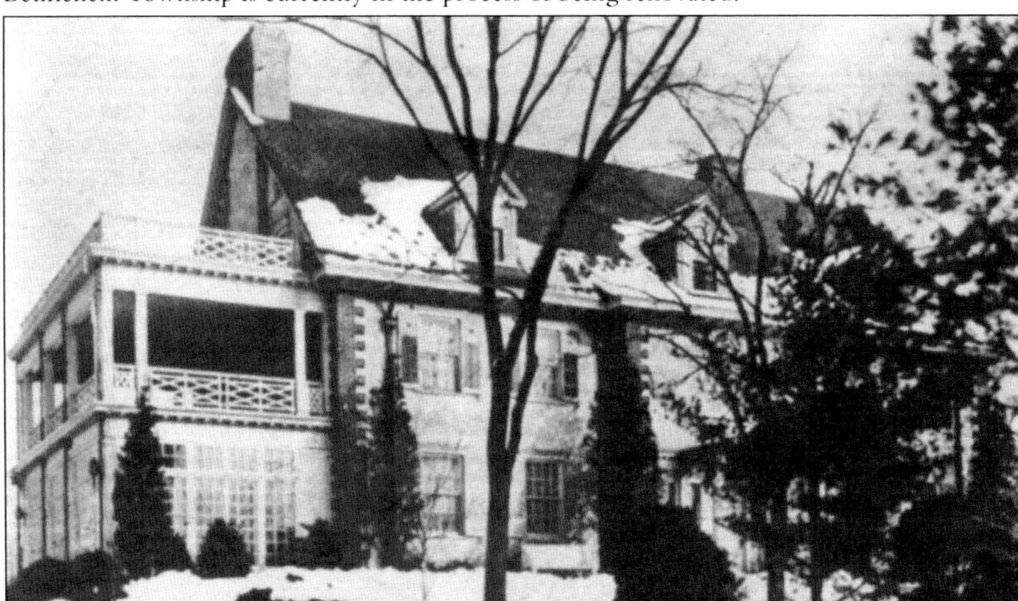

This is a view of the Archibald Johnston Estate in 1930. Bethlehem's *Globe Times* newspaper ran a feature of important estates. Johnston built his estate between 1921 and 1923 on 900 acres in Bethlehem Township. The mansion was designed by Bethlehem architect Curtis Lovelace. The estate compared with the best-designed parks of the time with a man-made waterfall, landscaped gardens, tennis courts, a boathouse, three pools, and a large picnic grove with a portable band shell.

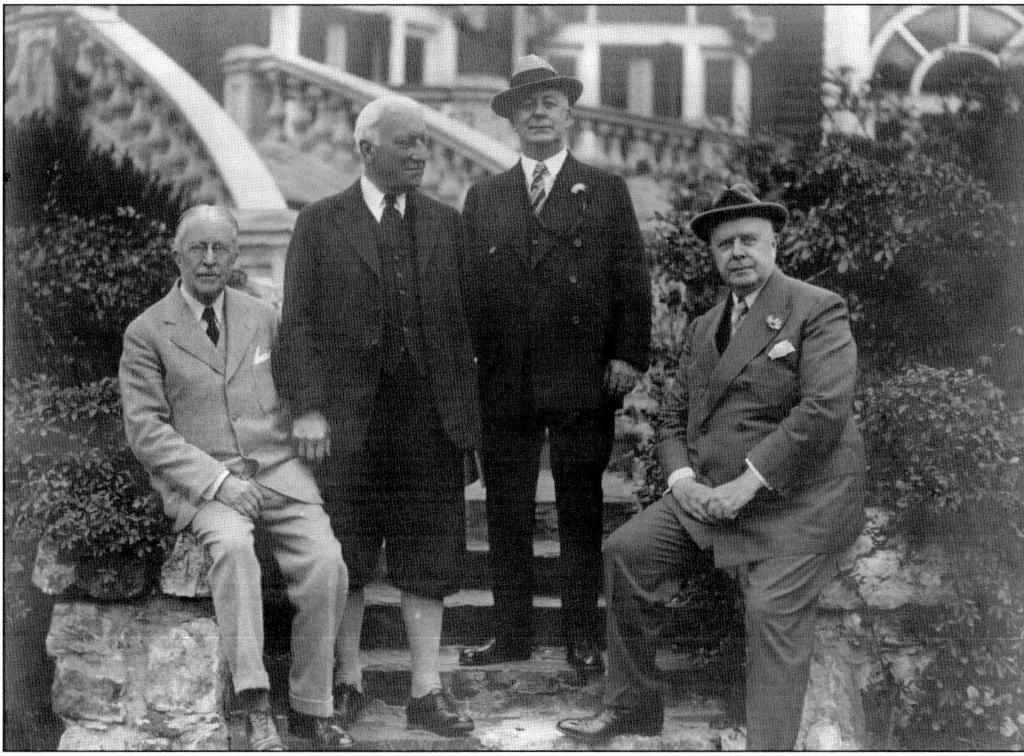

In October 1931, as they vacationed at the Homestead Resort in Hot Springs, Virginia, these four well-known, accomplished men had a photograph taken to commemorate their friendship. They called themselves "the Four Horsemen." From left to right are James T. Conway, George P. Adamson, Archibald Johnston, and Albert Brodhead. Conway owned Brooklyn Chair Manufacturing Company, Adamson owned Adamson Chemical Company, Johnston was the vice president of Bethlehem Steel Corporation, and Brodhead was a Bethlehem real estate magnate.

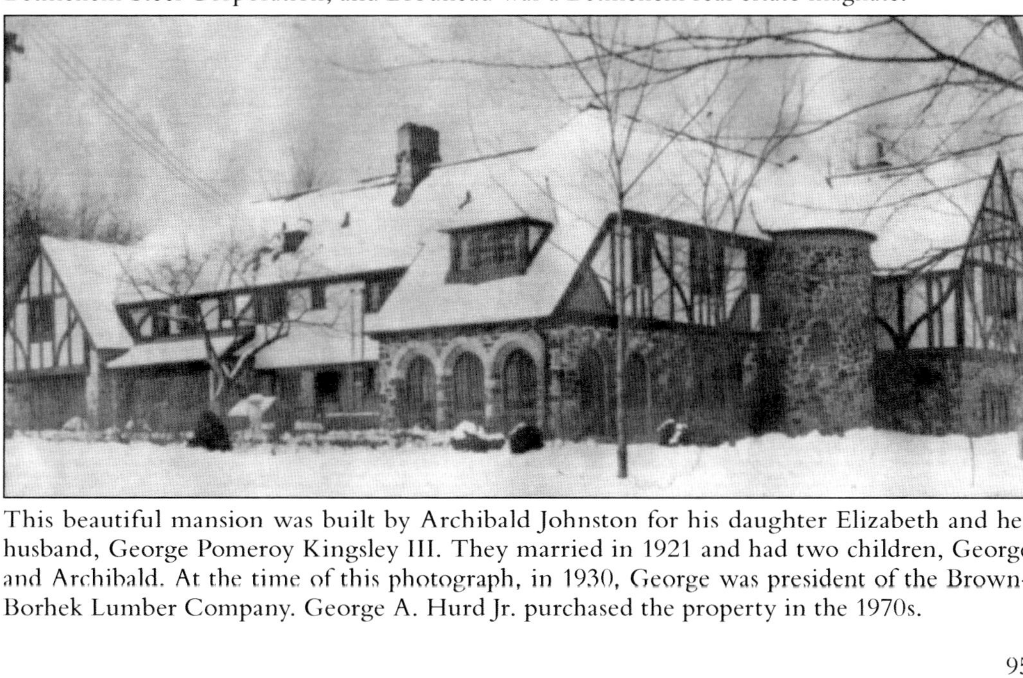

This beautiful mansion was built by Archibald Johnston for his daughter Elizabeth and her husband, George Pomeroy Kingsley III. They married in 1921 and had two children, George and Archibald. At the time of this photograph, in 1930, George was president of the Brown-Borhek Lumber Company. George A. Hurd Jr. purchased the property in the 1970s.

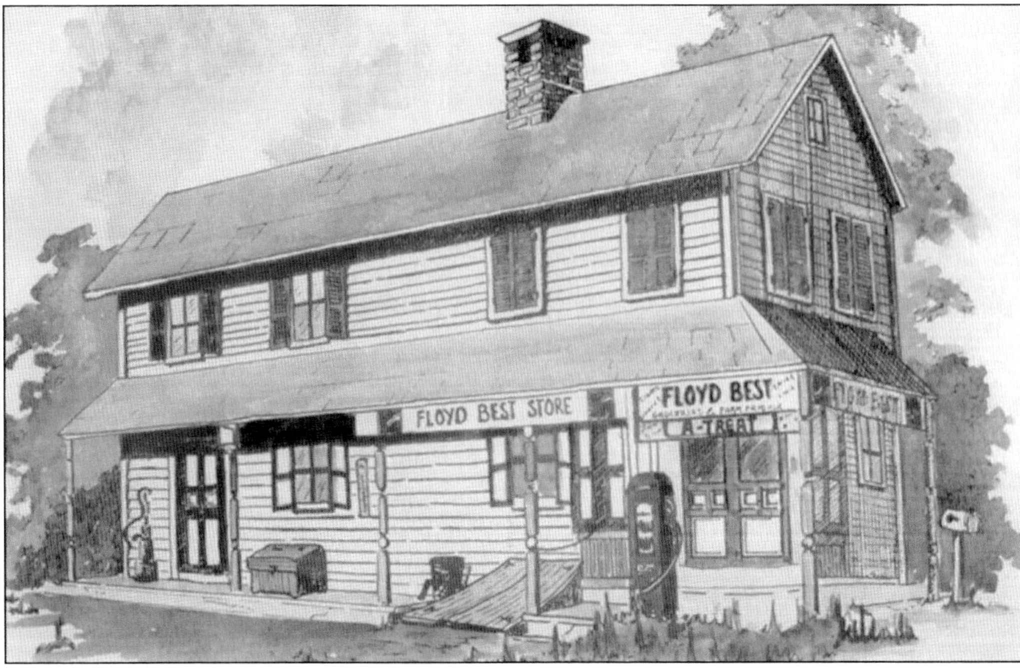

This painting of the Floyd R. Best General Store by Shirley Worsley captures the store when it was the center of the Macada-area farming community. The artist has included the gas pump, large thermometer, and water pump. The sign says groceries and farm produce. Floyd had expanded the business to include apple orchards, cornfields, a dairy, and a picnic grove for families and community groups.

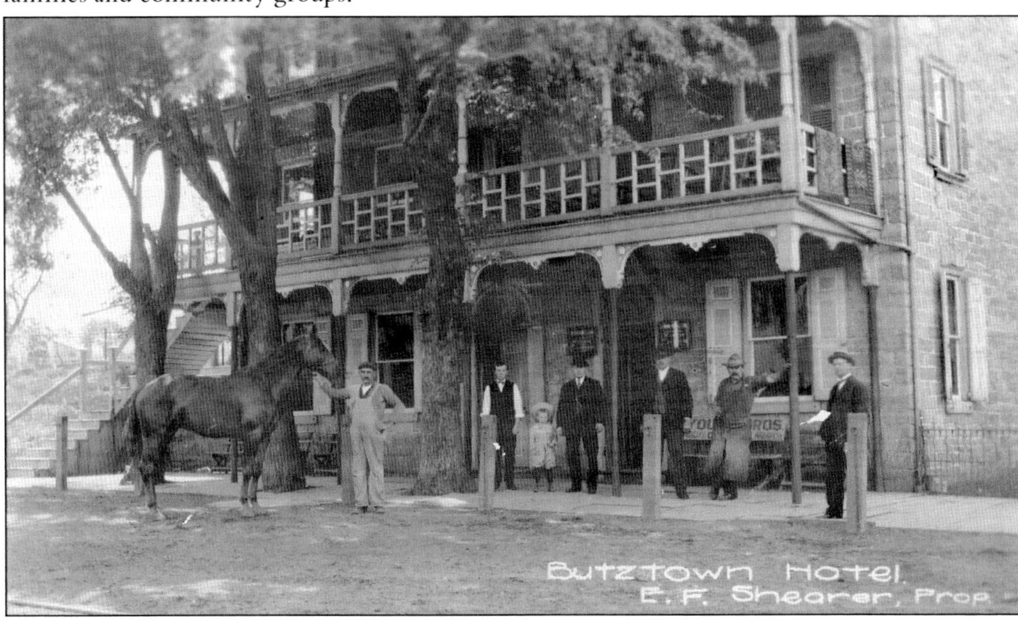

R.T. Schweitzer built the Butztown Hotel on the west side of Easton Avenue where it intersects Willow Park Road. E.F. Shearer was the proprietor when this photograph was taken in the early 1900s. Other proprietors have been Howard Searfass and Charles and Nancy Eyster. As of 2000, the building is called the Keystone Pub.

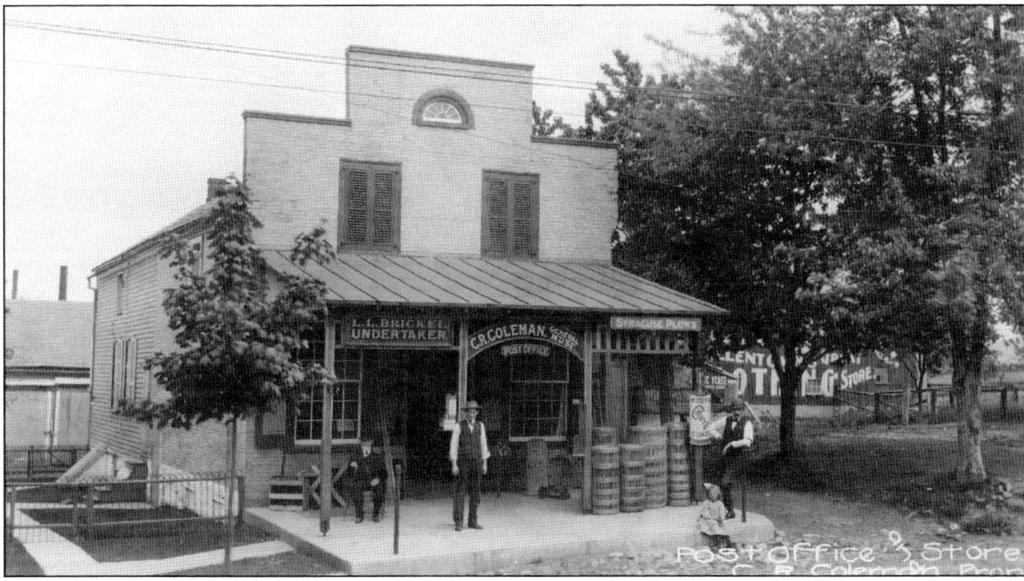

Pictured here are the C.R. Coleman General Store and Butztown Post Office. All of one's needs could be taken care of in one stop. Elsie Coleman, sister of William H. Coleman, mailed the postcard in 1909. She writes that William is standing on the right, leaning against the pole. A niece is sitting on the porch. Next-door is the L.L. Brickel Undertaker. Brickel began his career as a carpenter and eventually became an undertaker. His wife, Mary E. Brickel, carried on the business after his death.

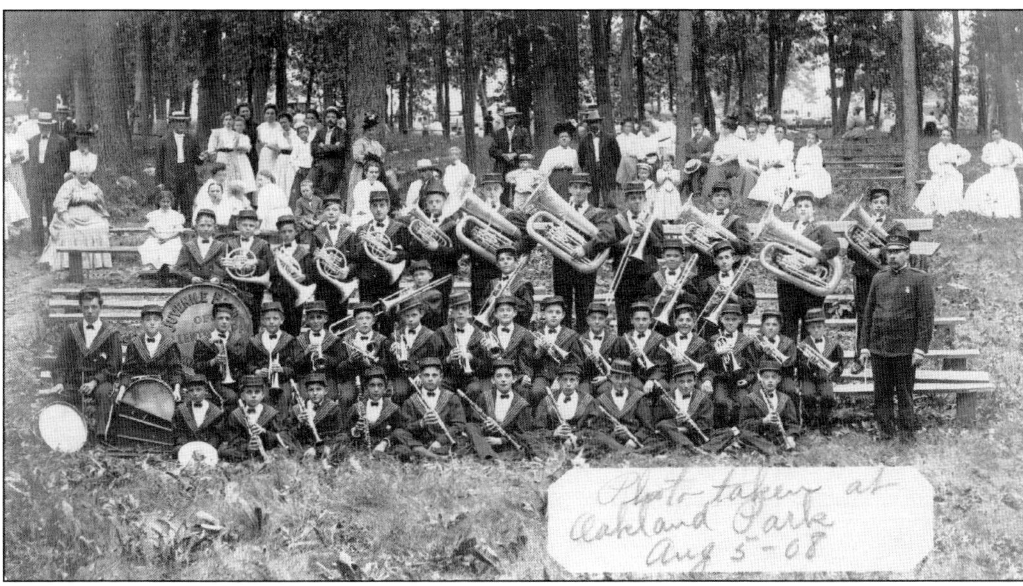

The setting of this hot summer day in 1908 is Oakland Park, located between Bethlehem and Easton off of William Penn Highway. Depending on which direction one was coming from, trolleys were available to ride to the park. A trolley could be caught at New and Broad Streets in Bethlehem at 35 minutes after the hour. From Easton, trolleys were available on the half hour. Only local cars stopped at the park, and the "limited cars" passed right by without stopping. The Juvenile Band of Allentown, Pennsylvania, posed for this photograph. The US Navy uniform inspired their uniforms, and their favorite composer was John Philip Sousa.

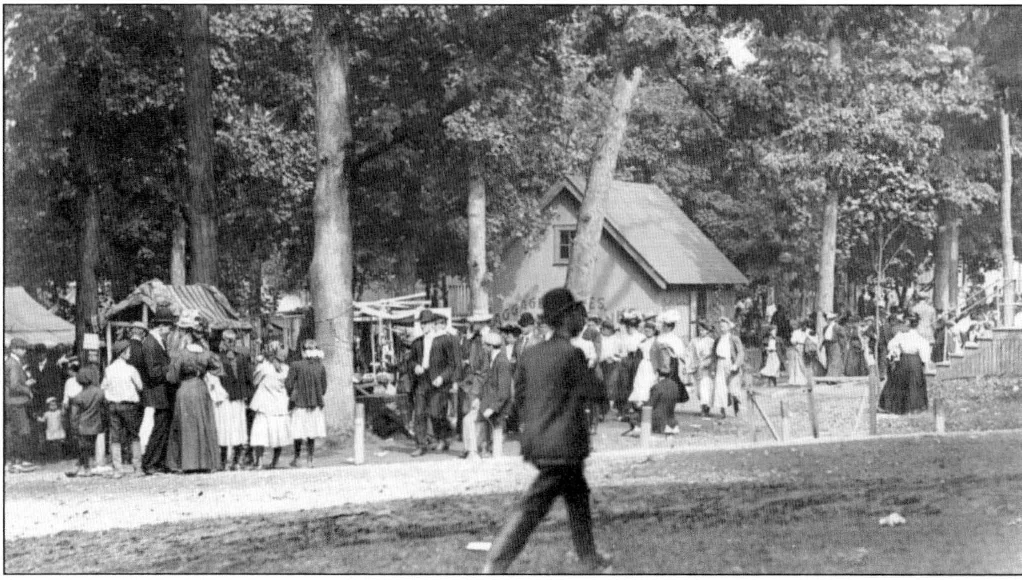

Oakland Park was a small family-oriented park. There was a large pavilion and several family-size wooden tables that could be moved around the beautiful grove. One could pack his or her own picnic or buy a light lunch at the refreshment stand. Although most people took trolleys, there was ample parking for automobiles. Children enjoyed the merry-go-round with a gold ring dispenser. If they were able to grab the ring, they received a free ride. The carousel had 46 wooden animals, carved by Muller and Leopold, and two band organs produced its music. There was also a large sandbox and a miniature Black Diamond train ride.

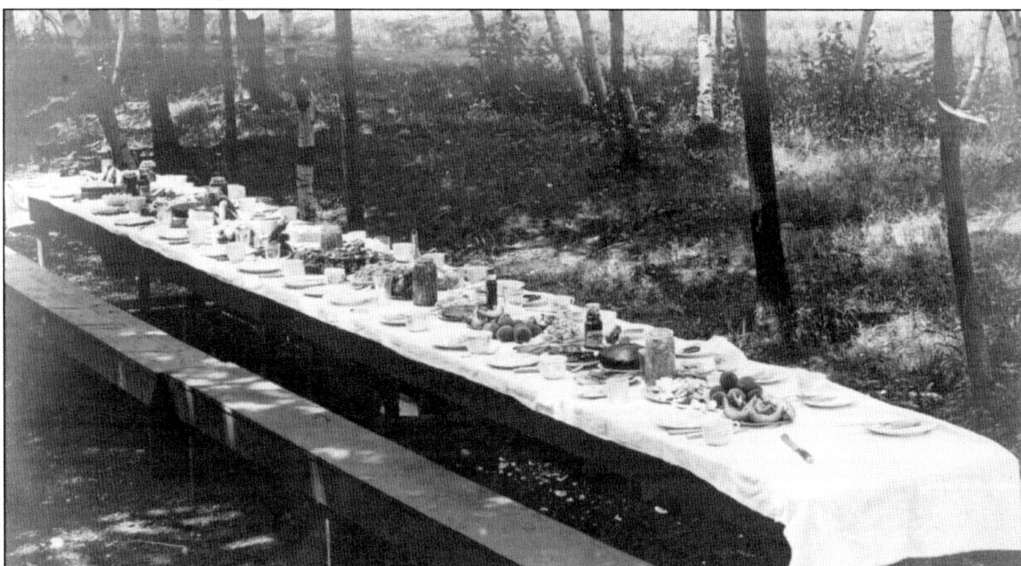

There were family reunions at Oakland Park every weekend. Local newspapers announced the reunions of family names, such as Laubach, Shimer, or Hummel. A group could reserve the large pavilion then place several tables end to end to allow everyone to sit down for a meal together. Note the glassware, porcelain plates and teacups, and silverware. Bananas, peaches, and freshly baked bread line the center of the cloth-covered table. The surrounding trees provided plenty of shade on a summer day.

Four

West Side Revisited

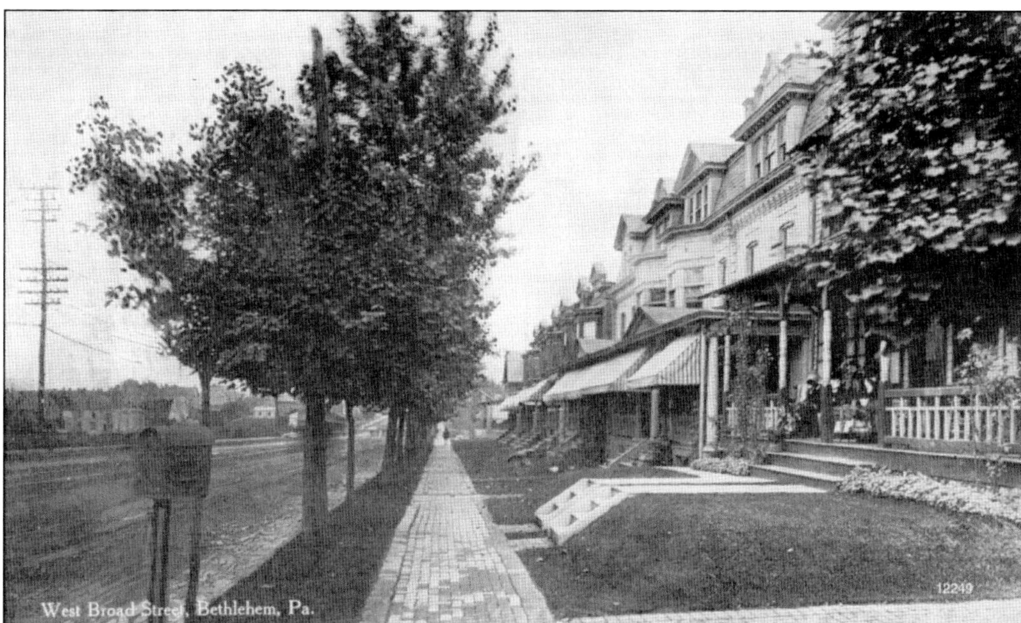

Here is a view of West Broad Street in West Bethlehem looking east on Broad from near Seventh Avenue. A woman is sitting on the porch on the far right. She is enjoying her beautiful garden surrounding her house. Although the homes are built close to each other, it must have been luxurious to move from the soot-filled city to the west. The wide streets and clear air were so much of a draw that the area became a borough in 1886. West Bethlehem Borough was annexed by Bethlehem in 1904.

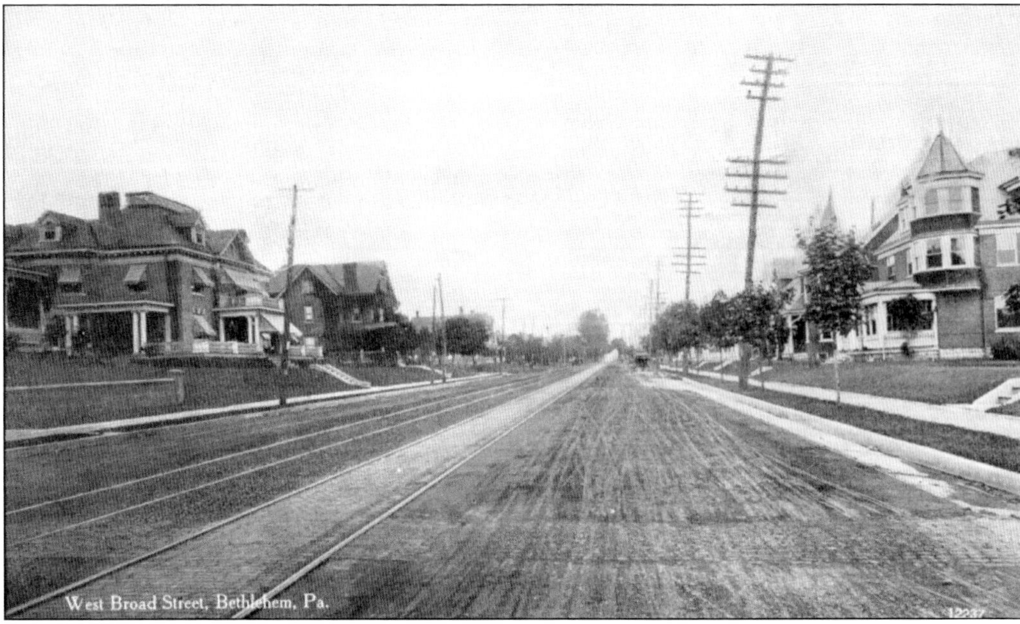

These residences along West Broad Street were built in the early 1900s as single-family homes on large lots with wide sidewalks, trees, and shrubs. The photographer was looking west in the 900 block of West Broad Street (between Eighth and Ninth Avenues). The first house on the left (south) side of the street is now known as the Bank Building at 925 West Broad Street. The houses on the right (north) side have been torn down and the location is now KNBT Bank and a parking lot.

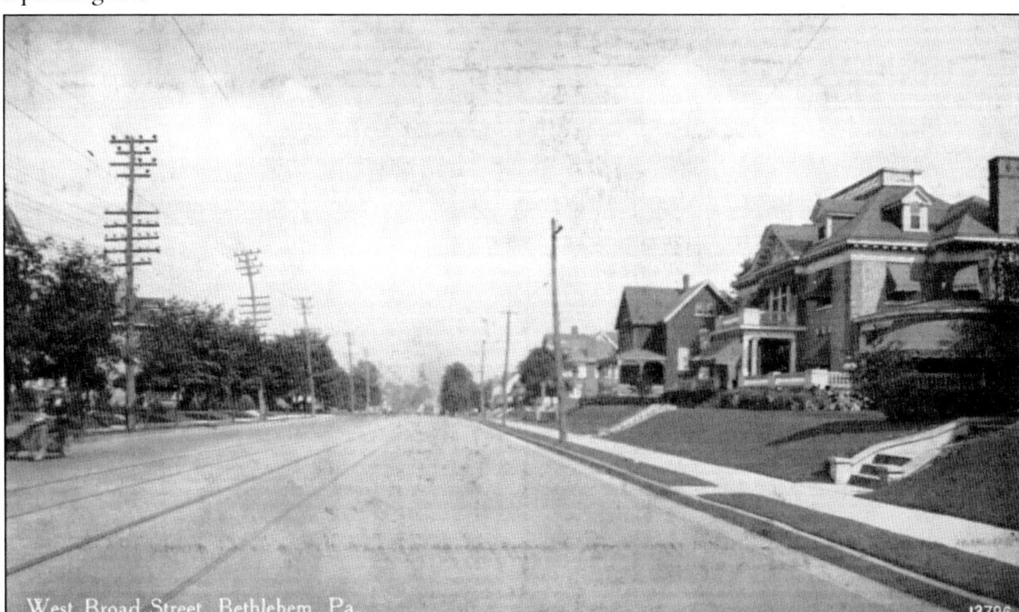

Along West Broad Street, one sees the trolley tracks that run between Allentown and Bethlehem. There is a car pictured on the left, which is not surprising because most of the residents of this neighborhood had their own cars. The picture was taken looking east from about Ninth Avenue, with the Banko Building on the right.

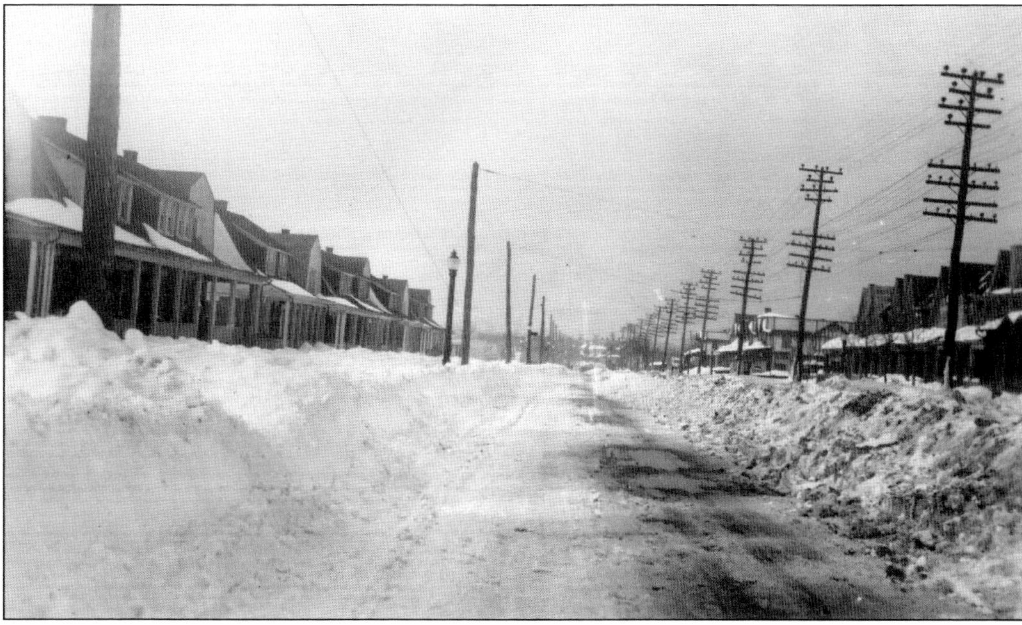

This view is looking west on West Broad Street in West Bethlehem. This was the fashionable place to live once the Broad Street Bridge was erected and made it accessible. This is the Mount Airy Historic District today. These residents owned cars, and it is very possible that the cars are buried in the snowbanks lining the street.

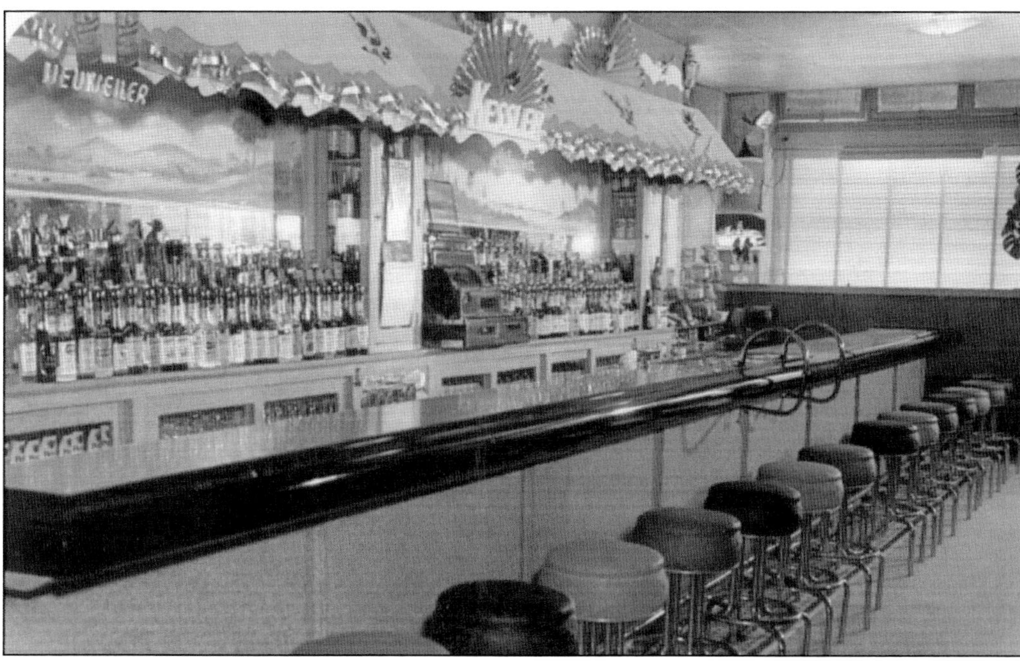

Here is an inside photograph of the well-stocked Liberty Tavern, located on the corner of Second Avenue and West Broad Street. The corner bar had a succession of owners, including Joe Ballek in the 1940s and Charles Chamberlain in the 1960s. Dreamscape Comics occupies the building now.

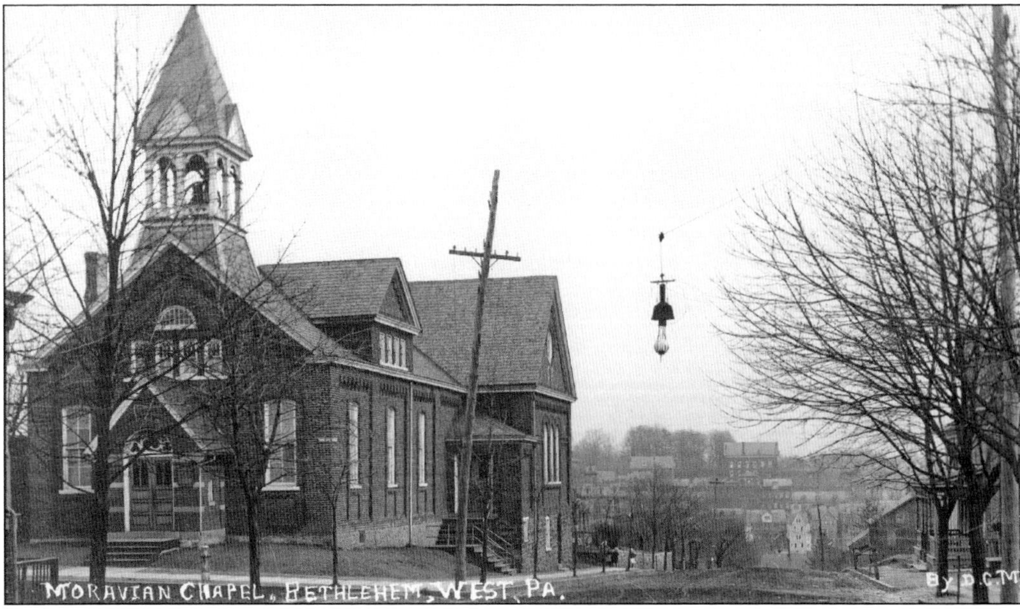

In 1883, Moravian Theological Seminary students, all under the age of 22, raised the funds to build the West Side Moravian Church, shown here. This was a 34-by-60-foot brick building located at the intersection of Prospect and Third Avenues. In 1884, the small church was dedicated. In 1890, an annex, larger than the original building, was built. The church still thrives today at that location.

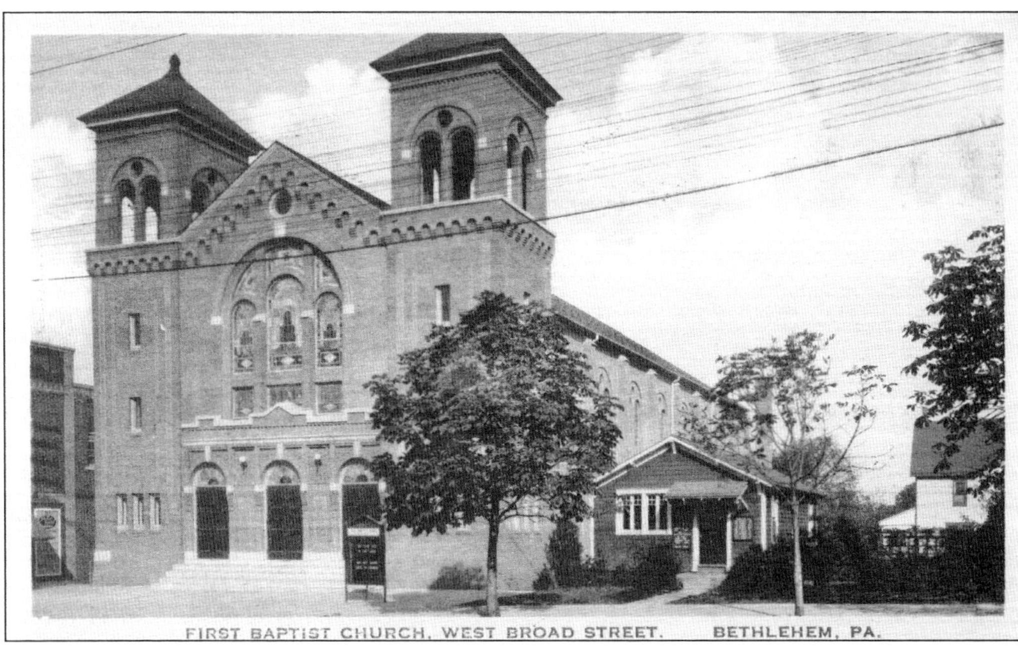

The First Baptist Church, located at Fourth Avenue and Broad Street in West Bethlehem, was built in 1922. This group has a long history in Bethlehem beginning in 1869. In that year, 12 people met in a room over a blacksmith's shop on North New Street to organize the church. They now worship in a newer church, built in 1972 on Linden Street. A modern bank sits on the original site today.

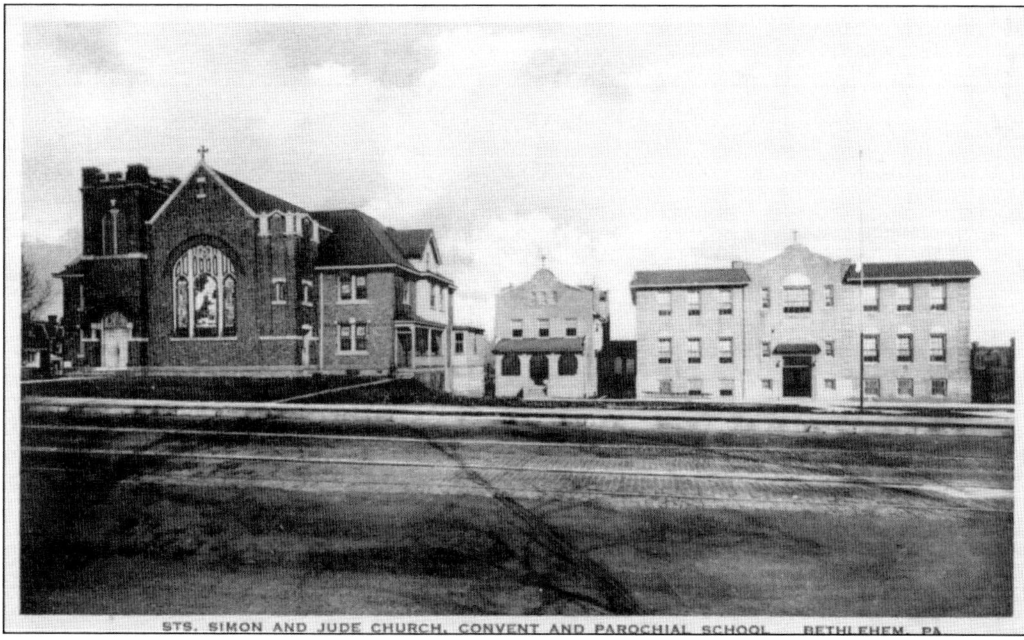

Ss. Simon and Jude Church was organized in 1917. The group purchased the Olivet Evangelical Church on West Broad Street between Sixth and Seventh Avenues in West Bethlehem in 1920. The congregation built a new church on the site in 1932. A new school and convent were built in 1966. The name of the school was changed to Seton Academy in 2006, and the school was closed in 2013.

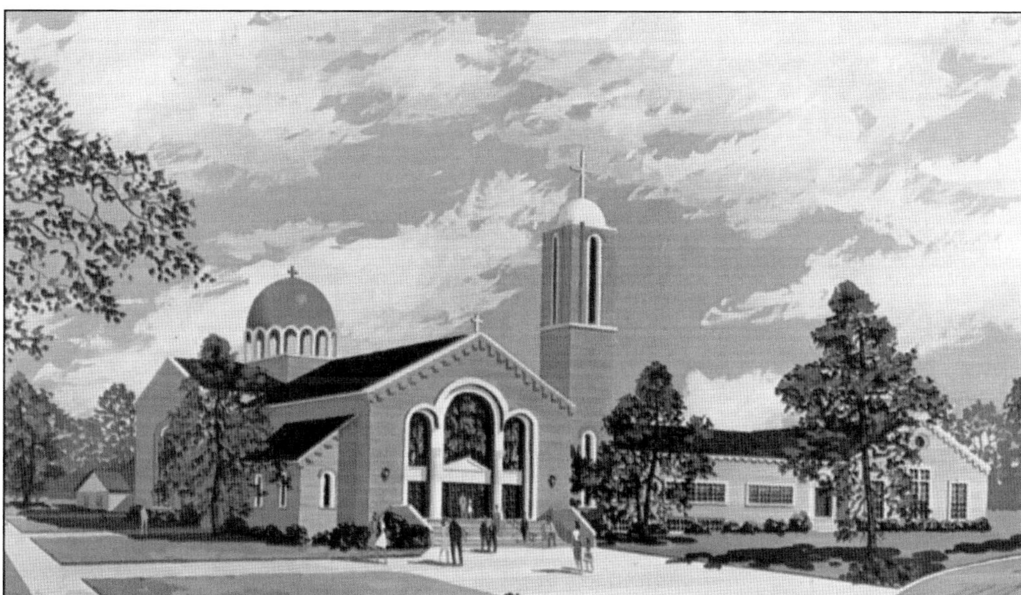

The Greek immigrants who arrived in Bethlehem in the early 1900s organized a church to preserve their religion, language, and customs. In 1916, they purchased St. Joseph's Episcopal Church on East Fourth Street. Over the years, they outgrew this church, and they purchased a lot on Union Boulevard in 1955. St. Nicholas Greek Orthodox Church, pictured here, at the intersection of Union Boulevard and Fifteenth Street, was completed in 1960.

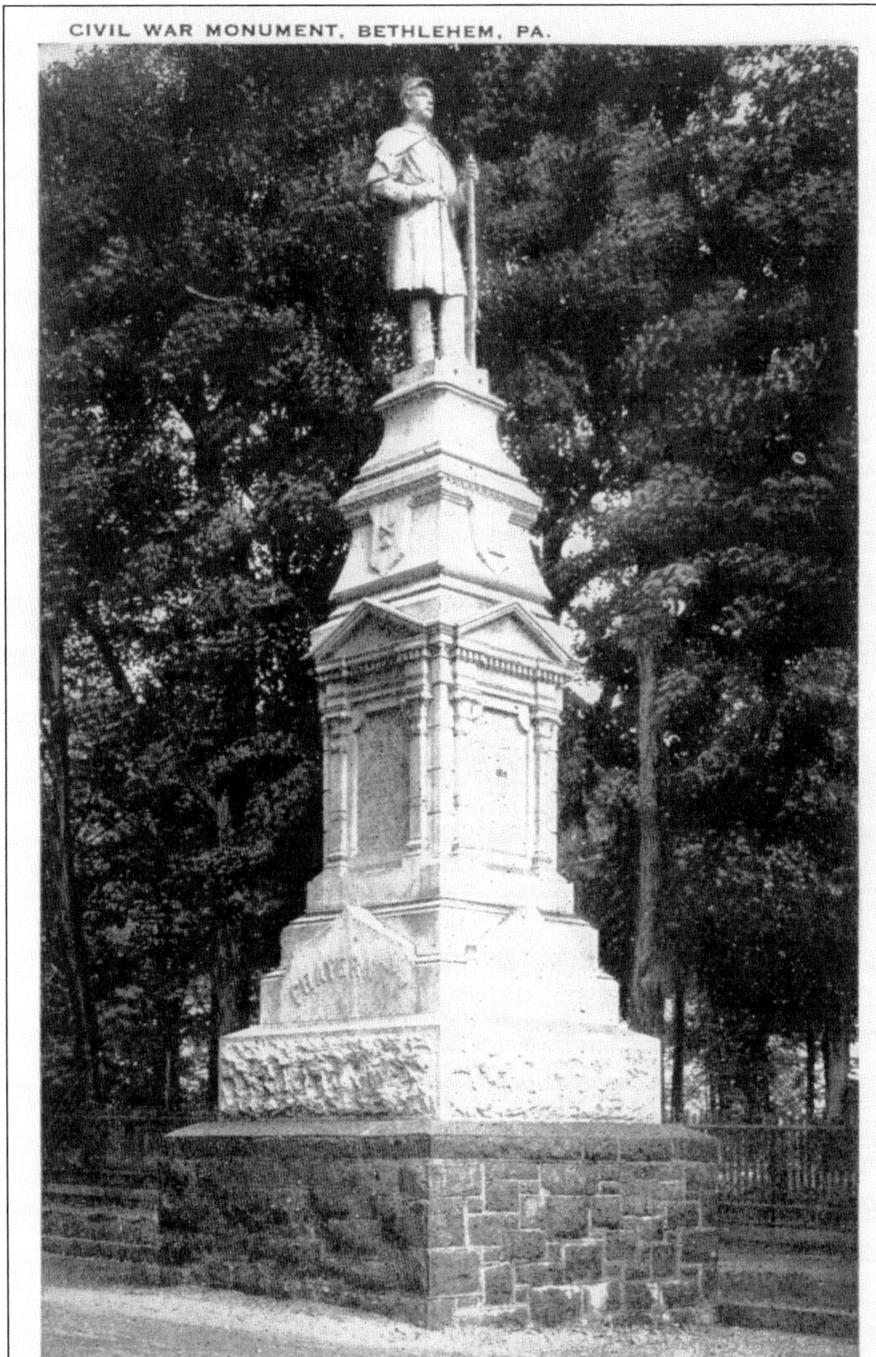

In October 1887, the Grand Army of the Republic J.K. Taylor Post unveiled, in memory of deceased soldiers and sailors of the Civil War, a monument. It was located on Market Street next to the Moravian Cemetery. Decoration Day ceremonies were conducted around the monument each year. As traffic increased on Bethlehem streets, the monument was moved in 1967 to the Bethlehem Rose Garden at Eighth Avenue, where it stands facing Union Boulevard today.

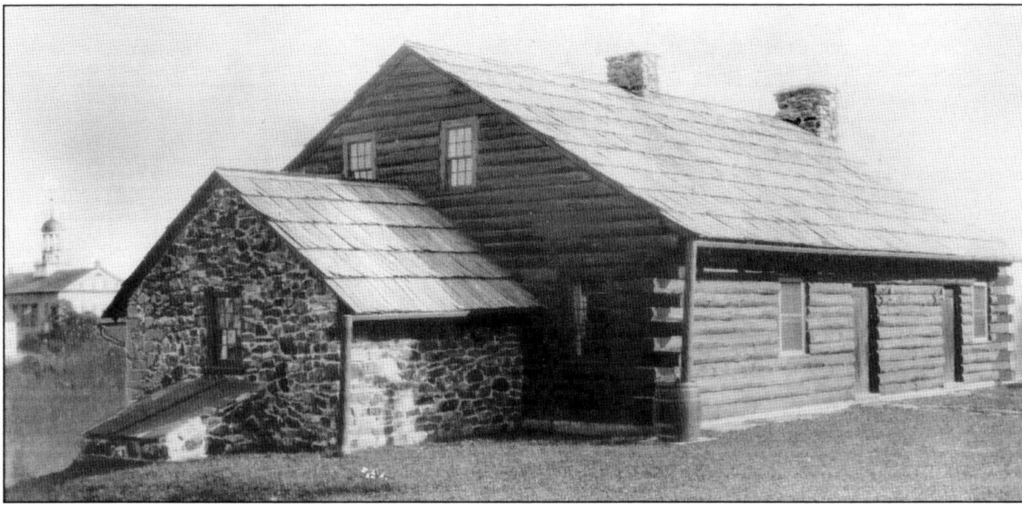

In 1931, the Bethlehem Chapter of the Daughters of the American Revolution built a replica of the first house that was built in Bethlehem. In 1741, Moravian settlers built a log cabin that measured 20 by 40 feet. A loft above the entire first floor provided sleeping quarters. The house stood along the bank of the Monocacy Creek, where the Hotel Bethlehem stands today. The replica house was built on First Avenue but was relocated in 1965, as the construction of Route 398 was routed through the property. The house sits in the Bethlehem Rose Garden on Eighth Avenue, where one can visit it.

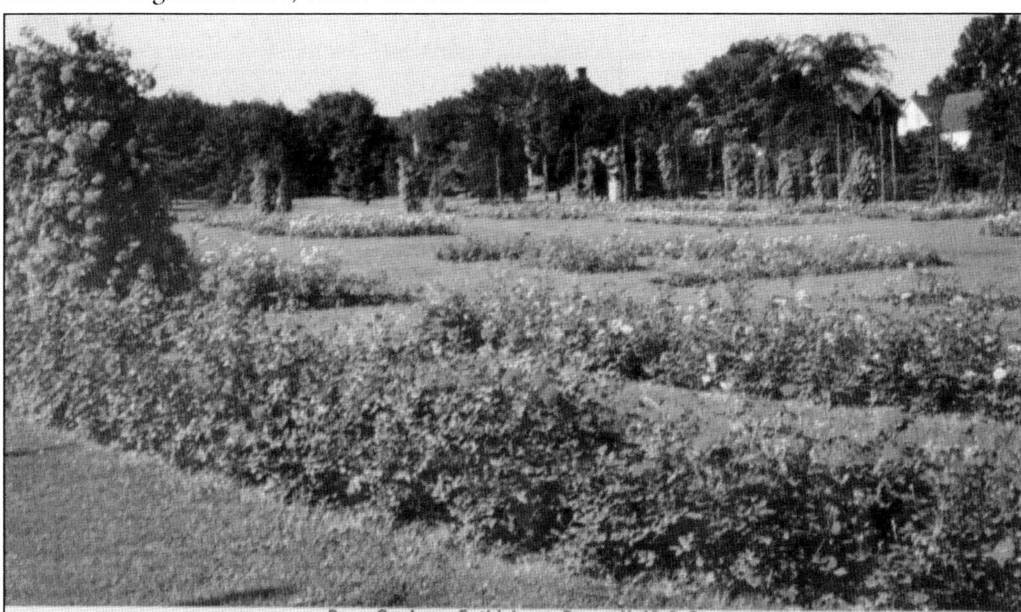

In the 1950s, Harold Becraft, a New York photographer, was drawn to the lovely Bethlehem Rose Garden between Eighth and Tenth Avenue. His Kodachrome film captured the bright reds and pinks of the roses. Becraft may have also wandered over to the portable bandstand to listen to the Bethlehem Municipal Band perform or paused to appreciate the Jonathan K. Taylor Post No. 182 Grand Army of the Republic (GAR) Monument. In the same park, he may have also admired the Daughters of the American Revolution (DAR) Memorial House, a replica of the first house built in Bethlehem. One can still enjoy all of the above in the park today.

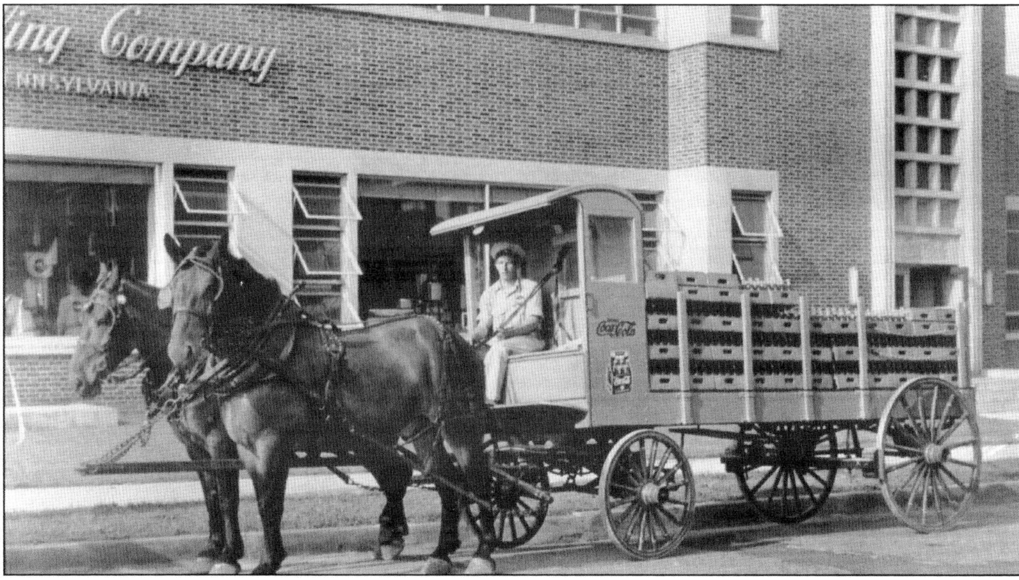

The Coca-Cola Bottling Company of Bethlehem was founded in 1917 and was located on Tenth Avenue. In 1941, the company moved to a new location on West Broad Street, pictured. The horse-drawn wagon in front of the building is the original wagon used by Melvin Klotz. The picture was taken in 1942 during World War II. Gas rationing at the time necessitated that horse and wagon deliver the bottles of Coca-Cola. The bottling company moved in 1981 to Industrial Drive, Bethlehem, and changed its name to Coca-Cola Bottling Company of the Lehigh Valley. (Courtesy of Kevin K. Klotz.)

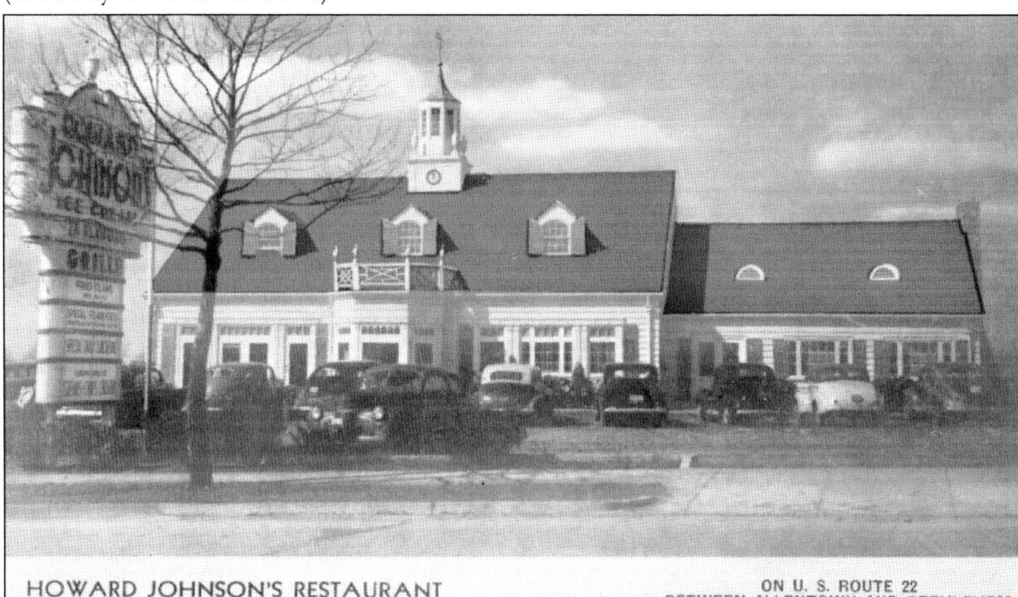

Howard Johnson's Restaurant on Union Boulevard opened in 1941. On April 6, 1948, Gen. Dwight David Eisenhower, former supreme commander of the Allied forces in Europe and future president (1953–1961), his wife, Mamie, and her mother, Mrs. John Sheldon Doud (Elivera), stopped by for lunch. There are no longer any "Ho Jo's" in the Lehigh Valley. A Wendy's restaurant occupies the former site today.

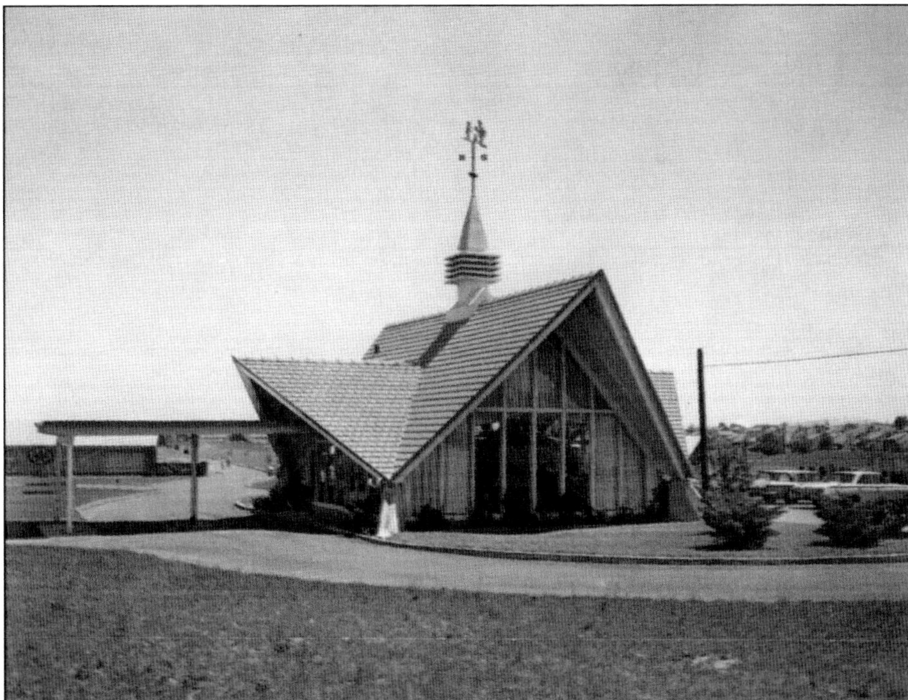

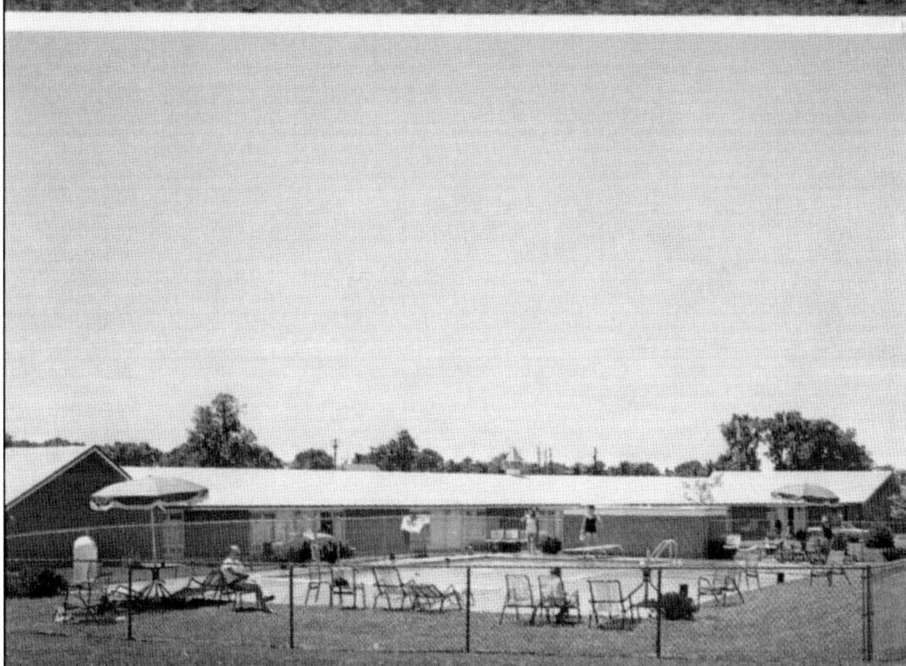

Here are views of the Howard Johnson's Restaurant (top) and Motor Lodge (bottom) located at the bend of Catasauqua Road where it meets Motel Drive. Applebee's restaurant (2109 Motel Drive) is currently on the site of the restaurant. The motor lodge has been torn down and replaced with Fairfield Inns and Suites (2140 Motel Drive).

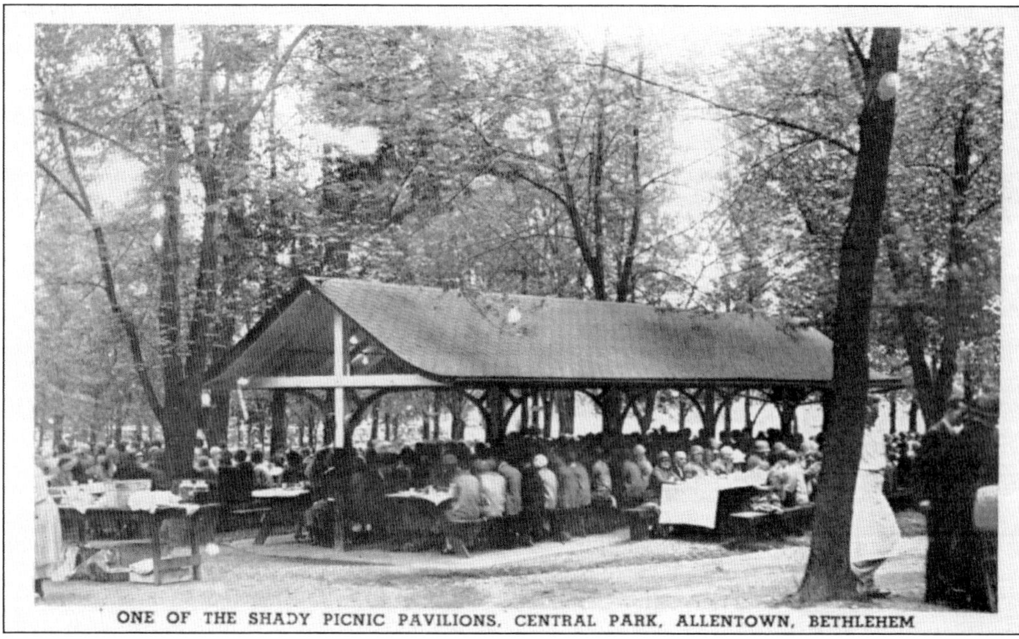

The Lehigh Valley Traction Company in Rittersville built Central Park where Broad Street met Hanover Avenue. The park opened on Saturday, July 2, 1892. The Fairview Band of Bethlehem gave a concert, and two consecutive baseball games were played at the park. Families and church groups organized large gatherings utilizing the numerous picnic tables.

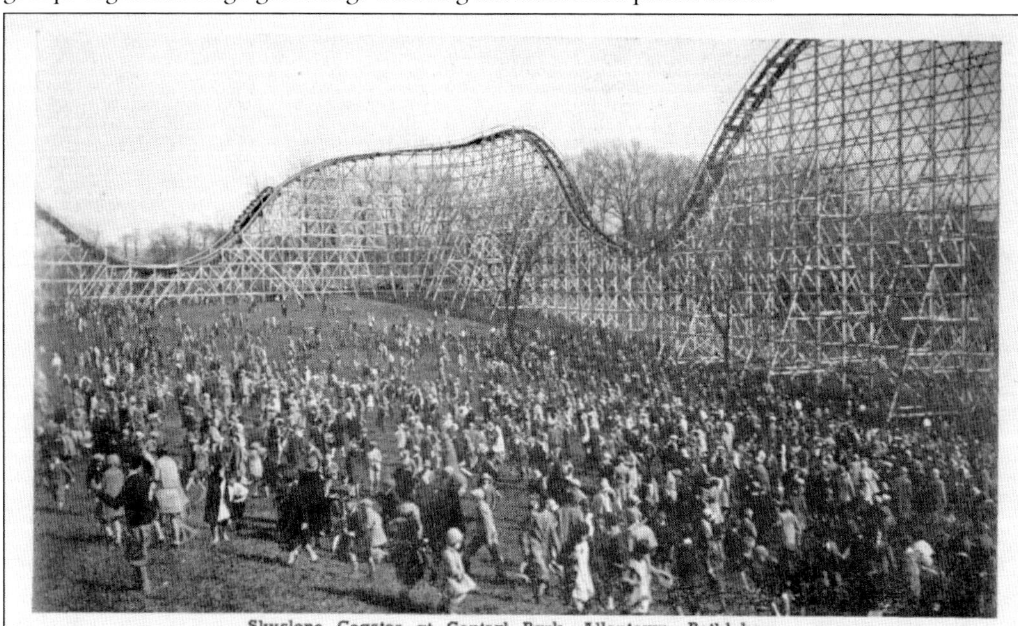

Central Park advertised its park as the "playground of the Lehigh Valley." Trolleys from Allentown, Bethlehem, and Easton brought crowds for picnics, family reunions, rides, and movies. In this postcard is the Skyclone Coaster, added to the park in 1929. It was known for its terrifying 90-degree turn. Over the years, the ride was rebuilt several times. It burned to the ground in 1935. The park opened in 1893 and was closed in 1957.

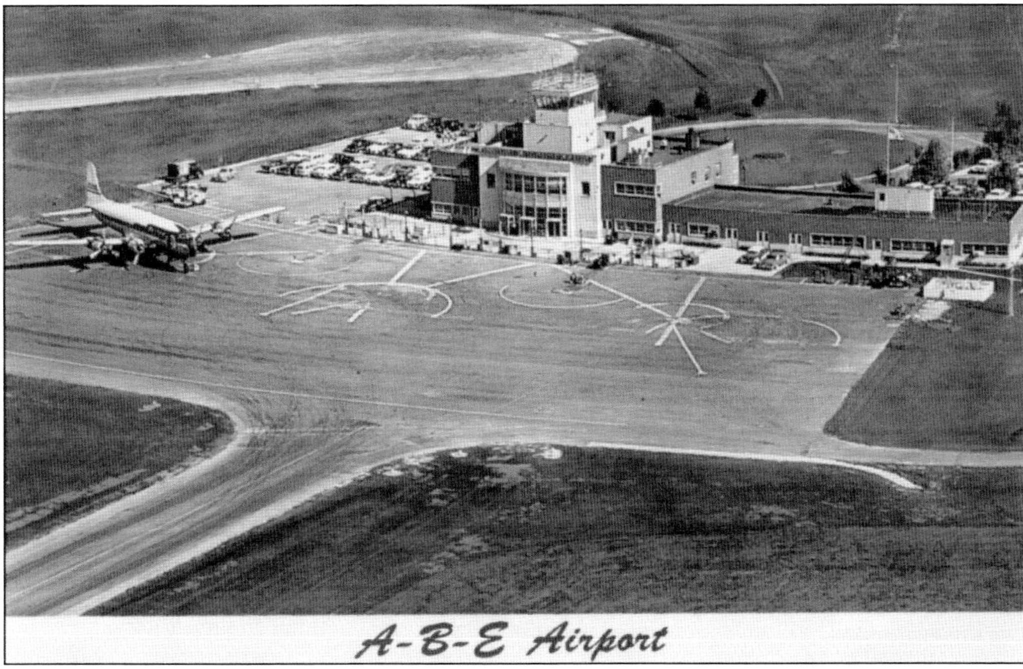

The Allentown-Bethlehem-Easton airport began in 1927, when the US Department of Commerce rented 50 acres of farmland in Hanover Township as an emergency landing airstrip for airmail pilots. This 1,500-foot grass landing strip was the first airstrip in the Lehigh Valley. Wilfred M. "Wiley" Post Jr. was manager of the airport from 1937 to 1983.

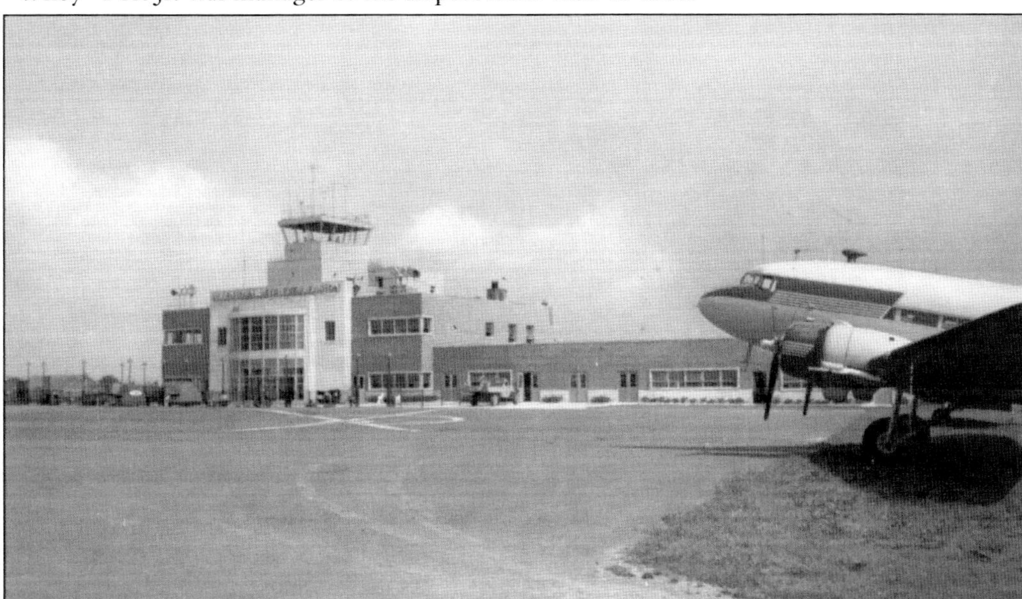

In 1948, the Allentown Airport Corporation was reorganized as the Lehigh-Northampton Airport Authority to become eligible for federal funds. At the same time, the name of the airport was changed to Allentown-Bethlehem-Easton Airport. In the same year, Trans World Airlines began providing flights from ABE to Newark and Pittsburgh. The second passenger terminal, shown here, was completed in 1950 for $1 million.

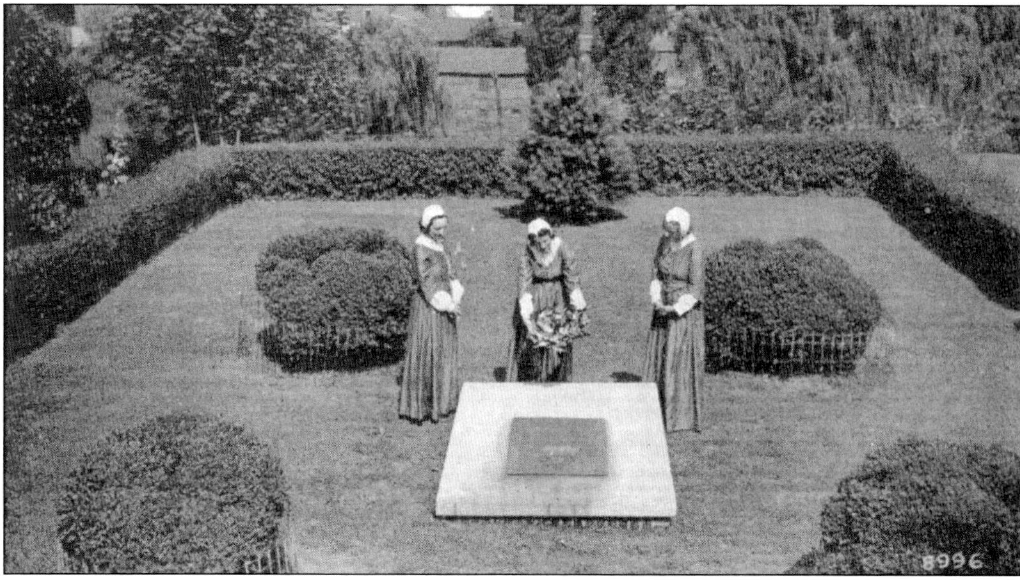

More than 500 Revolutionary War soldiers who died in the Continental Hospital in Bethlehem between 1776 and 1778 were buried in unmarked graves on this hillside that overlooks Route 378. These graves have been removed. The Tomb of the Unknown Revolutionary Soldier memorial, located at First Avenue and West Market Street, commemorates these soldiers. The women pictured by the grave are demonstrating the dress of the Moravian sisters who nursed the soldiers.

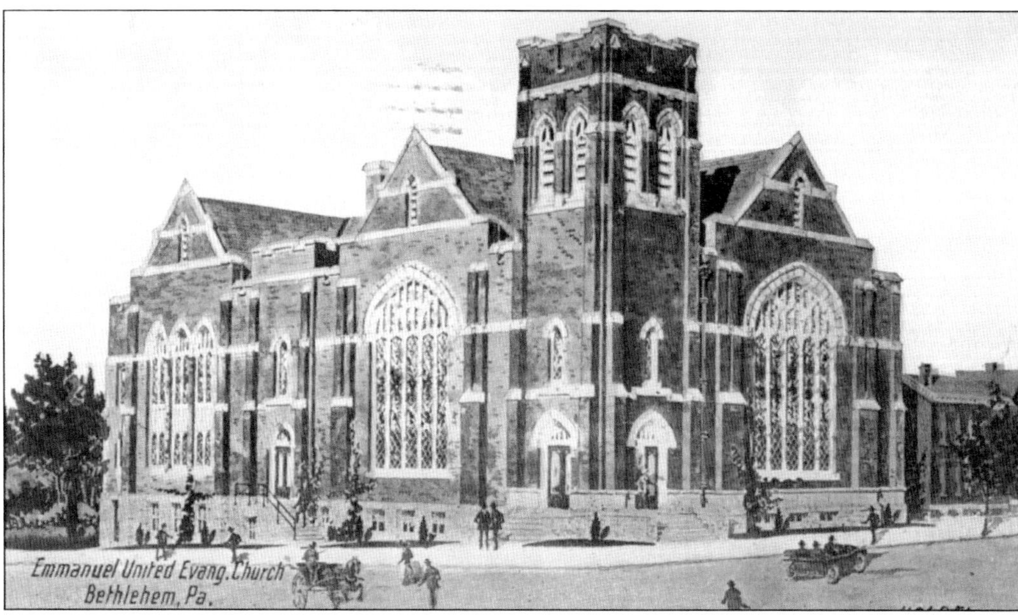

The Emmanuel Evangelical Congregational Church, shown here, was the second church on the same site. This church was located at the northwest corner of East Union Boulevard and North Center Street. In 1890, it changed its name from St. John's United Evangelical Church to Emmanuel Evangelical Church. In 1912, it built a larger church to accommodate increased numbers of members. Emmanuel has been a mother church to two newer Evangelical churches in the Bethlehem area.

Five

Bethlehem Steel Revisited

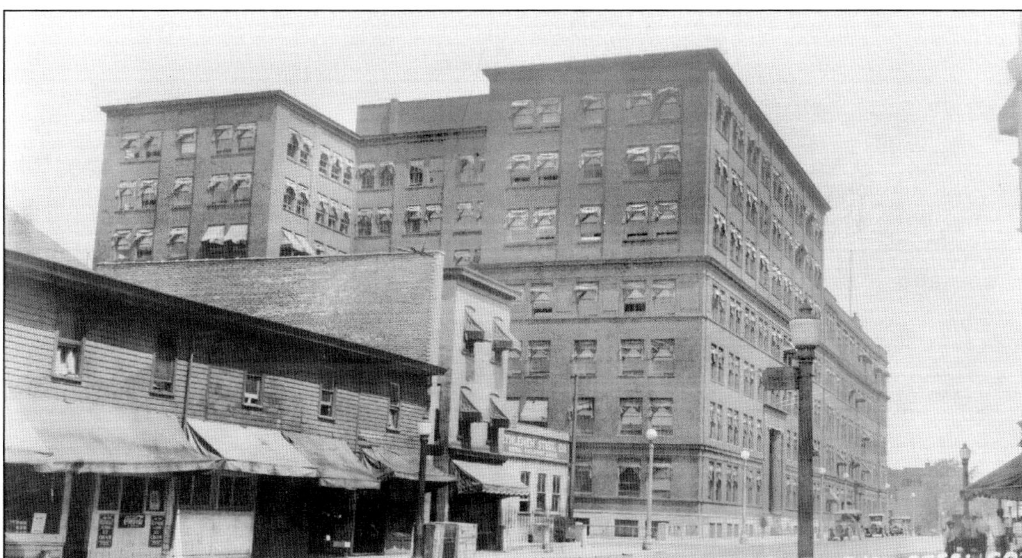

Here is an early-1900s photograph of the main office building of the Bethlehem Steel Corporation, located on Third Street. On the far left is a luncheonette and Klein's Bakery. These casual eateries were located all around South Bethlehem to feed the hungry mill workers. The early-20th-century automobiles parked along the street were becoming more prevalent. The luncheonette would later be demolished due to a fire to create a parking lot.

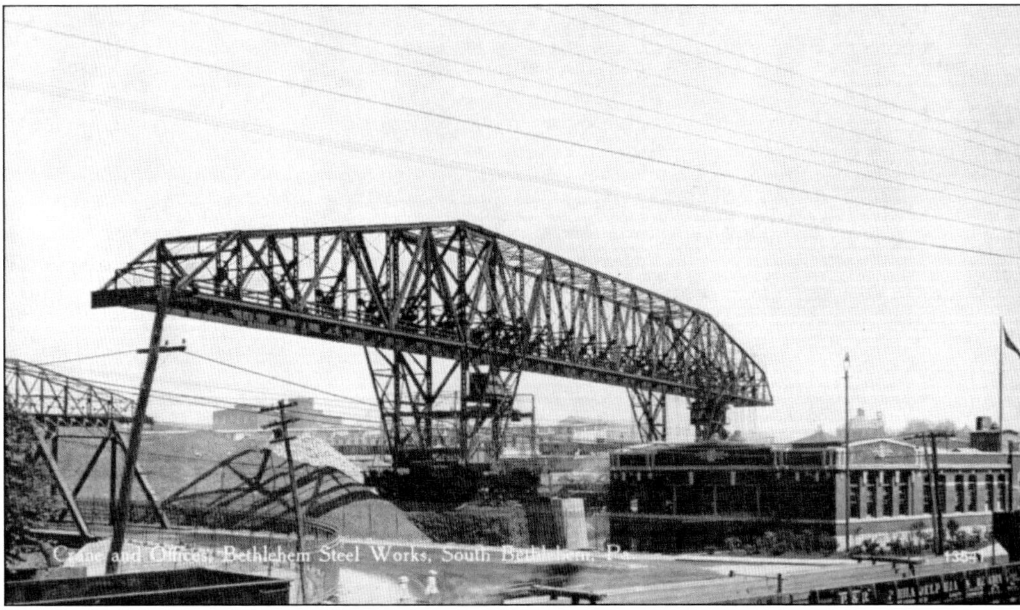

The ore crane pictured here weighed 20 tons and was capable of lifting 10 tons of ore 70 feet high. Bethlehem Steel used as much as 1,500 tons of iron ore a day. A clamshell-type bucket was operated from the crane. Bethlehem Steel conducted regular inspections to prevent collapse of the massively heavy crane. Bethlehem Steel operated two ore cranes. The one shown here was salvaged for the entrance to the Sands Casino. The casino sits on the site of the former ore yard.

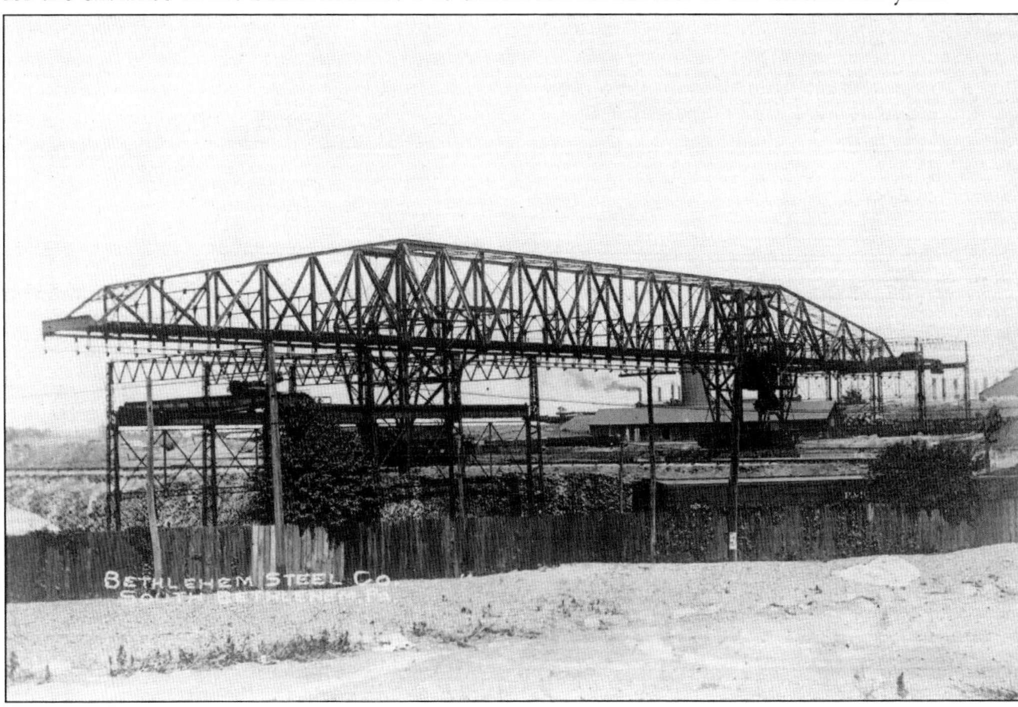

This crane, one of the largest in the world, ran a huge bucket shovel horizontally along the rails of the crane to scoop up iron ore and coke from mountains of the materials in the stockyard of the Bethlehem plant or from ore trains with open cars filled with piles of ore.

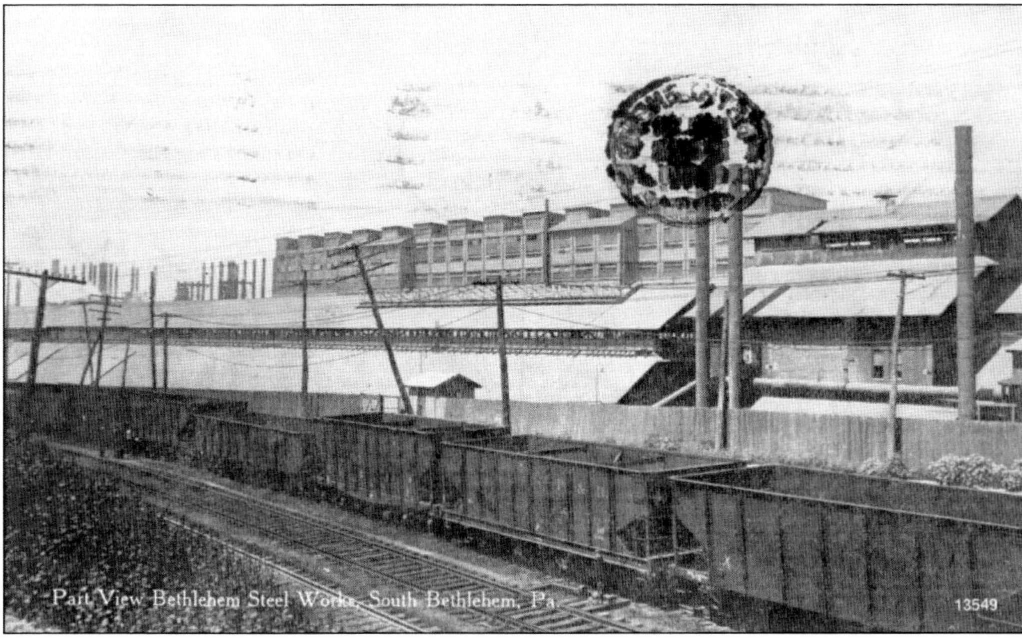

Here is the Bethlehem Steel Corporation plant in South Bethlehem. At the time of this postcard, the company owned iron mines in Cuba and several shipyards on both coasts. The new gray rolling mill, built in 1908, began producing one of the nation's first wide-flange structural sections, which revolutionized building construction.

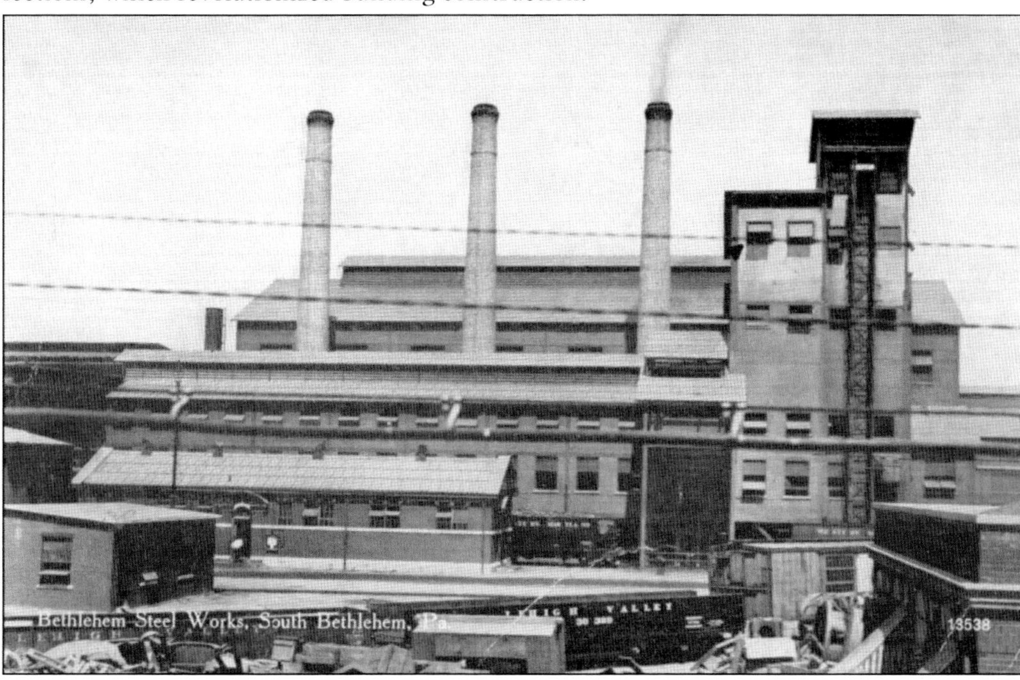

This photograph of the Bethlehem Steel Corporation shows a beehive of activity. The Lehigh Valley Railroad transports material to and from the gray rolling mill. At the time of this early-1900s photograph, Bethlehem Steel was the largest supplier of steel to building contractors in the United States.

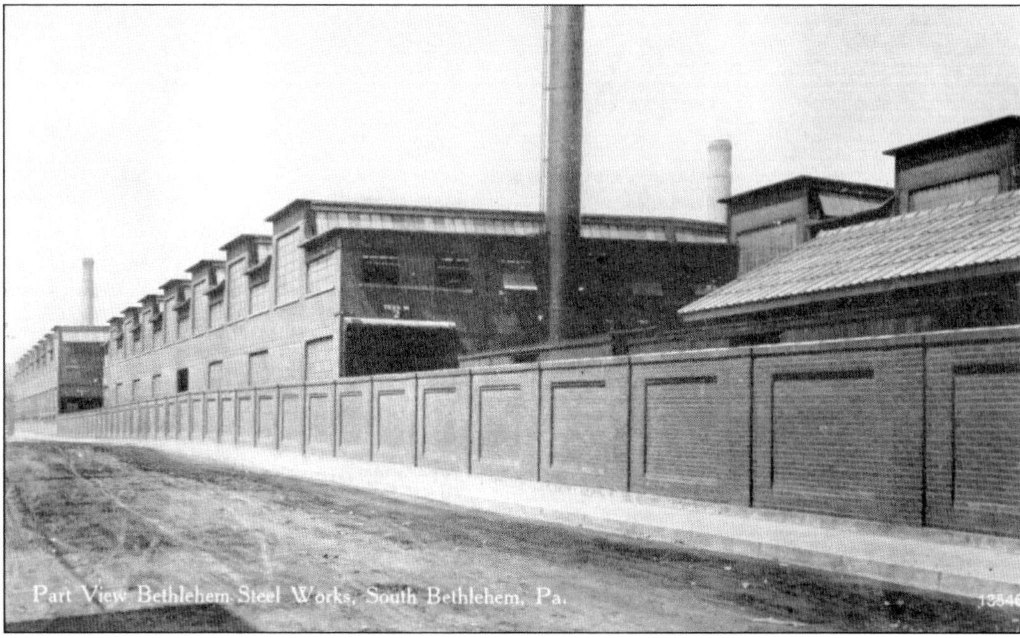

Initially, the Bethlehem Steel Plant was a producer of rails for the railroad industry. In 1904, Charles M. Schwab reorganized the business into Bethlehem Steel Corporation, becoming president and chairman of the board. The company provided steel for the Army during both world wars.

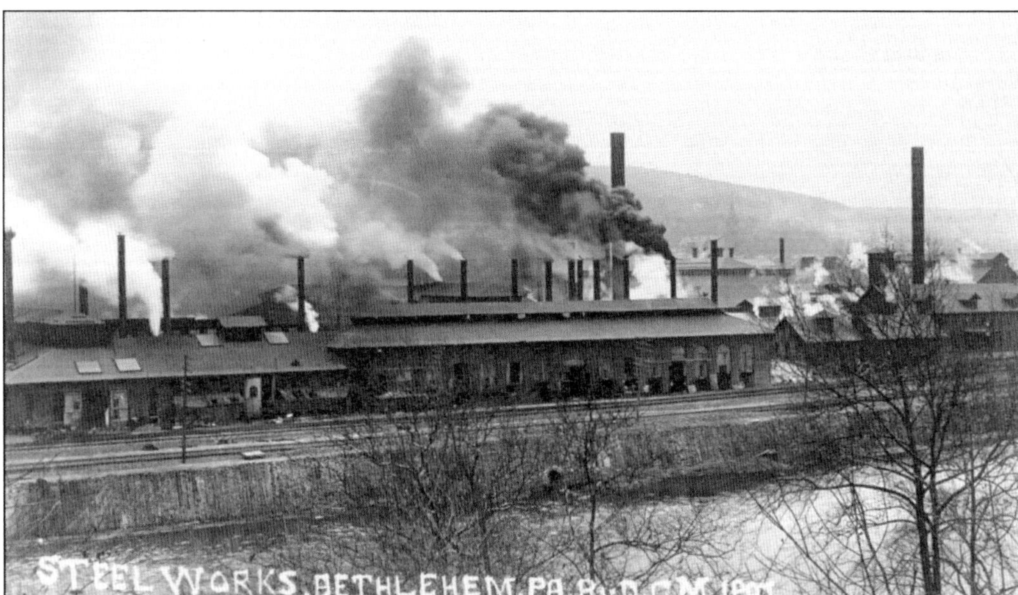

Historically, the city of Bethlehem's biggest polluter was the Bethlehem Steel Corporation. The corporation consistently violated the Clean Air Act until it closed its operations in 1995. The Bethlehem Steel plant also used more than 1 million gallons of water from the Lehigh River a day in its processing systems. It required 65,000 gallons to make a single ton of finished steel. The bed of the Lehigh River still contains high concentrations of cadmium and zinc from this industry.

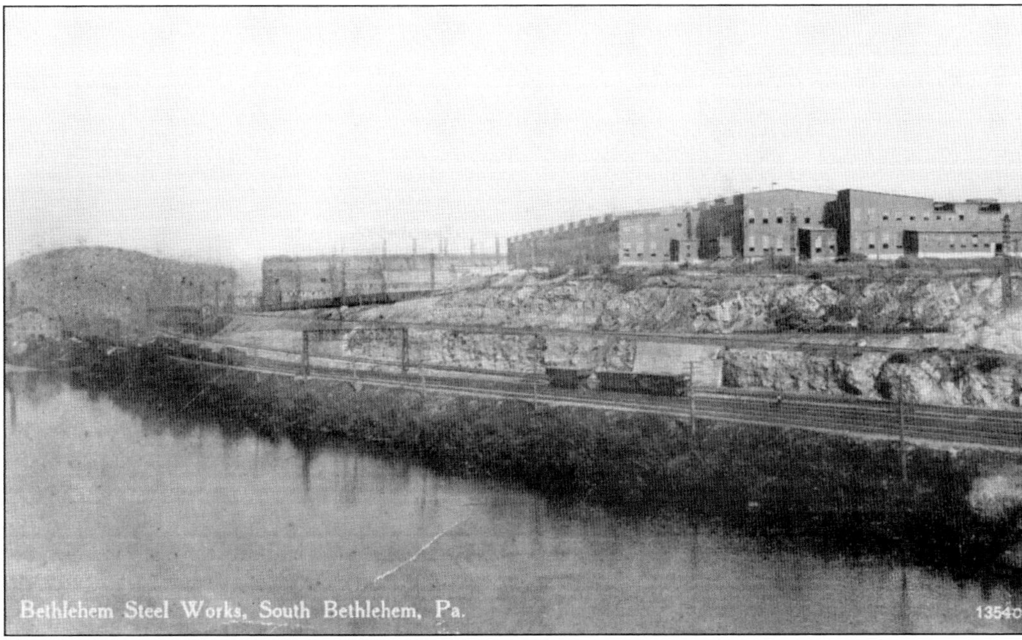

The mill was situated on a flat parcel of land along the Lehigh River. The original property was owned by the Moravian Church and purchased by Augustus Wolle, the organizer of the Bethlehem Rolling Mills. Charles Brodhead, a local businessman and colleague of Wolle's, convinced him to build near the junction of the Lehigh Valley and North Penn Railroads.

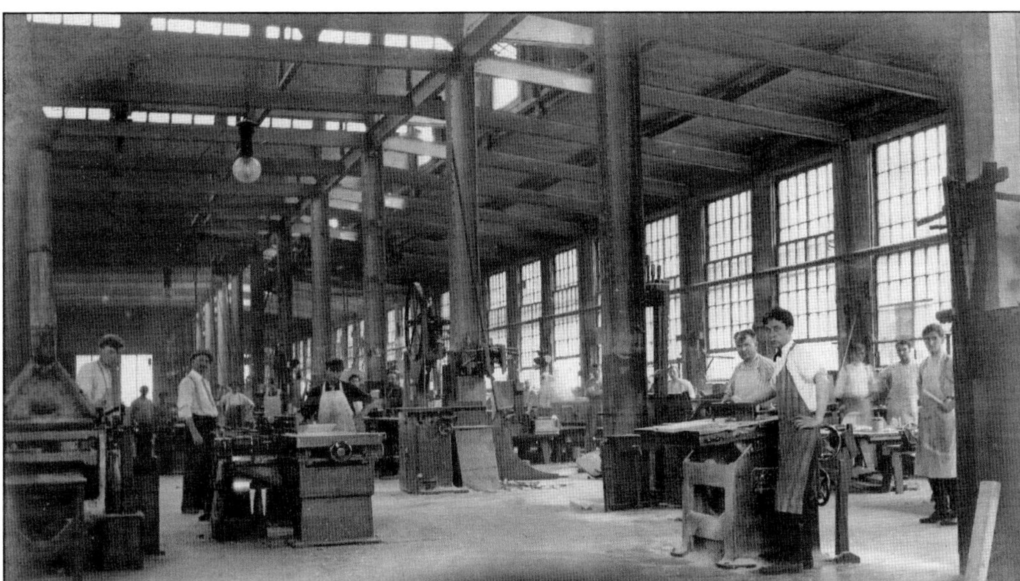

This photograph of the Bethlehem Steel Corporation pattern shop was taken after the shop was rebuilt in 1913. Charles M. Schwab included the pattern shop in an extensive modernization of the steel plant. In the shop, workers produced patterns for the production of ordnance, engine parts, and hydraulics. When the building next to the new pattern shop caught fire in 1915, Charles M. Schwab rushed back from West Virginia to evaluate the damage. The pattern shop still stands today and can be seen as a backdrop in the movie *Transformers: Revenge of the Fallen.*

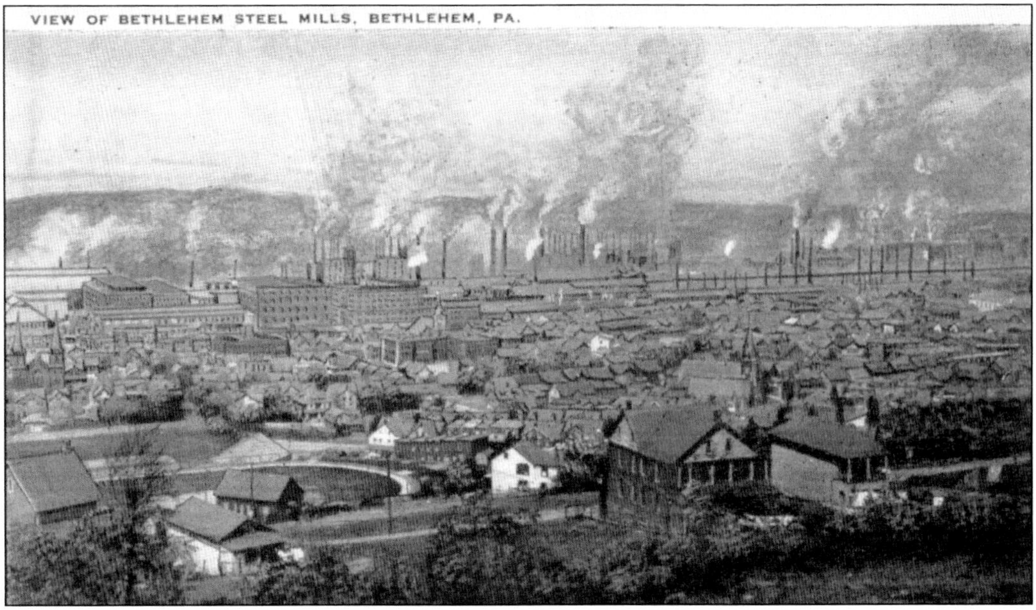

Bethlehem Steel produced the steel for iconic New York City structures such as Madison Square Garden, the Lincoln Tunnel, the Waldorf Astoria Hotel, the Chrysler Building, and the George Washington Bridge. Structures built elsewhere in the United States were San Francisco's Golden Gate Bridge; Chicago's Merchandise Mart; the Virginia Bay Bridge-Tunnel; Los Angeles City Hall; and DC's US Supreme Court and US Congress's Rayburn Buildings.

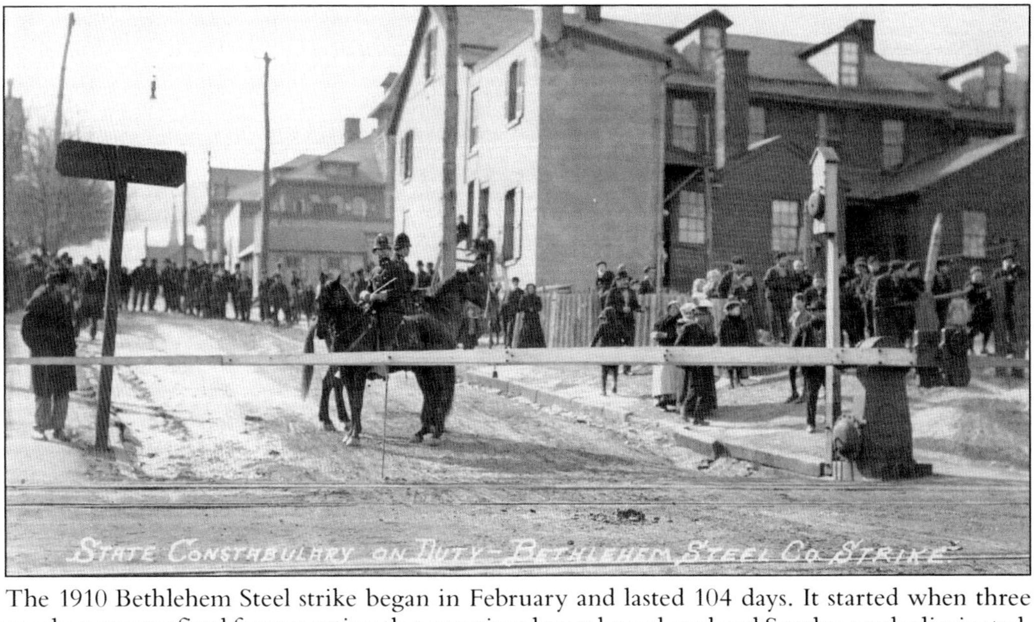

The 1910 Bethlehem Steel strike began in February and lasted 104 days. It started when three employees were fired for requesting that overtime hours be reduced and Sunday work eliminated. At the time, employees worked for 12¢ an hour, 12 hours a day, 7 days a week. Over 100 members of the Pennsylvania State Constabulary, the forerunners of the state police, were called in to control the strikers and their supporters. G.A. Conradi took several photographs during the strike. When he sold his images as postcards, Bethlehem Steel president Charles M. Schwab ordered that they all be removed from the public so they would not incite further support for the strikers.

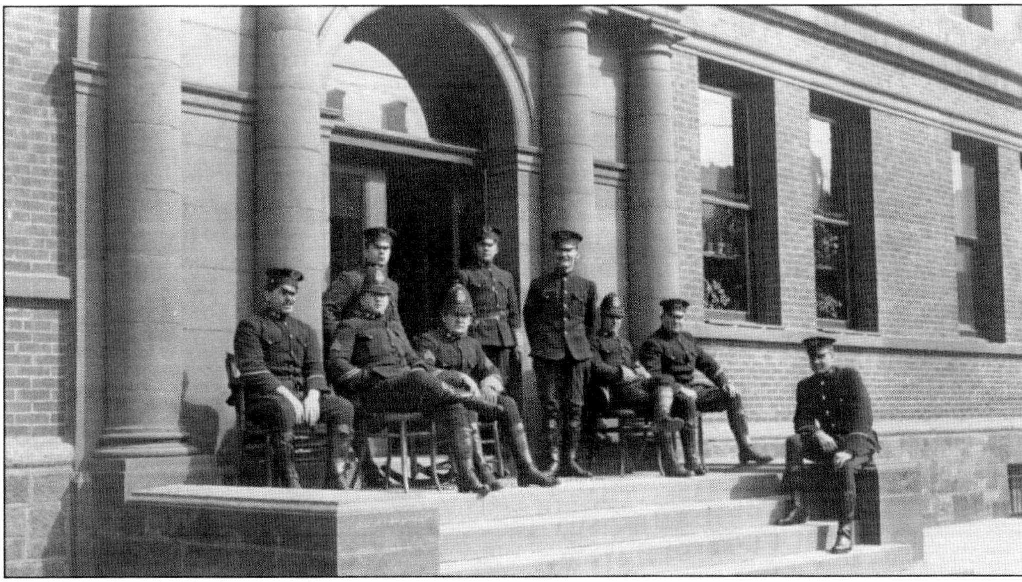

Here is the entrance to the Bethlehem Steel corporate office being protected by the state troopers. In this photograph, their demeanor appears relaxed, unlike the previous photograph, when crowds in the streets of South Bethlehem confront them. Their only mission was to protect the entrances to prevent trimers from threatening nonstriking workers as they entered the plant. When the troopers left the steel property and rode down the streets of South Bethlehem, they escalated the tensions of the strike.

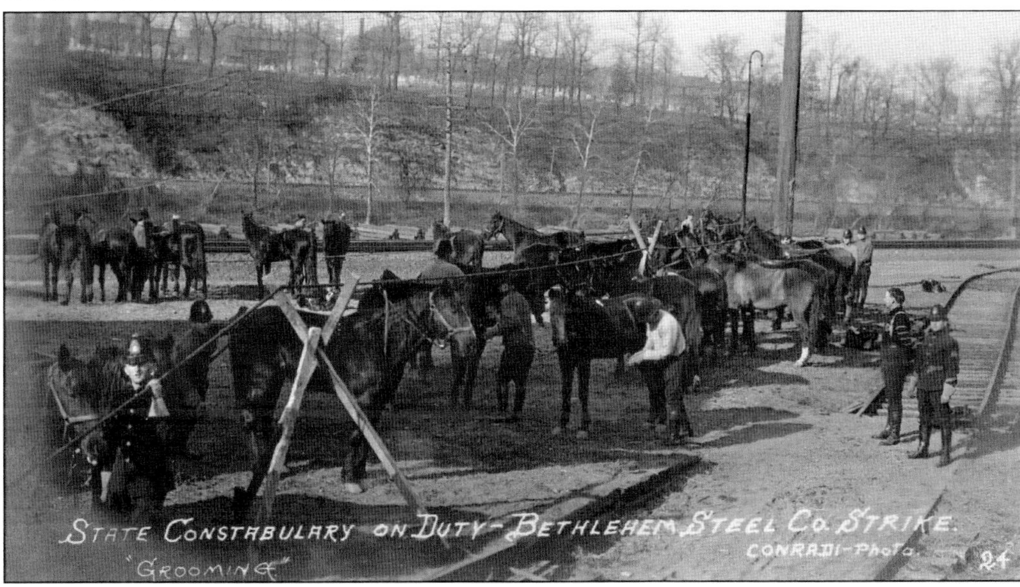

After riding on the Reading Railroad from Philadelphia to the Union Station in South Bethlehem, the Pennsylvania State Constabulary and their horses proceeded to the Bethlehem Steel Corporation plant. The horses were stabled in an enclosure in the plant. Just within the first day in South Bethlehem, February 26, 1910, troopers arrested 23 strikers for rioting, throwing bricks and stones, and drunkenness. The arrested strikers were imprisoned in the steel plant, as there was no other facility available. The horses pictured here were well trained to obey their riders and march into danger.

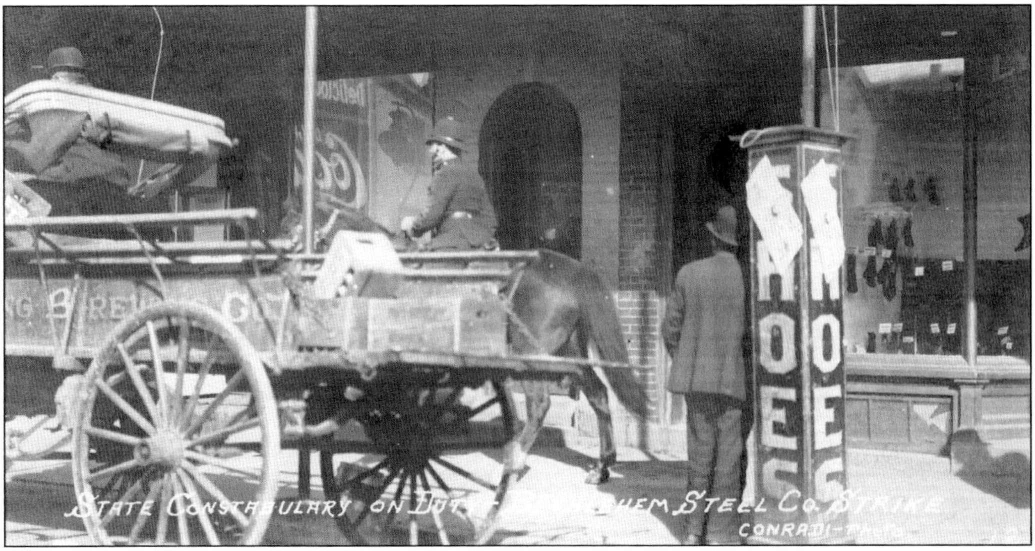

One effective way to move strikers off the sidewalk was to ride one's horse down the middle of it, as the Pennsylvania State Constabulary did in February 1910. Conradi captures this odd event on a busy South Bethlehem street. One person died during this strike when a trooper on horseback chased a striker along a sidewalk to the front of the Majestic Hotel. The trooper then fired into the hotel barroom and killed an innocent bystander. Although it is not known if this photograph documented that event, one can be sure that Conradi was taking photographs as confrontations between the strikers and the troopers escalated.

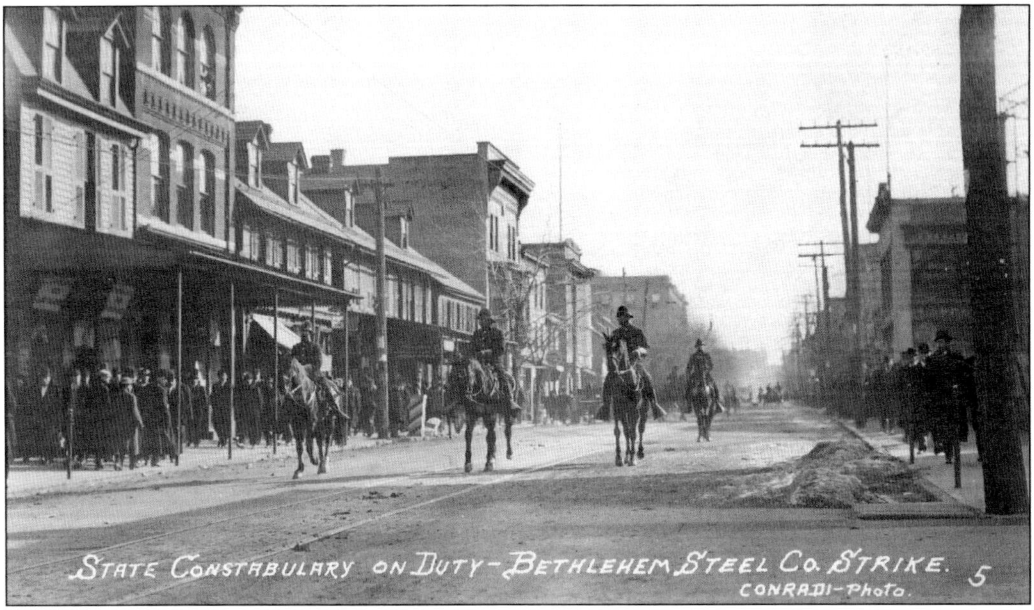

Gustav A. Conradi captured these rare images of the 1910 Bethlehem Steel Corporation strike and sold them as sets of postcards. Charles M. Schwab, president of the company, was not happy about distribution of these postcards so he attempted to purchase all of them to remove them from the public. People today are fortunate that a few postcards were rescued from Schwab's censorship. One can see the tension between the striking workers lined up along both sides of Third Street and the Pennsylvania State Constabulary on horseback.

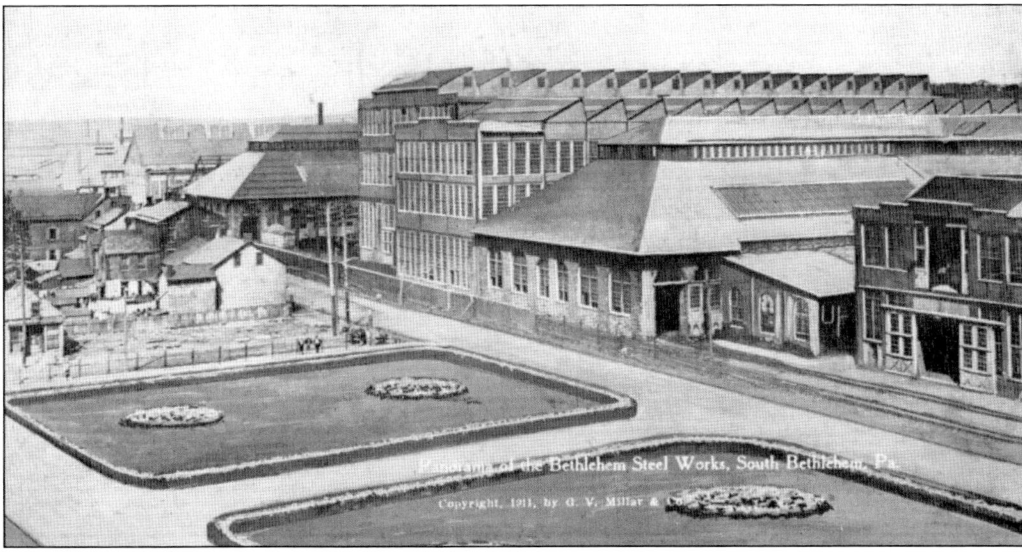

This photograph of Bethlehem Steel Corporation shows an attempt to grow gardens in a dirty, industrial space. In 1905, without company owner Schwab's permission, young superintendent Eugene Grace landscaped the steel yards with trees, plants, and bushes. Schwab was pleased and let the improvements stay. The area shown in this postcard is the oldest section of the mill, known as the Lehigh Plant. On the far left are residences with laundry hanging out to dry. By 1940, Bethlehem Steel had purchased all the property going east to New Street and built its alloy and tool steel division on the newly acquired properties.

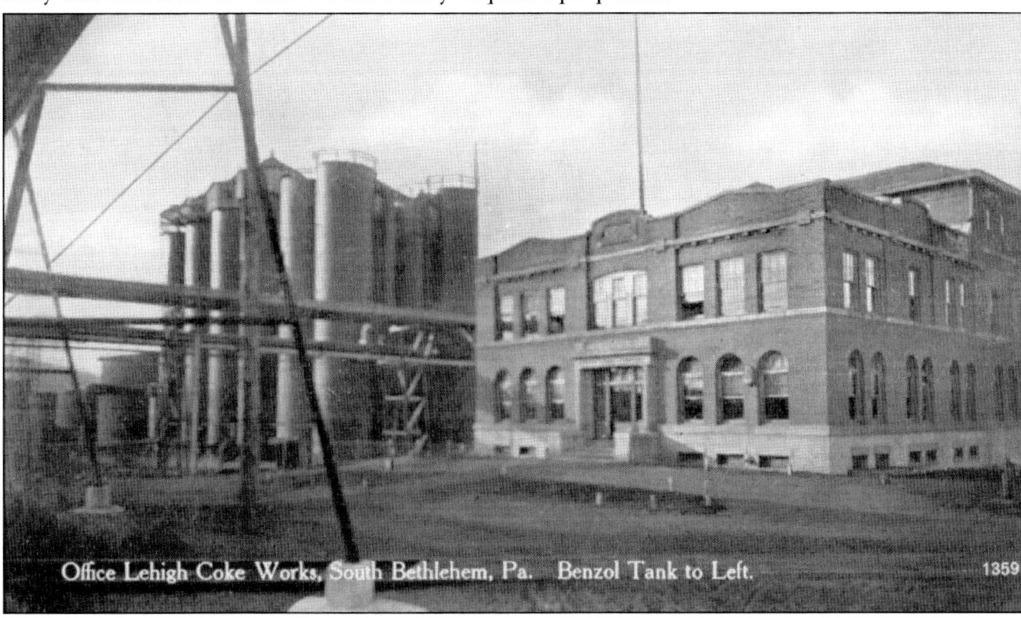

Here is an image of the Lehigh Coke Works and equipment. At the time this photograph was taken, the German company Didier-March, which began building the works in 1912, owned the coke works. Didier-March, concerned that it would lose the business if the United States entered World War I, sold its coke operation to Bethlehem Steel for $8 million. The coke plant annually produced about 1 million tons of coke, refined coal that fuels blast furnaces used in steelmaking. Bethlehem Steel Corporation closed its coke works in 1998.

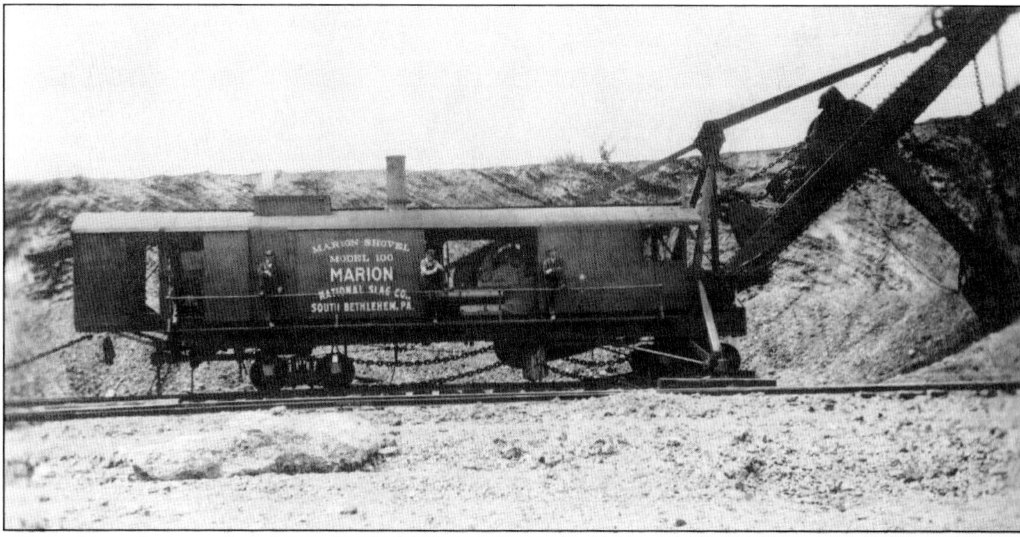

National Slag Company of South Bethlehem set up a reclaiming and crushing plant to recover the large slag dumps of the Bethlehem Steel Corporation. The company incorporated in 1909 for the production of crushed slag as an additive to cement. Bethlehem Steel Corporation tracks led to towering piles of slag along Route 412 on the steel property. The powerful Marion steam shovel model 100 weighed 137 tons and was the largest railroad shovel made. Today, the companies Waylite and Mineral Fiber Specialists are still processing these huge piles of slag for cement aggregate.

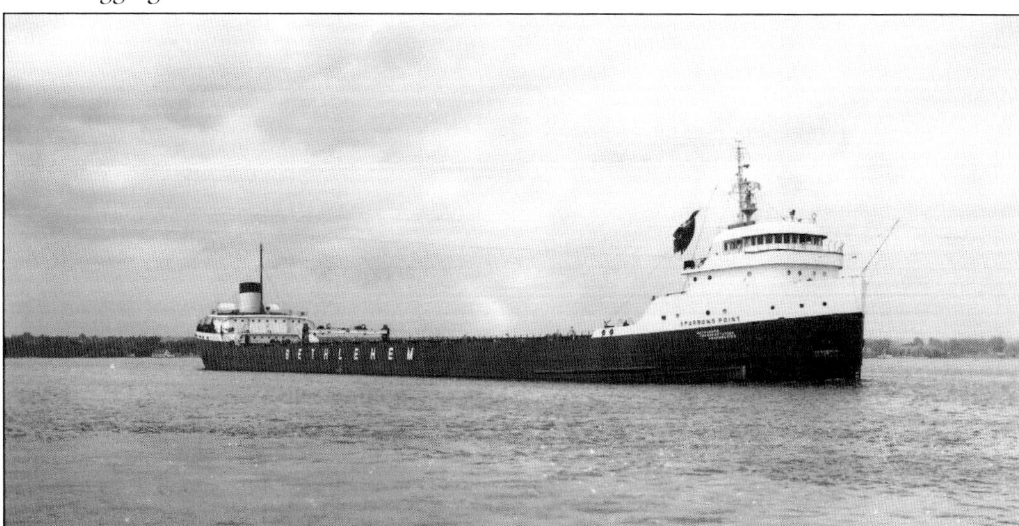

In 1904, Bethlehem Steel Corporation was organized and merged with seven shipyards with Charles M. Schwab at the helm. Later, Bethlehem Steel acquired Sparrows Point Shipyard, located on the Patapsco River in Maryland, in 1916. The shipyard and mills there serviced and repaired ships and manufactured industrial products. During the World War II years, it was the most active shipyard in the United States. Pictured here is the ship *Sparrows Point*, which was named in honor of the shipyard that built her. The ship served as a Great Lakes bulk carrier and was launched on April 18, 1952, entering service for the Bethlehem Steel fleet in November of that year. The *Sparrows Point*'s cargoes were focused in the iron ore trades, supplying Bethlehem Steel's lower Lake Michigan and Lake Erie mills with ore.

Six

Zum Nachtisch

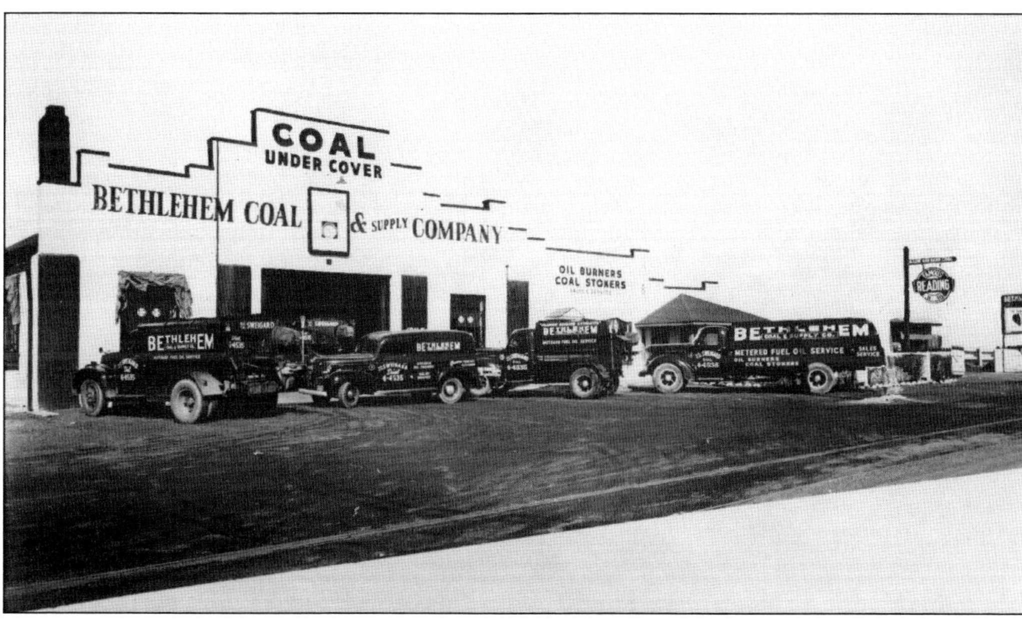

The Bethlehem Coal and Supply Company on Newton Avenue moved to a larger building by 1950. Charles B. Sweigard Sr. and his wife, Pauline S., operated it until they retired in 1967. They began supplying coal, oil, and firewood to Bethlehem customers in the late 1940s. They advertised selling "Famous Reading Anthracite and Esso Fuel Oils."

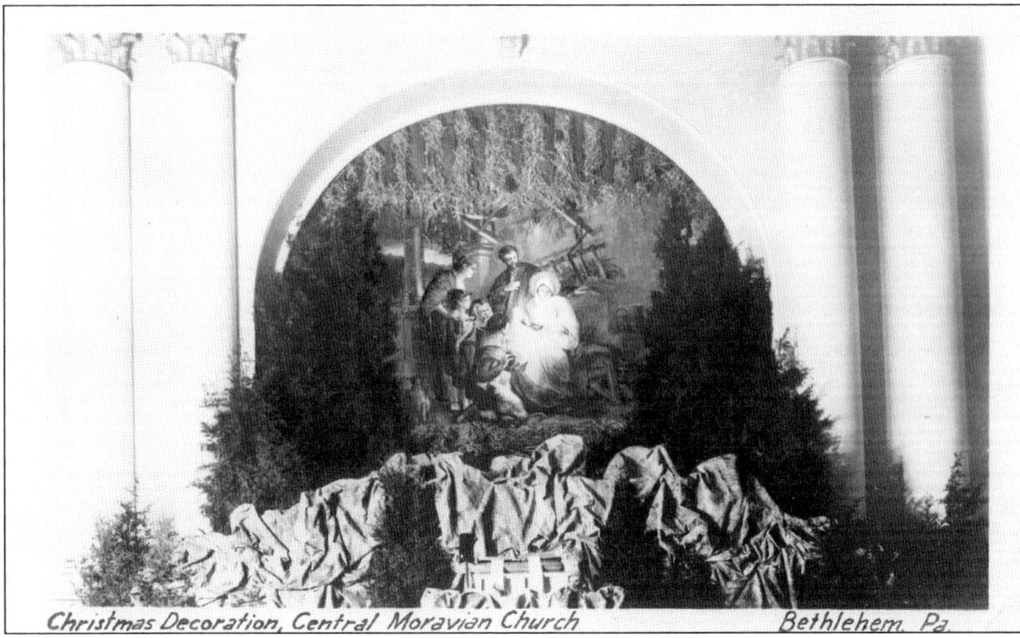

The elaborate and dazzling Christmas decorations of the Central Moravian Church attracted visitors from across the country. The message on this postcard mentions the beautiful display in 1948. Bethlehem's first settlers were known for decorating for the Christmas holiday in their homes from the time they settled here in 1741.

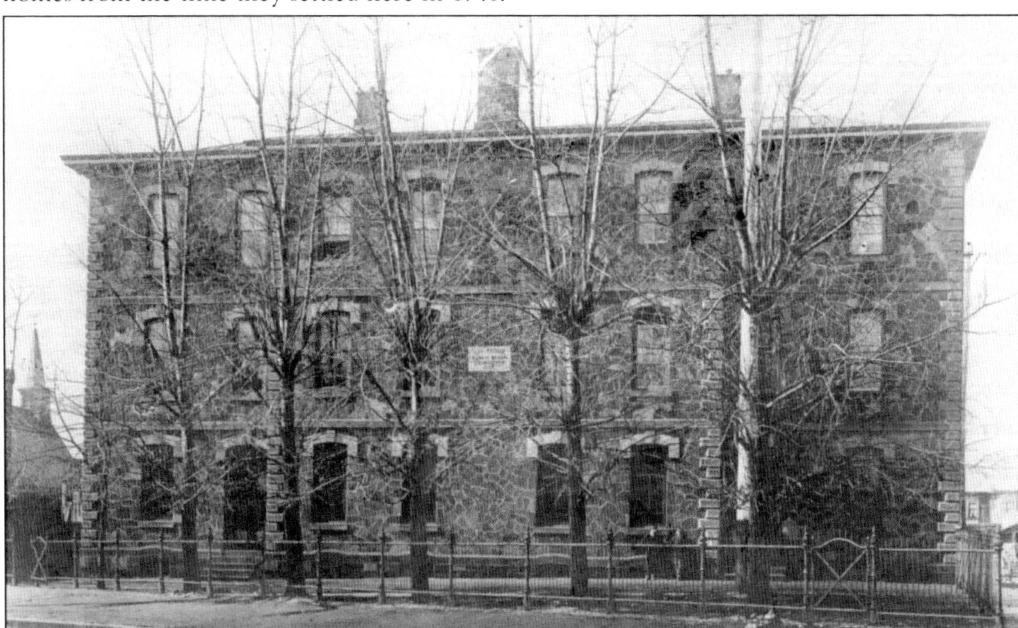

The Asa Packer School was built in 1890 at a cost of $15,473. It was located on the south side of Fourth Street, near Perry Street. In 1890, South Bethlehem's population was 10,386, and it would double in the next 10 years. In 1889, O.R. Wilt was the first superintendent to oversee the school district. Eventually, the school district sold the building, and it was converted into an apartment house, but it was demolished in the 1970s.

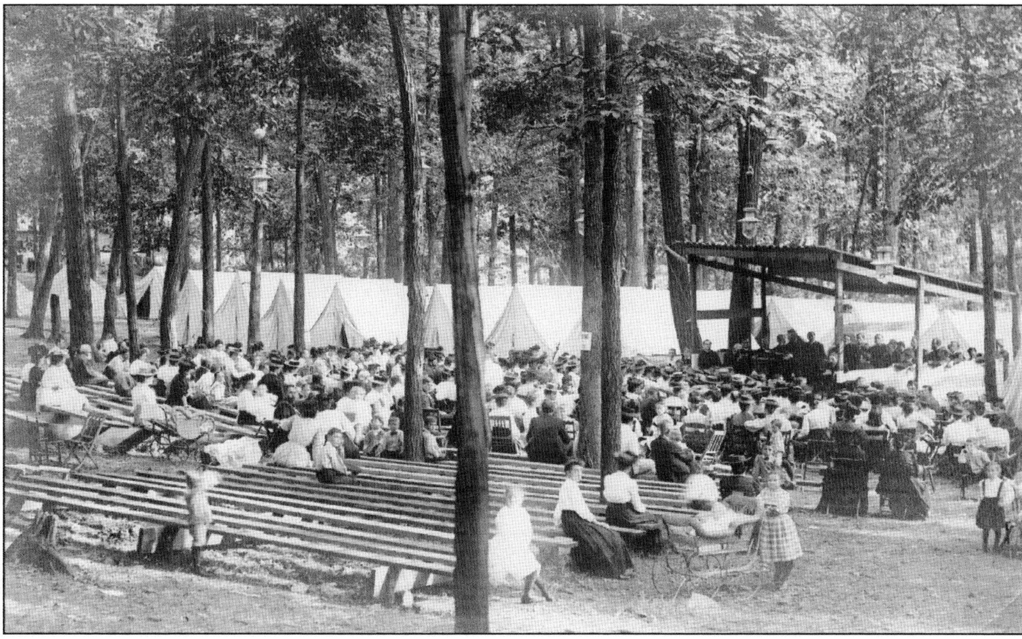

Here is a postcard of a United Methodist camp revival in Beulah Park in Rittersville, between Allentown and Bethlehem. During the 1800s and the first half of the 1900s, religious revival meetings were a popular way to gather congregations in an open-air location to hear prominent religious speakers.

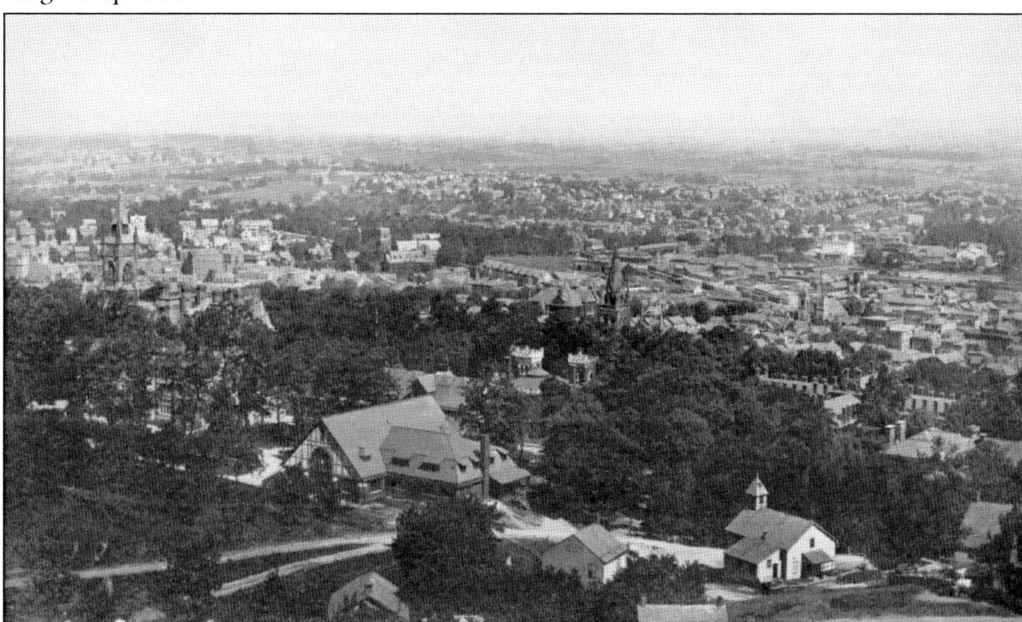

Here is a view of the Lehigh University campus and South Bethlehem from Prospect Point, also known by Bethlehem locals as the lookout, on top of South Mountain. The University Center or Packer Hall is on the far left. The tall steeple of Packer Memorial Chapel is located at center with the Linderman Library in front of the chapel. Off in the distance on the far right is the New Street Bridge over the Lehigh River.

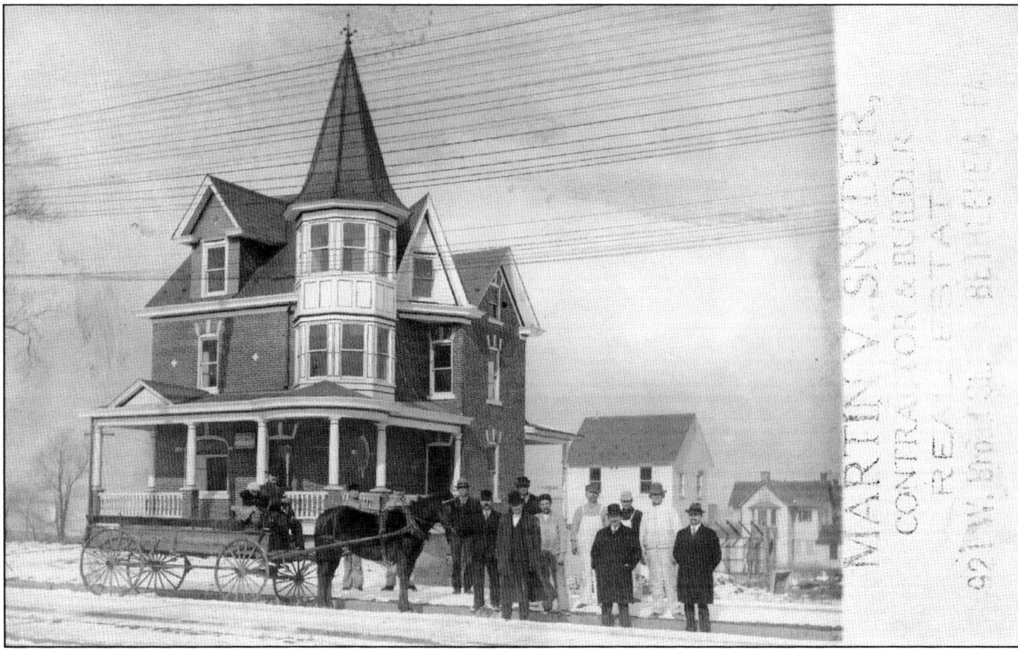

Here is Martin V. Snyder with family and friends in front of his home at Tenth Avenue and West Broad Street. Snyder built homes throughout the Lehigh Valley and employed as many as 30 men. Snyder owned large real estate holdings in West Bethlehem and Rittersville. He married Ella Long, known for her paintings.

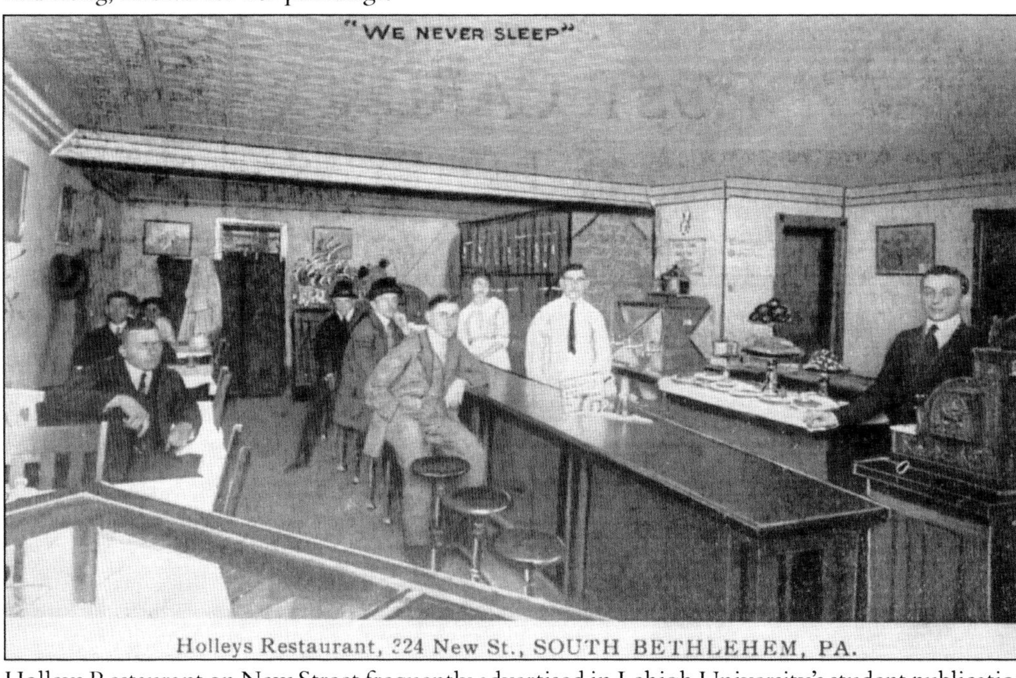

Holleys Restaurant, 224 New St., SOUTH BETHLEHEM, PA.

Holleys Restaurant on New Street frequently advertised in Lehigh University's student publication *Brown and White* to entice students to walk down the hill from their dorms for an after-school drink. The restaurant always included its slogan, "We never sleep." The small saloon was tucked into the Lehigh Steam Laundry building next to the E.H. Kresge Store.

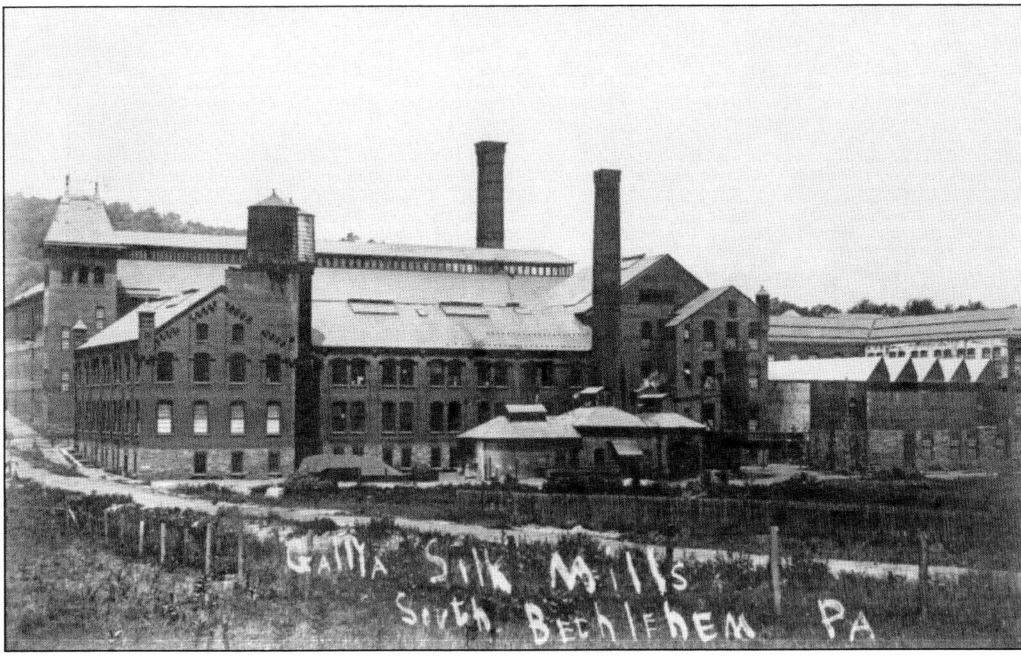

Pictured is the Gallia Silk Mills at 940–942 Seneca Street in Fountain Hill; Gavin Alexander was the superintendent at the time of this photograph. Alexander began working in a silk mill when he was 12 years old. Gallia Silk Mills was incorporated in 1908 by a group of New York investors led by Louis A. Stim. The mill employed 250 workers. Gallia closed in the 1930s as a victim of the Great Depression and the popularity of synthetic fibers.

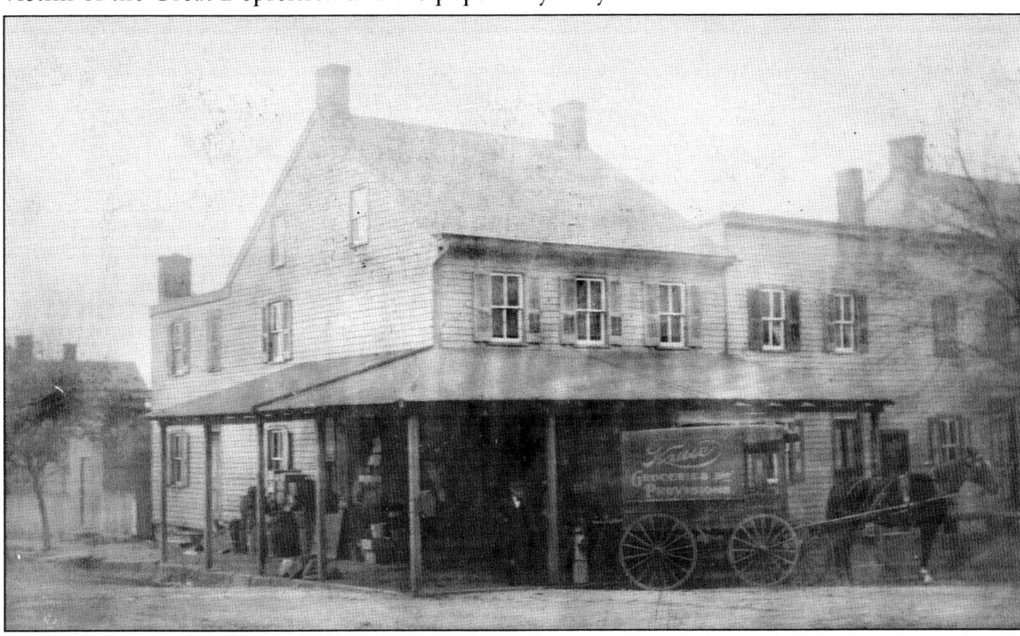

J.H. Kruse Grocery & Meats Store was at the corner of Center and Goepp Streets. John and Anna Kruse ran the store at that location and resided on the second floor until the 1940s. John's father, John J. Kruse, started the business in the late 1800s at the same location. Lump's Deli now operates out of the same building, making this store the oldest operating deli in Bethlehem.

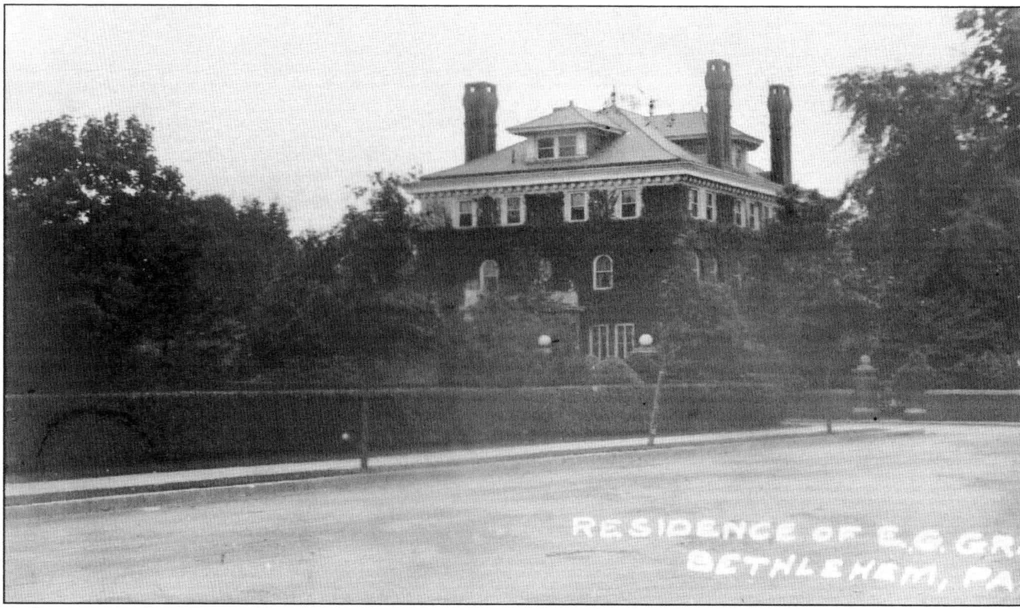

Eugene Gifford Grace (August 27, 1876–July 7, 1960) was the president of Bethlehem Steel Corporation from 1916 to 1945. In 1923, he purchased a mansion on Prospect Avenue in West Bethlehem, erected in 1917 by Prof. Edward Williams, along with several lots surrounding the home. Grace added an extensive addition to create a three-story brick home with a ballroom, 23 bedrooms, 15 bathrooms, and a basement with a game room. The home of Eugene Grace has become Holy Family Manor, a nursing home.

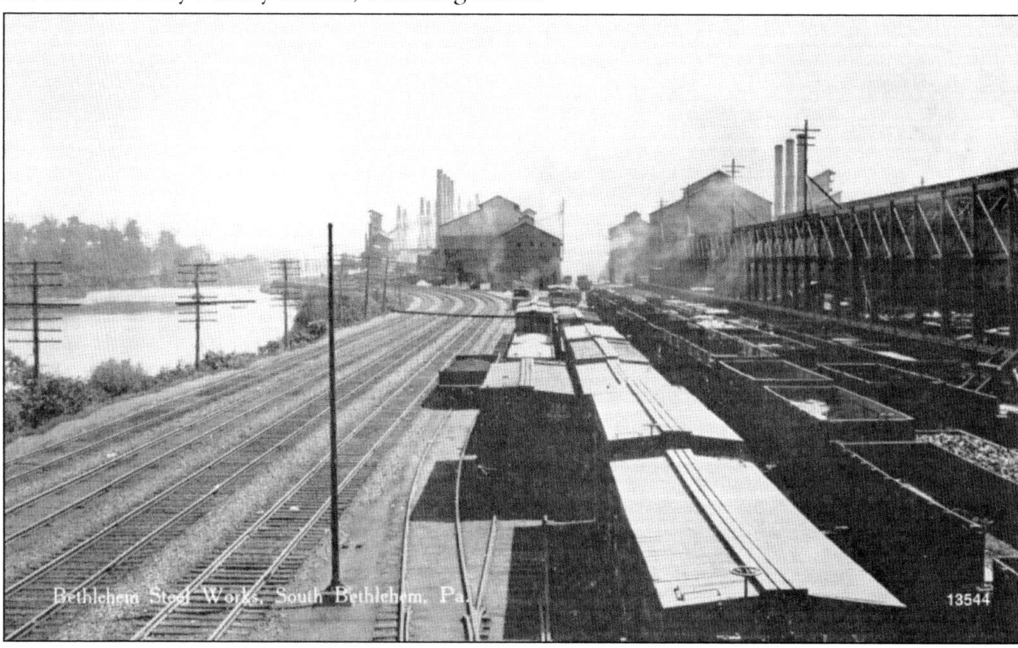

This early-1900s photograph of the Bethlehem Steel Corporation shows the soon-to-be second-largest steel maker in the world, under the guidance of Charles M. Schwab. He purchased Bethlehem Steel in 1901 for $7.2 million. It was a specialized small business that made heavy steel forgings for guns and marine engines and produced armor plate.

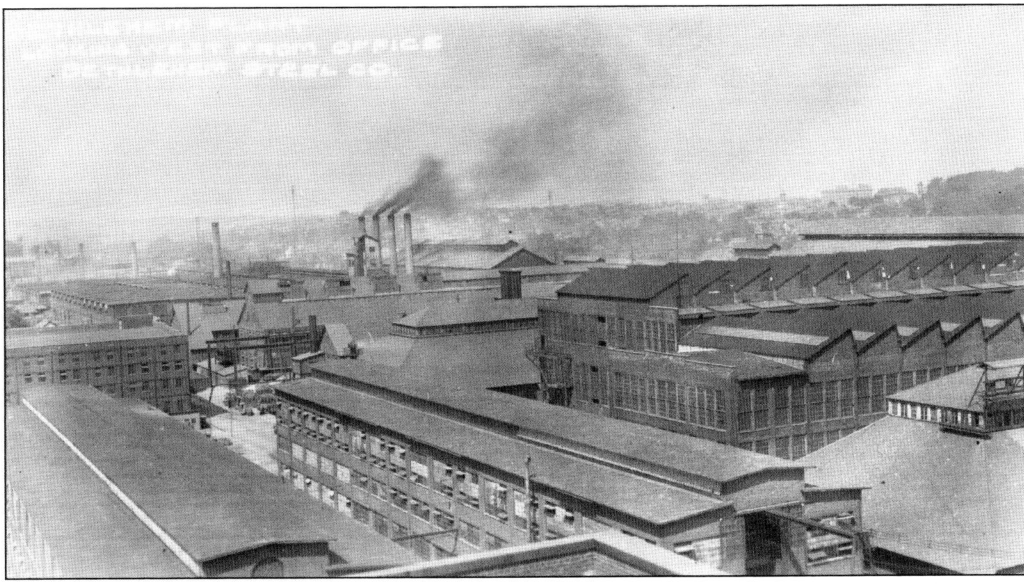

Looking west from the Bethlehem Steel Corporation offices is the gray rolling mill, built in 1907. Bethlehem Steel's shrewd adoption of the gray process allowed the plant to produce H-section steel beams that were lighter, wider, and cheaper than traditional beams. These beams were necessary for the building of taller skyscrapers and longer bridges.

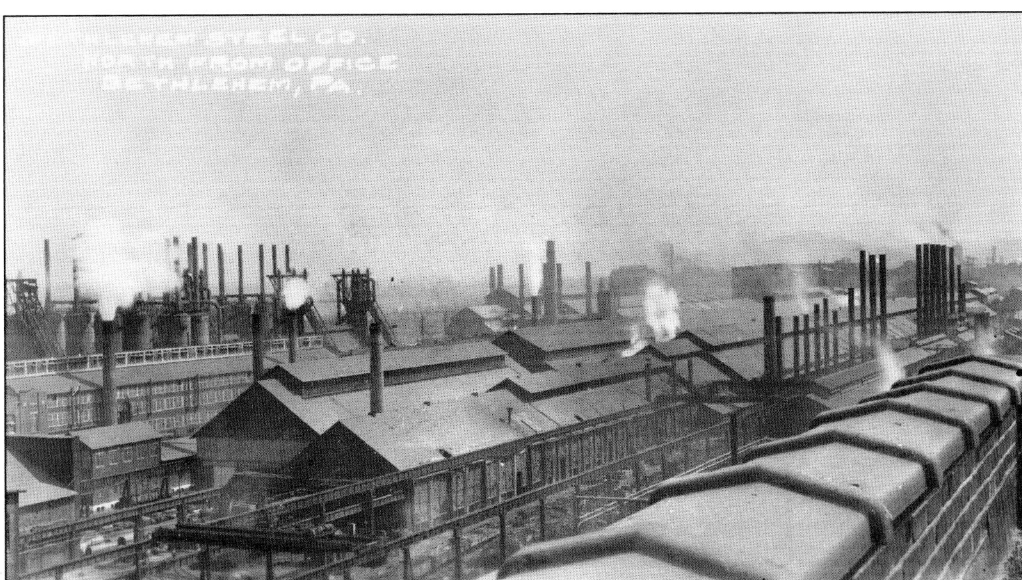

Looking north out of the main offices of the Bethlehem Steel Corporation shows the mill buildings along the Lehigh River. The corporation built east to Hellertown as it expanded. World War I was a few years away, and Bethlehem Steel was ready to become the largest ordnance and munitions supplier to the Allies.

Consistent with our mission to preserve history on a local level, this book was printed in South Carolina on American-made paper and manufactured entirely in the United States. Products carrying the accredited Forest Stewardship Council (FSC) label are printed on 100 percent FSC-certified paper.

MADE IN THE USA